The Language of Passion

Translated by Natasha Wimmer

Farrar, Straus and Giroux

New York

The

LANGUAGE

of

PASSION

❧ ❧

SELECTED COMMENTARY

❧ ❧

Mario Vargas Llosa

Farrar, Straus and Giroux
19 Union Square West, New York 10003

Copyright © 2000 by Mario Vargas Llosa
Translation copyright © 2003 by Natasha Wimmer
All rights reserved
Distributed in Canada by Douglas & McIntyre Ltd.
Printed in the United States of America
Originally published in 2000 by Grupo Santillana de Ediciones S.A., Spain,
as *El lenguaje de la pasión*
Published in the United States by Farrar, Straus and Giroux
First American edition, 2003

Library of Congress Cataloging-in-Publication Data
Vargas Llosa, Mario, 1936–
    [Lenguaje de la pasión. English]
    The language of passion / Mario Vargas Llosa ; translated by Natasha
Wimmer.— 1st ed.
        p.   cm.
    Includes index.
    ISBN 0-374-18326-0 (hc : alk. paper)
    I. Title.

PQ8498.32.A65 L4613 2003
864'.64—dc21
                                                          2002037909

Designed by Jonathan D. Lippincott

www.fsgbooks.com

1   3   5   7   9   10   8   6   4   2

Contents

Author's Note

Nearly all the essays in this book are selected from among those that appeared as installments of my column, "Touchstone," between 1992 and 2000 in the Madrid daily newspaper *El País* and in a number of affiliated publications. Unlike those included in a previous collection, *Desafíos a la libertad* (1994),* which were thematically related, the pieces here cover a broad range of topics, politics alternating with culture, social issues, travel, literature, painting, music, and current events.

The title, the same as one I gave to a short tribute to Octavio Paz, is not meant to suggest that these pieces were written in a state of passion or outrage. Since I know that a hot head is incompatible with clear ideas and good prose, I try to write as dispassionately as possible, though I realize I don't always succeed. In any case, these pieces are not entirely devoid of feeling, to judge by the reactions they've elicited in different parts of the world and from a varied slate of protesters, among them the archbishop of Buenos Aires, a worldly London sociologist, a Washington bu-

---

*Not published in the United States, though many of the pieces were included in *Making Waves. (Trans.)*

reaucrat, a Catalan ideologue, and a number of supposedly progressive but actually remarkably hidebound writers. I don't mean
to celebrate or condemn the controversy sparked by my articles; I
simply present it as proof of the independence and freedom with
which they were written.

I've included as prologue my acknowledgment of the José
Ortega y Gasset Journalism Prize, which was awarded to one of
these pieces, "New Inquisitions," in Spain in 1998.

In recognition of their help in preparing the contents of this
book, I would like to thank my colleagues and friends Rosario de
Bedoya and Lucía Muñoz-Nájar Pinillos.

London, August 2000

Touchstone

Ever since I was a boy, I've been fascinated by the idea of the touchstone. According to the dictionary, it is used to test the purity of precious metals, but I've never seen one and I'm still not sure whether it is real or imaginary.

The term occurred to me at once when it came time to name my newspaper column. In the column, every other Sunday, I try to comment on some current event that rouses, angers, or disturbs me, subjecting it to the test of reason and in the process weighing my convictions, doubts, and confusions. The column obliges me to attempt a clear picture of the tumultuous present, and through it I hope to help my readers form opinions about what is going on around them.

Writing it is difficult, but also extremely pleasurable, and I try to keep in mind Raimundo Lida's dictum: "Adjectives were made not to be used" (something that goes against my natural instincts). The process allows me to feel involved in the everyday life of the planet, and immerses me in history as it is being written, which is the particular province of journalism. I discovered this province when I was fourteen years old, working for the Lima newspaper *La Crónica*, and since then I have always belonged to it, as an editor, reporter, editorial writer, and columnist. Journalism has been the other side of my literary career; as I set off on purely imaginary voyages, it has kept pace with me, furnished me with material, and prevented me from losing sight of living, everyday reality.

"Touchstone," then, reflects my hopes and disappointments, what I am and what I'm not, and what I think, fear, and hate just as faithfully as my books, though more explicitly and rationally.

Sartre wrote that words were weapons and that they should be used to defend our best options (advice that he himself didn't always follow). In the Spanish-speaking world, no one put that theory into practice better than José Ortega y Gasset, a first-rate thinker capable of writing opinion journalism without oversimplifying his ideas or sacrificing his style. To win an award that bears his name is an honor, a satisfaction, and, above all, a challenge.

Paris, May 4, 1999

The Language of Passion

The Lady from Somerset

T he story is as decorous and discreet as she herself must have been, and as unreal as the romances she wrote and devoured until the end of her days. That it happened as it did and that it now forms part of reality is moving proof of the power of fiction, that beguiling lie which every so often comes true in the most unexpected of ways.

The beginning of the story is surprising, and quite suspenseful. Great Britain's Society of Authors was informed by an executor that a woman, recently deceased, had left it all her worldly goods—£400,000, some $700,000—in order that it establish an annual literary prize for novelists under the age of thirty-five. The winning work had to be "of a romantic or traditional, but not experimental, nature." The news hit the front pages instantly, because the prize thus created—$70,000 a year—was four or five times bigger than either the Booker McConnell or the Whitbread, the two most prestigious British literary awards.

Who was the generous donor? A novelist, of course. But the shamefaced directors of the Society of Authors had to confess to the press that they had never heard of Miss Margaret Elizabeth Trask. And despite their best efforts, they had not been able to find even one of her books in London bookstores.

Nevertheless, Miss Trask had published more than fifty romance novels since the 1930s under a nom de plume that shortened her given name and made it sound slightly less aristocratic: Betty Trask. The titles of the books suggest the nature of their content: *I Tell My Heart, Irresistible, And Confidential, Rustle of Spring, Bitter Sweetbriar*. The last appeared in 1957, and no copies of any of them were to be found at the offices of Miss Trask's publishers or the literary agency that handled her rights. In order to have a look at one, the reporters on the trail of the mysterious English literary philanthropist had to bury themselves in those odd neighborhood libraries which even today lend out romance novels for a modest yearly fee.

Thus the biography of the enchanting Miss Trask was reconstructed. Unlike her Spanish counterpart, Corín Tellado, she refused to adjust her moral standards to the times, and in 1957 she put down her pen, realizing that the gap between everyday life and her novels was growing too wide. Her books, which, judging by the money she left, were very popular, fell immediately into oblivion. This seems not to have mattered at all to Miss Trask, who outlived her work by more than a quarter century.

The most extraordinary thing about Margaret Elizabeth Trask, who devoted her life to reading and writing about love, is that in all her eighty-eight years she never had a single romantic experience. The evidence is conclusive: she died single and a virgin, body and soul. Those who knew her speak of her as a relic of another age, a Victorian or Edwardian anachronism lost in the century of hippies and punks.

Her family came from Frome, in Somerset; they were prosperous silk manufacturers. Miss Margaret received a strict and careful education at home. She was a shy, attractive girl with aristocratic ways who lived in Bath and Belgravia, London's most exclusive neighborhood. The family fortune dried up when her father died, but Miss Trask's habits, already frugal, weren't much altered by this change. She never enjoyed much of a social life, went out very infrequently, claimed a benign allergy to men, and never permitted any flirtatious compliments. The love of her life was her mother, whom she cared for devotedly after her father's death. This caretaking, and the writing of romances at the rate of two a year, were the sum total of her life.

Thirty-five years ago, the two women returned to Somerset and rented a tiny house on a dead-end street in their hometown of Frome. Miss Trask's mother died in the early sixties, and Miss Trask's life became a neighborhood enigma. She rarely ventured out, she was coolly and distantly polite, she neither received visitors nor made visits herself.

The only person able to speak of her with some familiarity was the director of the Frome library, to which Miss Trask belonged. She was an insatiable reader of love stories, though she also liked biographies of unusual men and women. The librarian made a weekly trip to her house, bringing her books and picking them up again.

As the years went by, the frail Miss Margaret's health began to deteriorate. The neighbors deduced this from the appearance of a National Health nurse, who began to come once a week to give her massages. (In her will, Miss Trask rewarded these attentions with the cautious sum of two hundred pounds.) Five years ago, her condition worsened until she could no longer live alone. She was taken to a nursing home, where, surrounded by the poor, she continued to live the austere, discreet, nearly invisible life she had always lived.

Her neighbors in Frome couldn't believe their eyes when they read that the spinster of Oakfield Road had left so much money to the Society of Authors and that she was a writer. What they found even harder to understand was why, instead of using her £400,000 to live more comfortably, she had given the money away to reward the writing of romance novels. They spoke condescendingly of Miss Trask to newspaper and television reporters, and said how sad and dreary life must have been for someone who never invited anyone over for tea.

Her neighbors in Frome were fools, of course, as are all those who believe that Margaret Elizabeth Trask should be pitied for her life of quiet routine. In fact, Miss Margaret lived a wonderful, enviable life, full of excitement and adventure. In it there were astounding deeds of derring-do, wild passions sparked by smoldering glances, and acts of generosity, sacrifice, nobility, and bravery like those in episodes out of the lives of the saints or novels of chivalry.

Miss Trask had no time to socialize with her neighbors or gossip about the high cost of living or the behavior of today's disrespectful youth because every minute of her life was concentrated on impossible passions: burning lips brushing lily-white fingers and causing young maidens to blossom like roses; knives buried with fierce tenderness in the hearts of unfaithful lovers. Why should Miss Trask have gone out to walk the stony streets of Frome? Could that miserably real little town have offered her anything like the sumptuous country houses, the farmhouses battered by storms, the haunted forests, the marble pavilions alongside lagoons that were the settings of her dreams and imaginings? Of course Miss Trask avoided making friends or talking to anyone. Why should she have wasted her time with people as ordinary and limited as the living? The truth is that she had many friends. They kept her from being bored for even an instant in her modest little house on Oakfield Road, and they never said anything stupid, out of place, or unpleasant. Who among the earthbound could speak with the charm, respect, and wisdom of the ghosts of Miss Trask's novels when they whispered in her ear?

Margaret Elizabeth Trask's existence was surely more intense, varied, and dramatic than that of many of her contemporaries. Propelled by a certain upbringing and her own particular idiosyncracies, she inverted the relationship that usually establishes itself in human beings between the imaginary and the real, or what is dreamed and what is lived. What generally happens is that people, caught up in their busy existences, "live" the majority of the time and dream the rest. Miss Trask went about it the other way. She devoted her days and nights to fantasy and shrank what we call living down to a bare minimum.

Was she happier than those who prefer reality to fiction? I think she was. If she wasn't, why should she have left all her money to encourage the writing of romance novels? Isn't that proof that she went to the next world convinced she was right to exchange the reality of life for the lies of literature? Though many see it as an outrageous document, her will is in fact a stern judgment on the odious world into which she was born and in which she contrived not to live.

London, May 1983

Shadows of Friends

ᴥ ᴥ

I've been noticing with some alarm that many of the friends I made and spent time with in Barcelona in the sixties are no longer with us. Hardly a trace is left, either, of the city I knew then. In those days Barcelona was down-at-the-heels, cosmopolitan, and international; now it is extremely rich, provincial, and nationalist. Before, it surged culturally toward the rest of the world; today it seems fascinated by its own navel. This self-absorption is fashionable in Europe, and it is the natural response of the conservative and traditionalist strain of long-established cultures to the growing internationalization of life and to the headlong rush of the modern world toward the dissolution of boundaries and confusion of cultures. But in Catalonia, the return to the "tribal instinct," whatever its deep political roots, contradicts another venerable tradition: universalism, so characteristic of the region's great creators, from Foix to Pla and from Tàpies to Dalí.

My friends were all citizens of the world. Gabriel Ferrater wrote his poems in Catalan because, he said, he could "kick better goals" in his native tongue than in Spanish (we were both soccer fans), but he wasn't a nationalist, or anything that required any kind of faith. All convictions and passions, except possibly litera-

ture, inspired in him a barbed and biting sarcasm, spiked with fe-
rociously cynical metaphors. Just as others squander time or
money, Gabriel squandered his genius writing book reviews and
encyclopedia entries, talking to friends, and consuming lethal
quantities of gin.

"Genius" is a big word, but I don't know how else to describe
the monstrous ability Gabriel had to learn everything about whatever he was interested in and become an instant expert on a subject. Then he'd lose interest, and move on. To call him a dilettante
suggests he was superficial, and there was nothing superficial
about the way he'd eviscerate Picasso in a discussion about art,
wave his arms like a windmill as he argued the linguistic theories
of the Prague Circle, or quote from memory in an effort to prove
that Kafka's German derived from police reports. I'm sure it's
true that he learned Polish in hardly any time at all just so he
could read and translate Gombrowicz. He could, after all, read all
the languages of the world, and he spoke all of them with a heavy
Catalan accent.

Maybe "excessive" is the term, along with "genius," that best
describes him. Everything about him was over-the-top, from his
voracious reading and learning to his long, restless hands, which,
after a first drink, would make the ladies around him jump. Because I voted for João Guimarães Rosa over Witold Gombrowicz
when we were on a jury together, he punished me by depriving
me of a year of his friendship. On the three hundred and sixty-
fifth day, I received a book by Carles Riba inscribed with the following lines: "Now that the year of punishment is over, we can
pick up where we left off, etcetera. Gabriel."

They say that he always claimed it was immoral to reach the
age of fifty and that this coy declaration explains why he killed
himself. It might be true: it accords very well with the strange mix
of anarchism, insolence, discipline, sweetness, and narcissism that

constituted his character. The last time I saw him it was ten in the morning, and he was at the Bar del Colón. He had been drinking for almost twenty-four hours and he looked flushed and exultant. With Juanito García Hortelano patiently listening, he was shouting hoarsely, reciting Rilke in German.

Unlike Gabriel, García Hortelano was reserved, even-tempered, obliging, and, above all, modest in the display of his intelligence, which he disguised behind a hearty, good-natured facade and a veil of humor. He wasn't from Barcelona, but it was in Barcelona that I met him and saw him many times, more often than in Madrid. The day we met, we went out together to buy a Catalan grammar book, and we confessed to each other our fondness for Catalonia. In my memory I can't dissociate him from Barcelona or the sixties, the decade in which his first novels were published—an era that, with everything that has happened since, has come to seem prehistoric.

When I was a child, I played with friends in Lima trying to guess which writers would go to heaven (if it existed), and it seemed to us that of the classic authors few would be chosen, and of contemporary writers none at all. I'm very much afraid that if that hypothetical Judgment Day comes, we'll be deprived of Juan, because he'll be whisked up instantly. Of all the men of letters I've known, he's the only one who qualifies. I'm joking, but at the same time I'm deadly serious. I've never met anyone among my colleagues who seemed so honest and upright, so naturally decent, so free from vanity and deceitfulness, so generous as Juan. Goodness is a mysterious and grating virtue, and one that, in my experience—dispiriting, I admit—has much to do with lack of imagination and simplicity of mind, and with a naïveté that comes across as candor. That's why it's not popular, and why, in rarefied cultural circles, it is regarded with distrust and disdain, as a proof of idiocy. And it is also why the good man who possesses a subtle mind and a refined sensibility is a disconcerting rarity.

It's true that bad people tend to be more fun than good people and that goodness is usually boring. But García Hortelano broke the mold here, too, because he was one of the funniest people in the world, a constant source of stories, inventions, intellectual games, nicknames, and plays on words that could keep the night patrons of the narrow Bar Cristal entertained for hours. With the same seriousness with which he assured us that Walter Benjamin was a pseudonym of Jesús Aguirre, I heard him swear once that he went to the red-light district of Las Ramblas at dawn only to buy the newspaper *La Vanguardia*.

Among the many things that I once planned to write but never will is a magic meeting with him on a foggy morning by the sea at Calafell. As in his novels, much was happening and nothing at all. We had listened to the debut record of a singer called Raimón, which Luis Goytisolo had brought with him; guided by our host, Carlos Barral, we had visited bars and restaurants, traipsed around boats and fishermen, and made a fire on the beach. For a long time, Jaime Gil de Biedma held us rapt with electrifying stories of evil deeds. At midnight we swam, in a fog that made ghosts of us. We got out, dried ourselves off, talked a little, and all of a sudden someone asked where Juan could be; he was nowhere to be found. Surely, we thought, he had gone to bed. Much later, I went to plunge again into the water and fog. Wreathed in wisps of mist, the writer appeared, shivering. What was he doing there, chilled to the bone? Teeth chattering, he told me that he couldn't find his way off the beach. Each time he tried, he seemed to be heading toward Sicily or Tunisia. And why hadn't he cried for help or called out? Cry for help? Call out? Only a bad novelist would do that.

Unlike Juan, Jaime Gil de Biedma was utterly lacking in modesty, and cultivated intellectual arrogance the way others cultivate their gardens or breed dogs. He started arguments in order to demolish his opponents, and when admirers of his poetry approached him full of unctuous praise, his retorts would leave them reeling. He did everything he could to seem unpleasant, arrogant, unapproachable. But he wasn't as bad as he would have liked to be, or as tough and cerebral as he made himself seem in his *Diario del artista seriamente enfermo* (Diary of a Seriously Ill Artist). Late at night, in conversation with a few close friends, he'd tire of posing and let the bad-boy mask fall, and the sensitive reader would appear, the man torn between his vocation and his work, the man of ambivalent sexuality, the vulnerable and tormented young writer of verse.

When he wasn't sunk in self-contemplation, his intelligence could be dazzling. He had an infallible ability to detect the original thought or exquisite shading in a poem or a sentence, and to pick out falseness and ostentation; one could trust blindly in his literary judgment. But although his poetry and essays may be read with pleasure, there is something in Jaime's work that struggles to show itself and seems repressed, something that never becomes more than a spark: the part of experience that is outside the intellectual orbit. Maybe because his aesthetic only had room for elegance and because his sentiments and passions are always a little precious, his poetry, like Borges's stories, has more thinking than living in it.

It was through Carlos Barral that I met Gabriel, Juan, Jaime, and almost all of my Spanish friends in Barcelona in the sixties. Carlos published my first novel, fighting fiercely to get it past the censors. He helped me win prizes, got my books translated into many languages, invented me as a writer. Everything has already been said that needs to be said about the breath of fresh air that his work represented in the stifling cultural climate of Spain thirty years ago. But enough will never be said about the charms of the persona he cultivated and the spell he was capable of casting back then, before the terrible ordeals he had to endure.

What will he surprise me with this time? I used to ask whenever I went to see him. There was always something: his dog, Argos, would bark hysterically if the poems he read aloud were bad; he had taken to wearing eighteenth-century capes and carrying sword canes on the streets of Barcelona's La Bonanova; or he would recite to me in Latin a list of two hundred timbers of a ship on which, according to him, Ulysses had sailed. With his grand gestures and phosphorescent adjectives, he was every inch a gentleman. His generosity was boundless, and though he sometimes posed as a cynic, since cynicism was in fashion then, he was good through and through. To seem wicked, he had invented a diabolical laugh—openmouthed, reverberant, gravelly, volcanic—that contorted his rail-thin, Quixote-like form from head to foot and left him exhausted. A formidable laugh, and one that still echoes in my memory.

He had literary fixations that one had to respect at the risk of losing his friendship: Mallarmé and the seventeenth-century Spanish poet and playwright Gabriel Bocángel were unmentionable, for example, and English literature was beyond the pale, except maybe for Shakespeare and Marlowe. But he could spend hours discussing the writers he liked, speaking brilliantly and quoting from memory with the passion of an adolescent. His love for form was such that in restaurants for a while he took to asking just for "oysters and cheese," because he liked how it sounded. He dreamed of having an ocelot to take for walks around Calafell, and I brought him one from the depths of the Amazon, at the cost of unimaginable hardship. But in the Barcelona airport, a Civil Guard washed it down with a hose and gave it chorizo to eat, sending the poor animal to its death. I still keep the beautiful letter I received from Carlos upon the demise of Amadís as one of my literary treasures.

Beneath the posing and the theatrics there was something

more lasting: a talented creator and an editor and literary promoter who left a deep mark on the entire Hispanic world. In today's Spain, open to all the world's currents, it is hard to conceive of his importance. But those who, like myself, arrived in Madrid in 1958 and discovered that the isolation and prudishness of cultural life in Spain were even worse than in Lima or Tegucigalpa know that Carlos Barral's efforts to topple barriers and familiarize Spanish readers with what was being written and published abroad, while saving the young or oppressed writers of the Iberian Peninsula from anonymity and persecution, were a decisive factor in the intellectual modernization of Spain. Then, too, of course, he brought Latin America to the attention of Spaniards, and Latin Americans to the attention of each other. How many of the young poets and writers of the New World who immigrated to Barcelona in the seventies and eighties and turned the city, for a time, into the literary capital of Latin America knew that the person who paved the way for them was the gaunt gentleman, now shed of his publishing houses and plagued with ulcers, who could still be seen with his cape, staff, beard, chains, and long hair walking his dog like an apparition along the streets of Sarriá?

Shades of the past, and friends long gone. But their presence is still felt.

Berlin, May 1992

The Morality of Cynics

❧ ❧

In a lecture on politics as a vocation (*Politik als Beruf*), given to the Free Student Association of Munich in 1919, Max Weber distinguished between two kinds of morality to which all "ethically oriented" human actions could be traced: the ethic of responsibility and the ethic of ultimate ends. This soon-to-be-famous formula was almost as instrumental in establishing the German sociologist's reputation as his studies anticipating bureaucratic government and charismatic leaders or linking the Protestant Reformation and the development of capitalism.

At first glance at least, the division seems precise, illuminating, and irrefutable. The man who follows the ethic of ultimate ends says what he thinks and acts on his beliefs without pausing to consider the consequences, because in his view authenticity and truth must always prevail and trump quotidian or circumstantial concerns. The man who follows the ethic of responsibility adjusts his convictions and principles to a conduct attuned to the effects of what he says and does, so that his actions don't provoke catastrophes or bring about results contrary to an overarching design. For the former, morality is above all personal and associated with God or with fixed ideas and beliefs that are abstract and dissociated from the collective human experience; for the latter, morality cannot be divorced from concrete matters, social life, efficiency, and history.

One ethic is not superior to the other; they are different in nature and can't be ranked in a hierarchical system of values, although in a few ideal cases they are confused in one individual or act. It is more common, however, that they stand in contrast to each other and be incarnated in different people, whose paradigms are the intellectual and the politician. Among these people, certain figures appear who best illustrate cases at either end of the spectrum. In these figures the difference and irreconcilability of these two ways of acting are revealed with luminous eloquence.

If the Dominican friar Bartolomé de Las Casas had taken into consideration the interests of his country or his monarch when he set out to chronicle the evils of the conquest and colonization of America, his denunciations—from which stemmed the Latin American narrative of resentment of Spain, or the "Black Legend," as it is known—would not have been so fierce. But for Las Casas, the typical follower of an ethic of ultimate ends, the truth was more important than the Spanish empire. Nor did Sartre care if he caused France to "lose face" during the war with Algeria when he accused the French army of torturing Arab rebels. It didn't matter to him that he was judged unpatriotic and a traitor by the majority of his fellow citizens when he made it known that he would have no qualms about carrying "suitcases full of arms" for the FLN (National Liberation Front) if he were asked, since he believed that the anticolonial struggle was just.

General de Gaulle could not have behaved with such Olympian disdain for his personal popularity without failing miserably as a leader and launching France into an even graver crisis than the one that precipitated the collapse of the Fourth Republic. The model of the responsible moralist, he came to power in 1958, disguising his true position on the explosive colonial question with ambiguous rhetoric and clever misunderstandings. In doing so, he brought peace and order to a society on the verge of anarchy. Once in the Elysée, the man who a majority of French citizens trusted to save Algeria employed silences, half-truths, and half-lies to push the stubborn public toward a shift in opinion, artfully leading them to resign themselves to the idea of decolonization, which de Gaulle would ultimately undertake not just in Algeria but in all of France's African possessions. The happy conclusion of decolonization retroactively transformed what had once seemed government inconsistencies, contradictions, and betrayals into coherent episodes in a long-term plan, evidence of the wise strategizing of a statesman.

Where Las Casas, Sartre, and de Gaulle are concerned, and in other, similar cases, all of this is clear because the integrity underlying individual actions gives consistency to seemingly erratic behavior. The weakness in this conception of the divide between those who follow an ethic of responsibility and those who follow an ethic of ultimate ends is that it assumes an essential integrity in everyone and does not take into account the impostors, the scoundrels, the irreverent, and the insincere.

There is, after all, an unbridgeable moral gap between a man like Bertrand Russell, who went to jail for being eccentric—for practicing the pacifism he preached—and one with the convictions of a Dalí, whose strident remarks and bizarre habits never made him run any kind of risk and in fact helped sell his paintings. Should the *maudit* extravagances that drove Antonin Artaud to alienation and the madhouse be equated with those that made Jean Cocteau the darling of high society and a member of the Academy of Immortals?

But it is above all among politicians that the ethic of responsibility splits into conducts which, though they seem to resemble each other, are revealed to be at odds when considered more carefully. De Gaulle's lies to the activists of French Algeria—"Je vous ai compris"—acquire a certain grandeur when considered in perspective, judged and understood in the context of his full time in office. Are they comparable, in moral terms, to the myriad lies leaders tell every day, aiming only to keep their hold on power or to save themselves trouble? For minor reasons, that is, without the least hint of historical transcendence?

This query is not academic, but has to do with a matter of tremendous present-day importance: What will the future of liberal democracy be? The collapse of totalitarianism in Europe and parts of Asia has, in theory, infused democratic culture with new vitality. But this is true only in theory, since in practice we are witnessing a profound crisis of the system in countries like France and the United States, where it seemed firmly rooted and inviolable. In many societies liberated from Marxist rule, democracy doesn't work properly, as in Ukraine, or is a caricature of itself, as in Serbia, or seems to hang by a thread, as in Russia and Poland. And in Latin America, where the authoritarian beast seemed vanquished, it has lifted its head again in Haiti and Peru and tirelessly besieges Venezuela.

The sad fact is that almost everywhere the majority values democracy only in contrast to what works less well, not for what it is in itself or one day could be. When compared with the fundamentalist satrapy of Iran, the dictatorship of Cuba, or the despotic regime of Kim Il Sung, democracy seems preferable. But how many would be willing to put their lives on the line—to risk everything—for a system that shows an increasing inability to solve problems and in so many countries seems paralyzed by corruption, routine, bureaucracy, and mediocrity?

The discrediting of the political class, which is accused of having expropriated the democratic system for itself and of governing in its own interests, behind the backs and in defiance of the common citizen, is discussed everywhere and to exhaustion. This chorus, which has allowed Jean-Marie Le Pen and the neofascist National Front to claim a considerable swath of the French electorate, has also been taken up by the apprentice dictator of Peru, Alberto Fujimori, who rails against "party-ocracy." It is the hobbyhorse of the Texan Ross Perot, too, who could surprise everyone in the upcoming U.S. elections and overthrow the country's traditional parties for the first time in history.

The exaggerations and demagoguery of critics like these aside, there is still plenty to find fault with, and this bodes ill for a system that, despite its flaws, has been the greatest champion in history of prosperity, liberty, and respect for human rights. The most serious problem democratic societies now face is the distance—sometimes great and sometimes enormous—separating those who govern from those who are governed. The main reason for this divide and lack of communication between the common citizen and those who decide from executive offices, ministerial cabinets, or parliamentary seats how common citizens live (and sometimes die) is not government's growing complexity (the bureaucratization of the state, so well analyzed by Max Weber). The main reason is a loss of confidence. The electorate votes for those who legislate and govern, but with ever rarer exceptions it doesn't believe in them. Voters go to the polls at fixed intervals and cast their ballots mechanically, as if resigning themselves to a ritual stripped of all significance. Sometimes they don't even take that trouble: abstention, a widespread phenomenon of liberal democracy, reaches dizzying levels in some countries.

This lack of participation is obvious at election time, but it is even more endemic and critical in the daily functioning of political parties, which are key institutions of democracy. Democracy is not conceivable without parties, associations formed, on the one hand, to ensure the pluralism of ideas and proposals and, on the other, to maintain a permanent dialogue between officials and citizens on a local and a national level. The democratic parties play that role less and less frequently because almost everywhere—in democracies young and old—fewer members take an active role and popular disaffection turns parties into professionalized bureaucracies or coteries of power brokers, with few if any ties to the bulk of the population from which they must receive their lifeblood.

A number of explanations are offered as to why there is such a broad lack of enthusiasm for our institutions when the health of a democracy depends in good measure on their constant renewal and creativity. But many of the explanations tend to confuse cause with effect. For example, it is claimed that political parties fail to inspire loyalty because they lack competent leaders, leaders endowed with the kind of charisma Weber described (never imagining the type of charismatic leader who would very soon be visited on Germany). The truth is the inverse, of course: it is because the citizen masses lose interest in the parties and in political life in general that such leaders do not appear. (Not long ago I read a survey of the career choices of students graduating with the highest grade point averages from North American universities: the great majority of them elected to work for corporations, and the next-largest group chose various liberal professions; only an insignificant minority chose politics.)

The common citizen's lack of faith and loss of confidence in his political representatives—the result of which is the general loss of authority of the political class—have come about, in essence, because reality has made the ethic of responsibility into a shameful farce, the luxury of the irresponsible. A kind of consensus has been established that reduces political activity in democratic societies to playacting. The things said or done are shorn of conviction and obey motives and designs unrelated to those explicitly stated by those who govern; the worst mischief and trickery are justified in the name of efficiency and pragmatism. In truth, the only justification for such mischief is society's tacit understanding that politics is a separate and cloistered space (similar to that which Johan Huizinga defined for games) with its own rules, its own discourse, and its own moral code, outside the boundaries and free of the rules that regulate the behavior of ordinary men and women.

This divide between two increasingly impermeable worlds is weakening democracy, causing many citizens to become disenchanted with their governments and making them vulnerable to the xenophobic and racist siren songs of a Le Pen, the authoritarian rabble-rousing of a Fujimori, the nationalist demagoguery of a Vladimír Meciar, and the anti-party populism of a Ross Perot. It also allows many beneficiaries of democracy to keep alive their romantic solidarity with Third World dictatorships.

That is why it is a good idea, as a first step toward the rebirth of the democratic system, to abolish the ethic of responsibility, which, in practice—where it matters—only serves to provide cynics with alibis. We must also demand of our representatives not the half-truths of responsibility but the full and unadorned truth, dangerous as it might be. Despite the obvious risks involved for the politician who chooses not to lie and instead imitates Churchill—offering blood, sweat, and tears to those who elect him—the odds will always be better in the middle and the long term for the survival and rebirth of the democratic system. There are not two moral systems, one for those who shoulder the immense task of guiding society and the other for those who suffer or gain from what is decided for them. There is only one, with its shared uncertainties, challenges, and dangers, in which conviction and responsibility go together like voice and word, or the two sides of a coin.

Berlin, July 1992

Postmodernism and Frivolity

❧ ❧

In an excellent and polemical collection of essays titled *On Looking into the Abyss* (1994), the historian Gertrude Himmelfarb attacks the culture of postmodernism, especially Michel Foucault's structuralism and Jacques Derrida's and Paul de Man's deconstruction, currents of thought that seem frivolous and artificial to her when compared with the traditional schools of literary criticism and historical study.

Her book is also an homage to Lionel Trilling, the author of *The Liberal Imagination* (1950) and many other works of cultural criticism that greatly influenced postwar intellectual and academic life in the United States and Europe and that today are scarcely remembered and almost never read. Trilling wasn't a liberal in the economic sense (his theories in that sphere were closer to social democratic), but he was a political liberal, as evidenced by his persistent defense of tolerance, which he considered the supreme virtue, and of the law as instrument of justice. Above all, he was a cultural liberal who believed deeply in ideas like the inevitability of progress and was convinced that great works of literature enrich our lives, make us better people, and are the bedrock of civilization.

To a postmodern critic these beliefs seem either preternaturally naïve or utterly idiotic, so much so that no one even bothers to refute them. Although only a few years separate the generation of Lionel Trilling from that of Derrida or Foucault, Professor Himmelfarb shows us that there is a vast abyss between the two. Members of the former are convinced that there is one human history, that the pursuit of knowledge is all-encompassing, that progress is truly possible, and that literature is an exercise of the imagination with roots in history and projections into a moral sphere; members of the latter relativize conceptions of truth and value to such an extent that they turn them into fictions, establish as axiomatic the belief that all cultures are equal, and dissociate literature from reality, confining the former to a separate world of texts which make reference to other texts without ever relating to human experience.

I don't fully share Himmelfarb's disdain for Foucault, because, despite all the sophisms and exaggerations for which he may justly be taken to task (his theories, for example, about the supposed "power structures" implicit in language, which always transmits the words and ideas that privilege powerful social groups), he must be recognized for having done more than most to give certain marginal experiences (of sexuality, social repression, madness) a place in cultural life. Nevertheless, Himmelfarb's criticisms of the way deconstruction has ravaged the field of the humanities seem irrefutable to me. It is to the deconstructionists that we owe, for example, the fact that today it is practically impossible to speak of the humanities—which is a symptom of intellectual decrepitude or scientific blindness.

Each time I've tackled Derrida's obscurantist prose and suffocating literary or philosophical analyses, I've felt I was miserably wasting my time. Not because I believe that all works of criticism must be useful (so long as they are entertaining or stimulating I'm satisfied) but because if literature is what Derrida believes it is—a succession or archipelago of isolated, impermeable "texts" that have no possible contact with outside reality and are therefore immune to all value judgments and all connection to the development of society and individual behavior—then why bother to deconstruct them? To what end those laborious efforts of erudition, of rhetorical archaeology, those arduous linguistic genealogies, which compare and contrast one text with another until one of those contrived intellectual deconstructions, like an animated void, is achieved? There is something deeply incongruous about a critical work that begins by proclaiming the essential inability of literature to influence life (or be influenced by it) and to transmit any kind of truths related to the human dilemma, and then turns so eagerly to the task of demolishing those monuments of useless words, often with unbearably pretentious intellectual self-congratulation. When the medieval theologians disputed the sex of the angels, they weren't wasting their time: as trivial as it seems, the question was somehow linked for them with matters as important as salvation or eternal damnation. But to dismantle verbal objects whose construction is at best considered an intense formal game—a wordy and narcissistically gratuitous action that teaches nothing about anything except itself and is devoid of moral sense—is to make literary criticism an exercise in masturbation.

Considering the influence that deconstruction has had on so many Western universities (especially in the United States), it comes as no surprise that literature departments are losing students (and filling up with con artists) and that fewer and fewer nonspecialist readers tackle works of literary criticism (which must be searched for with a magnifying glass in bookstores: it is not uncommon to find them in dusty corners between judo and karate manuals or Chinese horoscope books).

Trilling's generation, on the other hand, believed that literary criticism dealt with questions central to the human endeavor. This generation regarded literature as a perfect testament to the ideas, myths, beliefs, and dreams that make society work, and glimpsed in literature the secret frustrations and impulses that explain individual conduct. The faith of Trilling and his contemporaries in literature's power over life was so great that in one essay of *Beyond Culture* Trilling asks himself if the teaching of literature doesn't actually denaturalize and impoverish the object of study. His argument is summed up in this anecdote: "I asked them to look into the Abyss, and, both dutifully and gladly, they have looked into the Abyss, and the Abyss has greeted them with the grave courtesy of all objects of serious study, saying: 'Interesting, am I not?' " In other words, the academy neutralizes, trivializes, and renders abstract the tragic and unsettling humanity contained in works of the imagination, depriving them of their powerful vital force, of their capacity to change readers' lives. Professor Himmelfarb reviews with sadness all that has come to pass since Trilling worried that turning literature into an object of study would strip it of its soul and force, noting finally the cheerful nonchalance with which de Man, twenty years later, could use literary criticism to deconstruct the Holocaust: an intellectual act not so very different from that performed by the revisionist historians determined to deny the extermination of six million Jews by the Nazis.

I've reread Trilling's essay on the teaching of literature many times, especially when I myself must teach, which I am doing now in Washington, D.C., for a few months. It's true that there is something deceitful and paradoxical in subjecting works of the imagination to a pedagogical display which is inevitably schematic and impersonal (and involves homework, which—the final straw—must be graded). These works, after all, grew out of deep and sometimes heartrending experiences and real human sacrifices, and their true valuation must be decided not from the lectern but from the private and concentrated intimacy of reading, and must be measured by the effects and repercussions of reading on the private life of the reader.

I don't remember having any teachers who made me feel that a good book could bring us to the brink of the abyss of human experience and its potent mysteries. Literary critics, on the other hand, have done just that. I remember one especially, from the same generation as Lionel Trilling, who had the same effect on me as Trilling seems to have had on Professor Himmelfarb. This critic imbued me with his belief that the worst and the best of the human adventure were always present in books and that books helped us live. I refer to Edmund Wilson, whose *To the Finland Station*, an extraordinary essay on the evolution of socialist ideas and literature from Michelet's discovery of Vico to Lenin's arrival in St. Petersburg, fell into my hands in my student days. In those pages of crystalline prose, thinking, imagining, and inventing with the pen were revealed as magnificent ways of taking action and making a mark on history; in each chapter Wilson showed that great social upheavals were viscerally linked to the intangible world of ideas and literary fictions.

Edmund Wilson wasn't faced with Trilling's pedagogical dilemma, since Wilson never wanted to be a university professor. In fact, his tenure was much broader than that limited by the bounds of a university. His articles and reviews were published in magazines and newspapers (something a deconstructionist would consider an extreme form of intellectual degradation), and some of his best books—like the one on the Dead Sea Scrolls—were originally essays for *The New Yorker*. But writing for the general public didn't lessen his rigor or intellectual daring; rather, it made him strive always to write responsibly and clearly.

Responsibility and clarity go together with a certain conception of literary criticism, with the conviction that the realm of literature spans all of human experience since literature reflects experience and helps shape it. Along the same lines, this conception holds that literature should belong to everyone, since it draws upon the common resources of the species and we can always return to it to seek order when we seem buried in chaos, hope in moments of discouragement, and doubt and uncertainty when the reality that surrounds us seems too safe and predictable. On the other hand, if one believes that the role of literature is only to contribute to the rhetorical inflation of a specialized realm of knowledge, and that poems, novels, and plays proliferate with the sole object of producing formal tangles in the linguistic oeuvre, the critic may, like so many postmodernists, abandon himself with impunity to the pleasures of conceptual folly and muddy expression.

Washington, D.C., March 1994

Tragicomedy of a Jew

❦

As is true of Cervantes, Goethe, and Dante, everything there is to say and more has already been said about Shakespeare, which means that all new analyses or interpretations are almost automatically stale, further exercises in erudition or triviality added to the heaps of literary criticism that surround and sometimes seem to stifle great works. And yet the book that John Gross has devoted to Shylock, one of Shakespeare's most enduring characters, may be read with the kind of pleasure and interest aroused by genuinely original works.

A literary character is immortalized and passes into legend when, like Don Quixote, Hamlet, or King Arthur, he embodies a condition or ideal formed over time by men and women of very different origins who see expressed in his image and deeds certain fears and ambitions or experiences that they need in order to live or that they cannot liberate themselves from. The moneylender of Venice, intent on collecting his pound of flesh from Antonio, who isn't able to pay his debt in time, belongs to that mysterious genealogy of mythical characters born out of the prejudice, fear, and fascination with cruelty that have persisted through centuries and cultures without fading and whose appeal is as fresh today as it was when they first appeared on the vanished stages of Elizabethan theater.

The anti-Semitism that produced Shylock was, in Shakespeare's time, religious. In the years immediately prior to the creation of *The Merchant of Venice*, there was a political scandal in England in which the queen's doctor, a Portuguese Jew accused of trying to poison his mistress, was hanged, drawn, and quartered. General hostility toward the Jews, with its ancient medieval roots, was heightened by this episode, and critics see an echo of it in, for example, Christopher Marlowe's *The Jew of Malta*, whose protagonist is the epitome of evil. When Shakespeare, working from an ancient legend with both Roman and Italian versions, set out to write his play, he did so with the intent—no matter how you look at it—of exploiting his contemporaries' anti-Semitic sentiments, revived by the affair of the Portuguese doctor.

The final result was not, however, simply a caricature or a crystallization of religious prejudice into gruesome fiction; it was much more complex and difficult to classify. As John Gross demonstrates in his book, it is ridiculous to try to deconstruct *The Merchant of Venice* by reading between the lines and discovering in it a denunciation or rejection of anti-Semitic prejudice. That prejudice is present in the text in its original version, and to deny it is to distort the work just as surely as it was distorted in Germany in the 1930s, when the Nazis used it to illustrate and justify their racist theories. In reality, the racial angle does not come into play at all in Shylock's story; his daughter, Jessica, and he himself, at the end of the play, become ordinary members of society, which is to say they are integrated into the Christian flock. In Hitler's view, the Jewish condition was irreversible, which is why the Jews had to be physically liquidated.

Whether religious or racial, anti-Semitism is always repugnant, one of the most destructive manifestations of human stupidity and evil. What is profoundly expressed in it is man's traditional mistrust of the man who is not part of his tribe, that "other" who speaks a different language, whose skin is a different color, and who participates in mysterious rites and rituals. But it is a generic sentiment, lumping together in its blindness and hatred all those who form part of the other tribe and making no distinctions or exceptions. Is Shylock a generic character, representing all those who, like him, deny the divinity of Christ and still await the coming of the Messiah? He is, but only in brief flashes, when he reminds his adversaries that Jews have eyes and hands too and that if they are pricked red blood comes from their veins. But he isn't when, mad with rage at the flight of his daughter, who not only has run away with a Christian but has robbed him as well, he clamors for vengeance and vents his resentment and anger on Antonio, who is turned by the circumstances into a sacrificial victim. And he isn't when he demands before the judges of the court that the law be applied literally and without mercy and reminds them that contracts, like regulations and decrees and ordinances, are made of concrete words and ideas translatable into acts, not emotions or virtuous gestures.

As a jealous father, as a duped moneylender, as a cold defender of the strict enforcement of the law (any law), Shylock attains terrible heights of inhumanity, but in his aggressive behavior we recognize many varieties of human expression that have nothing to do with Judaism. We witness the particular reaction of one man driven to violence by simmering hatred, a thirst for vengeance, and feelings of rejection and anger from which no Christian is exempt. The basic humanity of Shylock's inhumanity, which all those who see *The Merchant of Venice* can't help but recognize to some degree in themselves (though with a shudder), is perhaps the most extraordinary attribute of the character and the primary reason for his perennial appeal.

The counterpoint to these upwellings of humanity in Shylock

is the abundant evidence of scarce or nonexistent humanity, and even of inhuman conduct, in the Christians of the play. Except for Antonio, who is portrayed as a generous man, ready to help a friend even at the cost of his own life, the characters are hardly paragons of virtue. The wily Portia practically sells her love to the highest bidder, and Bassanio, the husband whom fate assigns her, goes looking for a rich woman and woos her with the help of a loan from his friend Antonio. And the love of Lorenzo and Jessica, which inspires the most beautiful lyrical speech of the play— isn't it the product of an escape/kidnapping and a theft committed by a daughter who breaks her father's heart?

In its fascinating catalogue of the transformations that the figure of Shylock has undergone, and its chronicle of nearly five centuries of the character's terrible history, John Gross's book reveals how each era, society, and culture extracted a very different lesson from that sinister tangle of conflicts and moral contradictions, and relates the different (sometimes radically different) political and ideological intentions with which *The Merchant of Venice* has been staged, while maintaining that this diversity of variations has never betrayed the basic nature of the work.

There is at least one aspect of Shylock's behavior that today's spectators are able to judge with greater understanding than their predecessors. The role that money and commerce play in the drama was seen very differently by Shakespeare's contemporaries. Business claims a central place in the story of the "pound of flesh," let us not forget. The disdain that the Christian gentlemen of Venice feel for Shylock is inspired as much by his profession—a usurer who loans money in exchange for interest—as by his religion. Making a profit from money lent, as Shylock does and as all the bankers of the future would do, seems to the noble Antonio and his friends a shameful act, a dastardly transgression. Shylock's sarcastic commentary in which he warns Antonio that if he keeps lending money without charging interest he will be ruined could seem repugnant in its pragmatism to upright Christians of the six-teenth century. Today we know that Shylock, in saying what he says and working to build his assets, is a herald of modernity, put-ting into practice a basic principle of economic activity—the quest for profit or capital gains—that is the starting point for the cre-ation of wealth and societal progress.

It is also true that this practice, if freely indulged and not mod-erated by a culture of solidarity and a certain ethic of responsibil-ity, can be taken to monstrous extremes. That is allegorically anticipated in *The Merchant of Venice* in the borrower's unholy agreement to give the moneylender a pound of his own flesh if he defaults on his loan. The two aspects of the Janus-faced capitalist system, which produced enormous inequalities of income and tremendous sacrifices in certain social sectors and at the same time launched the unstoppable development of the West, are foretold in the terrible trials of the Venetian Jew.

Recent literary criticism, especially in its academic form, has become difficult to read, its hieroglyphic deconstructions turning literature into a contrived unreality and its linguistic obsession re-ducing poetry, drama, and the novel to grammatical experiments, disdaining anything ideological, psychological, or historical, as if all of that didn't also form a substantial part of literature. The work that John Gross has devoted to the inexhaustible Shylock joins the great European critical tradition linking literary and artistic creation to all social and personal experiences. In it we fol-low the trail of the sources that Shakespeare used to construct the character and the historical and social context that shaped the story, the fascinating trajectory of the work from its first stagings to its most recent ones, and the play's mutations in space and time, as well as the good and bad uses to which it has been put by reli-gion, social doctrine, fanaticism, and politics.

Madrid, June 1994

God Will Provide

☙ ❧

Many people were surprised when it was announced that the Vatican will ally itself with Islamic regimes like the Iranian government and fundamentalist institutions like Cairo's Azhar University to oppose next week's United Nations conference in Egypt, which will study the impact of population growth on the future of humanity. This surprise was due to the widely held belief that there is an essential incompatibility between modern, civilized, tolerant Catholicism and the kind of obscurantist, intransigent, and primitive faith that catapults all the societies it controls back to the Middle Ages, as has happened in Iran and Sudan.

Those who believe in this incompatibility are victims of a confusion that, though explicable and quite common, has serious consequences when judgments must be made about conflicts with religious roots, like those still troubling Northern Ireland and Israel or devastating the former Yugoslavia. As far as origins, doctrine, and tradition are concerned, there is no distinguishing between modern and primitive, flexible and inflexible, or democratic and authoritarian religions. All (including benign Buddhism, which seems the most ethereal of beliefs) are dogmatic and self-contained, convinced that they alone possess the absolute truth and the moral authority necessary to impose that truth on the rest of the world, even if doing so requires bloodshed.

If the pincers and grills of the Inquisition have rusted and Catholicism no longer burns heretics at the stake, while in some ways fundamentalist Islam keeps such practices alive and shamelessly flaunts them (as Salman Rushdie and Taslima Nasrim can attest), that is because, unlike Muslim societies, which are still deeply religious, Christian societies have undergone a secularization—the separation of religion from general cultural life and political power—that ties the Church hand and foot and obliges it to act within the confines of a legal system that it may influence but doesn't devise or control. Thanks to this long process, which began with the Protestant Reformation and reached a high point with the French Revolution, there is such a thing as democracy and we are able to speak of a culture of freedom.

Please don't deduce from this that I agree with the anarchists (or with the original Marxists, who believed that religion was "the opiate of the masses") that society must be liberated from all churches in order for man to achieve his full potential, even if that means burning convents and killing priests and nuns. On the contrary, although personally I am agnostic, I am firmly convinced that religion plays a very important role in society and that it provides an essential spiritual life and moral guidance for the immense majority of human beings, who are plunged into confusion and dangerous moral anomie by an exclusively secular culture (contemporary Western reality provides plentiful proof of this). So long as there is a clear separation between church and state that allows the latter to restrain the former when it oversteps the bounds of the spiritual and pretends to set itself up as a temporal power, religion is a basic ingredient of civilization.

The separation of church and state is not always easy. It requires maintaining and constantly readjusting a precarious balance, and if that balance is not preserved, basic tenets of individual sovereignty and human rights are threatened, and the very foundations of our precious culture of freedom may collapse. Nothing proves that better than the very prickly subject of birth control, or "the woman's right to choose," as it is euphemistically called in the document the United Nations has prepared for the Cairo conference, where birth control will be the target of a relentless offensive by the Catholic-Islamic alliance newly established for that purpose.

The Catholic Church has every right in the world to ask its members to abstain from using methods of contraception other than "biological" ones, to condemn abortion, and to devise public campaigns to make its prohibitions law, but it doesn't have the right to prevent citizens from using birth control if the law permits it or to prevent them from fighting for legalization. The conflict has no solution because in this case the law of Caesar and the law of God—or, less apocalyptic, reason and dogma—are categorically opposed: the Church can't be asked to approach the matter rationally and subject what it sees as a question of faith to deliberation and a vote.

No matter how solid and overwhelming the rational arguments for contraception may be, they always collapse when countered with divine pronouncements. If God himself has decided that man and woman may only make love in order to conceive and that the ultimate function of the female body is sacred procreation, what use are thousands of miserably pedestrian statistics that show that the practical end result of this belief is the condemnation of hundreds of millions of women to a life of animal servitude; the peopling of the earth with miserable children, most of whom die of hunger and terrible illnesses before they reach the age of reason; and the miring of Third World nations, all saddled with galloping population rates, in underdevelopment and poverty? Could the scientific fact that the 5.6 billion people living on the earth today will have become some 12 billion by the middle of the twenty-first century if effective birth control is not adopted immediately on a worldwide scale have any effect on an ineluctable decision made at the beginning of time by a Supreme Being—even if it is shown that such a rise in population will multiply today's suffering and social disasters and generate unspeakable holocausts and apocalypses for the poor, who will be the earth's great majority?

The problem is complicated further when the Catholic Church, instead of arguing against birth control simply on the basis of a dogmatic (and irrational) truth revealed by a God who in his infinite and mysterious wisdom has decided to make physical love solely a genetic investment and women permanent reproductive machines—an argument only valid for believers, and one the Church doesn't have to pretend that nonbelievers should accept—insists on bolstering its case with sociopolitical considerations and secular ideologies that are meant to possess universal credibility. It is in the name of the dignity and sovereignty of the people of the Third World that the Vatican critics of the upcoming Cairo conference now oppose any kind of agreement on population control, claiming that the world's rich nations intend to impose the use of contraceptives and abortion on Third World countries in an imperialist and neocolonialist attempt to destroy their cultures and make them easier to exploit.

This is demagoguery, and it should be understood as a cover-up for what is ultimately no more than a religious and dogmatic argument, a mere strategy intended to seduce uneducated and unwitting audiences who have been prepared by Third World rhetoric to swallow anything that seems anti-Western. It is just like the comical reasoning that Islamic fundamentalists use to justify *shari'a*, the Koranic law that legitimizes authoritarianism and makes women second-class citizens or objects: in their defense, Muslim societies claim they are only protecting their "cultural identity," which the debased Western countries of Europe and America would like to corrupt.

In fact, the document prepared by the United Nations for the Cairo conference is remarkably judicious. It gives all the pertinent information on world population growth and its tragic consequences in the Third World, but it avoids making unilateral pronouncements on specific birth-control policies. Rather, it emphasizes a fact that modern history corroborates over and over again: population growth slows or stops when women are no longer discriminated against and exploited and are given equal access to education, work, and social responsibility. In other words, support for women's rights and the struggle to topple the legal and cultural (or religious) obstacles that limit their freedom and decision-making ability is the most critical and productive way to contain the population explosion.

It is clear that besides emphasizing women's rights, all birth-control plans should categorically exclude any kind of coercion, like the policy of forced sterilization established in India under Indira Gandhi, and should also shun legal force or intimidation tactics, like those used now in China and other Asian countries, which take jobs and benefits away from couples who have more than one child. All governments are obliged to provide their citizens with a strong legal framework, information, and services that allow them to plan their families responsibly, in accordance with their convictions and means. No state should force anyone to have fewer children than she wants or more than she wants or is able to care for. This simple policy, dictated by common sense, is nevertheless a utopian ideal in societies that have not yet embraced democracy, and that is why there is reason to fear that the crescent moon and the cross will have more success in their reactionary and antifeminist conspiracy than they deserve at the Cairo conference.

Fuschl, August 21, 1994

Aid for the First World

❧ ❦

I was moved when I saw photographs of the three hundred tents set up in front of the Ministry of the Economy on the Paseo de la Castellana in Madrid by the activist members of the 0.7% Movement: students and hippies, the young and the old, professionals and housewives, artists, workers and the unemployed, all camped there day and night to pressure the government to devote 0.7 percent of Spain's gross domestic product to help the Third World. They've announced a hunger strike in support of their effort, and all their declarations, as well as the slogans on their banners, exude the purest selflessness, generosity, and idealism. I send them my thanks for their honorable gesture.

This thanks I offer not in the name of the poor countries of the world but in the name of the rich ones—that is to say, the great Western democracies, among which Spain happily now figures— which are urgently in need of such movements and campaigns. Demonstrations like the one organized by the 0.7% Movement are revitalizing and morally enriching, and show Spaniards (and Europeans) something that many now find difficult to believe: that civic action and political life aren't just vehicles for the unscrupulous and the power hungry, dishonest professionals and plodding bureaucrats, but can also channel the solidarity, decency, imagination, and altruism of those who want to combat injustice and make the world a better place.

That said, I should also make clear that even if the 0.7% Movement achieved its goal and 0.7 percent of Spain's income was pledged to aid poor countries, the fate of those countries would not change significantly. In fact, even if the United States, Japan, and all the prosperous countries of Europe decided to follow Denmark's magnificent example and give not 0.7 percent but an astounding 3 percent of their GDP to developing countries, it would make little difference.

This is because there is no direct link between the two economic realities, despite what is believed by the admirable idealists—"the Comanches," as my friend Rosa Montero charmingly calls them—who are ashamed by the First World's prosperity and feel guilty when they compare it with the misery of African or Latin American or (now only some) Asian countries. It's not true that rich countries are rich because other countries are poor or, conversely, that the misery of the Third World is the result of the affluence of the First. This was true, though only in a relative sense, in the past. In the present, it is simply false. And nothing does more harm to backward and wretched countries than this false belief that frees them from all blame for their condition and shifts the responsibility for the suffering and hunger of their poor onto the shoulders of developed countries, which are accused of bleeding them to death, sucking all the wealth out of them like vampires. If this were so, there would be no hope for them, and they would have no alternative but to cry and lament their fate or berate the unfortunate West while waiting passively with hand outstretched for their tormentors to take pity on them, stop tormenting them, and lift them out of their misery.

The truth is that today poverty is "produced" in the same way as wealth and that both are options within reach of any nation. It is also true that many underdeveloped countries, because of the infinite corruption of their ruling classes, the wild squandering of their resources, and the foolish economic policies of their governments, have become efficient machines for producing the atrocious conditions in which their people live. But take note: I refer here to the people, not their rulers, who often enjoy an *Arabian Nights*–style opulence. For example, the outrageous wastefulness and thievery of the populist governments of Venezuela (not just a rich country but an extremely rich one) have managed to ruin the nation, with the majority of its people getting a little poorer each day while its millionaires spirit their millions abroad.

In a Zaire decimated by famine and epidemics, the great Mobutu keeps governing unperturbed in the middle of disease and death, always sporting his jaunty leopard-skin cap: his personal wealth, deposited in Swiss banks and entirely the product of pillage, is calculated to be between three and four billion dollars. This sum is on a par with that filched from the Philippine nation by another famous Third World head of state, the deceased president Marcos. And how much must the Duvalier family fortune be worth, amassed by Papa Doc and increased by Baby Doc, who is now drinking the bitter champagne of exile on the Côte d'Azur? Low estimates put it at hundreds of millions of dollars and high estimates at five times that: either way, it represents a true commercial and financial feat, considering it had to be squeezed out of Haiti, the poorest country in the world. And how to calculate what percentage of the astronomical sums that Fidel Castro received from the Soviet Union (between five and ten billion dollars a year, over three decades) was squandered in military escapades and mad experiments in social engineering and collectivism, making Cuba a nation of beggars?

Moving on to a more positive topic, what nation has produced the most billionaires over the last twenty years? The United States? Japan? Germany? No: Mexico. This statistic could be construed as encouraging (if those billions were honestly earned) or sinister (if they came from commercial privilege and from political trafficking). I learned it barely two days ago from Kevin Rafferty, a leading British economic reporter who covers the East and for years has documented in his stories the flip side to the Third World's impoverishment at the hands of its bloodsucking rulers; that is to say, the formidable economic development of countries like South Korea, Taiwan, Hong Kong, Singapore, Thailand, and Malaysia, thanks to the opening up of their economies and their entry into the world market.

Real help for the Third World can't come in the form of handouts, noble or well intentioned as they might be. The sad reality is that in the great majority of cases, this money doesn't reach the people for whom it was intended (the starving, the sick ravaged by disease and without access to hospitals, the peasants lacking seeds or tractors) but goes straight into the bottomless pockets of the Mobutus and the Marcoses or serves to enrich petty military bosses or faction leaders. What these minor warlords don't steal and return to the Western banks where they keep their private accounts, they spend purchasing arms with which to kill each other, trying to seize power or maintain themselves in power forever.

The best aid the democratic West can give the oppressed and ravaged nations of the Third World is help in liberating them from their oppressors and ravagers, since these are the chief obstacles to breaking the infernal cycle of poverty. The West must also do business with the Third World: those borders of Europe, Japan, and the United States that are still shut must be opened or at least partially opened to admit products from developing countries. The West's protectionism and Western governments' complacency toward—in many cases, complicity with—Third

World despots must be combated. The governments of democratic developed nations should be urged to cut all ties with dictatorships and impose diplomatic and economic sanctions on
them; at the same time, they should actively help those fighting to
establish law-abiding, independent civil governments in their
countries, and foster cooperation and business exchanges with
democratic regimes.

The message to be sent from the European Union to the nations of Africa, Latin America, and Asia is this: escape from
poverty is possible, and it depends above all on each country's own
efforts. To counteract the curse of underdevelopment and move
from producing poverty to producing wealth, as so many Asian
countries have done and some countries in Latin America are beginning to do, certain basic conditions must be established. Respect for the law and freedom must be ensured, and reforms must
be enacted that transfer responsibility for production to civil society and take it away from the state (always the principal source of
corruption), that reward competition and private enterprise, and
that open the borders to outside market forces (the quickest way
to rescue and modernize an economy no matter how primitive it
is initially).

If such is the situation, why cheer a campaign like the 0.7%
Movement's, which seems to be based on a wrongheaded idea
about the true needs of poor countries? I've already said why, and
now I'll say it again: what the "Comanches" are doing may not
help the Third World much, but it does help Spain and Europe.
Democratic culture—which is now also Spanish culture—needs
nothing quite so much these days as a renewal of civic enthusiasm,
clarity of purpose, and faith in the system and in peaceful methods
of altering government policy, all values embodied in those who
defy pneumonia and aching backs in their three hundred tents on
the Castellana. What they are doing stands in refreshing ethical

contrast to the ugly, suffocating images of the democratic system on display in recent years in countries like France and Italy: wealthy men in power fleeing with their ill-gotten gains, bankruptcy bankers treated like heroes by the gossip rags, the constant report of sordid little underhanded deals carried out in the government's long shadow. One may disagree with the "Comanches," but only with the utmost respect and admiration.

London, October 1994

Italy Is Not Bolivia

❧ ❧

On October 3, in response to accusations by opposition critics that Italian prime minister Silvio Berlusconi was acting outside the constitutional framework, Giuliano Ferrara, spokesman for the Italian government, exclaimed indignantly at a press conference: "What country do you think this is? Bolivia?" Ferrara repeated the offense with another outburst a few days later, as I read in the October 21 issue of *L'Espresso*, criticizing Italy's Supreme Court by calling it a body "worthy of a South American country: *piú precisamente, di una Repubblica delle banane*" (more precisely, of a banana republic).

Simply put, this is what Ferrara meant to say on both occasions: "Don't forget, please, that Italy represents civilization, and therefore neither its government nor any other of its institutions can or should behave like those of certain little republics that exemplify barbarism." While acknowledging his right to criticize the many instances of barbarism that crop up everywhere in Latin America, I maintain that this spokesman of the Italian government is either a man behind the times in sore need of a political update or someone whose intelligence is impaired by stereotypes that cloud his vision.

Latin American countries are still plagued by many problems, but one of their triumphs is that none may be called a banana republic anymore. Only Cuba comes close to deserving that shameful sobriquet, because of the pterodactylian nature of the regime that has kept the island in thrall for thirty-four years and because Fidel Castro is the last survivor of a dynasty of all-powerful despots that once included Anastasio Somoza, Rafael Trujillo, Fulgencio Batista, and Alfredo Stroessner. But not even Cuba now depends on a foreign power or an economic conglomerate, as was true half a century ago, when, for example, the United Fruit Company was the true power in at least half the countries of Central America and determined what laws would be passed, what ministers named, and who would win elections. That reliance on foreign companies has ended even in Central America, thanks to the gradual opening up of its countries' economies. Participation in the world of competition and diversity has returned a measure of independence to the region that was inconceivable when its principal resources were monopolistically exploited by single companies—a modest measure, certainly, since these are still poor countries and true independence is only guaranteed by prosperity (although one could claim that in today's interdependent world, not even the richest countries enjoy total sovereignty).

It seems Ferrara is unaware that after a handful of Asian countries, Latin America is the most dynamic economic region of the world, judging by the high rates of its production of wealth and the volume of foreign investment it attracts—5.5 billion dollars last year, including sums from a growing number of Italian investors—to such an extent that some countries, like Chile and Argentina, are beginning to take steps to slow the pace, fearful that the hemorrhage of capital might spark the inflation they sacrificed so much to contain. Naturally, this promising reality—confirmed once more a few weeks ago by the International Monetary

Fund and World Bank reports and by the most recent world economic balance sheet prepared by *The Economist*—doesn't mean that anyone believes poverty has disappeared in Latin America, which is the idiotic accusation voiced by certain entrenched progressives when they hear, for example, that economic development in Chile is so effective that it has created a million jobs in under five years. It is evident that despite the country's impressive advances, intolerable pockets of poverty persist in Chile. But it is also clear, and this is of paramount importance, that thanks to the reforms and the economic model on which the Chilean nation has passed sentence in two elections, Chile has stopped producing poverty and has started to produce wealth at a fast clip and the benefits now reach even the most depressed sectors of society, though not in equal proportion.

What is happening in Chile is also beginning to happen in a dozen other Latin American countries, and most opt for privatization of their economies, entry into the world market, and balanced budgets: in sum, the establishment of market economies, which is what allowed Chile to take off in a way that has earned it the well-deserved respect of the rest of the world. Twenty years ago Chile was begging for assistance from international organizations to stave off collapse, and today its businesses are financing the development of Peru, Bolivia, and Argentina. Of course, there are exceptions to the rule, blots on a continent that seems to be in the midst of a renaissance after doing everything possible to stagnate or slip backward for much of its history. One of those blots is Venezuela, a country astoundingly rich in natural resources that is rapidly losing ground as a result of the kind of populist policies—nationalizations, the government's increasing interference in economic life, controls, and subsidies—that pushed Latin American poverty to near-apocalyptic extremes in the 1960s and 1970s.

What surprised me most about Ferrara's misinformation is that a good number of Latin American countries have already accomplished (and without making too much fuss about it) what his own government—headed by Berlusconi—has been trying to accomplish in Italy, without success. Every time the Italian prime minister speaks, doesn't he declare that if the public sector is not drastically shrunk, the country's fiscal deficit will never be reduced, and that if Italian businesses don't open themselves up to competition, they will never be able to face the challenges of a globalized world economy? Well, many of the countries that Ferrara calls banana republics have grasped that, have proceeded accordingly, and are just now beginning to reap the first rewards of their reforms.

One of those countries is Bolivia. I'm absolutely certain that if Ferrara knew what has happened there, he would profess the same respect and admiration for the country that I do. Until fifteen years ago Bolivia was, in political terms, purely barbaric: since 1835 the average period its presidents had lasted in office was one year, and its history as a republic, besides boasting more than a hundred coups d'état, claimed the sad distinction of featuring a handful of dictators who broke all records for savagery and eccentricity on a continent where, as everyone knows, such traits were common. In 1982, President Hernán Siles Suazo introduced a number of extremely foolish and destructive economic policies, comparable to the political misdeeds of Mariano Melgarejo (the celebrated petty tyrant who, with great geographic befuddlement, declared war on England, which caused Queen Victoria to order that Bolivia be wiped off the British world map). In other words, he began to print money frenziedly in order to fund the no less frenzied populist measures that he adopted to satisfy everyone. As a result, inflation in Bolivia reached a staggering 50,000 percent, and its industrial infrastructure fell to pieces, while its poor, the vast majority of the nation's population, became destitute and began literally to die of hunger. Without understanding what was happening, and still claiming that sinister imperialism had caused the tragedy, the pathetic demagogue found himself obliged to call early elections. And this was how Victor Paz Estenssoro came to power—for the second time in his life. His credentials were dangerous: during the 1952 revolution, which brought the MNR (Nationalist Revolutionary Movement) to power, he expropriated the tin mines, the country's main source of income, and nationalized much land, as well as practicing a more orthodox form of populist politics in the social sphere.

But with time the old fox had become wise and pragmatic. In the first week of his second administration he adopted a package of audacious and extraordinarily far-reaching measures, which, along with deadly inflation, wiped out the public companies—in other words, the tin mines, the major source of the immense fiscal deficit that the Bolivian state had been shouldering for four decades. While putting the public finances in order, he also stabilized the currency, trimmed the deficit-ridden public sector, opened his country's borders to international trade, and came to an agreement with international credit organizations to relieve Bolivia of the condition of pariah country—"non-eligible," in IMF jargon—to which it had been reduced by previous governments.

Even more notable than the radicalism of these reforms is that they were made democratically, with respect for the freedom of the press and the rights of a political and union opposition, and that for the most part, thanks to his prestige and power of persuasion, Paz Estenssoro won the support of the Bolivian people and forged a consensus that gave the country a stability that has lasted now for almost ten years. The government of Jaime Paz Zamora, which followed that of Paz Estenssoro and had the support of the former dictator Hugo Banzer, respected Paz Estenssoro's model of reform, and now the government of Gonzalo Sánchez de Lozada (Paz Estenssoro's minister of the economy in 1985) is perfecting it and has given fresh impetus to the modernization of the

Bolivian economy, integrating it into world markets. The country's gigantic sacrifice is beginning to show results: after coming through an incredibly difficult period of stabilization, Bolivia is now growing steadily and is one of the Latin American countries that proportionally attracts the most investment. After centuries of paralysis, political chaos, and systematic impoverishment, Bolivia today is free from inflation, a country with a balanced budget, a genuinely democratic government, and more or less solid institutions that seems firmly embarked on its battle with underdevelopment.

It is true that an examination of its political class reveals some conspicuous scoundrels, like the ex-dictator Luis García Meza—the first drug-trafficking head of state in the hemisphere—but he is in prison in Brazil, and the judges there have agreed to extradite him to Bolivia, where he will doubtless spend many years behind bars. And even so, Bolivia's politicians seem in general quite a bit more respectable than, shall we say, their Italian counterparts, among whom one would hunt in vain, even with the aid of powerful searchlights, for someone to respect as much as the octogenarian Paz Estenssoro, who, poor as a church mouse and revered by his fellow citizens, is whiling away his last years watering the garden of his modest little house in Tarija. None of Bolivia's politicians or ex-politicians is the match for Bettino Craxi, who ceaselessly transfers black-market money and gold bars into secret Swiss bank accounts, or for any of the many Italian ministers and ex-ministers being investigated today for their links to the Mafia and other shady activities.

So, in a sense, the misguided Giuliano Ferrara was absolutely right: Italy isn't Bolivia, luckily for the Bolivians.

Rome, October 1994

The Death of the Great Writer

꒜ ꒛

In a recently published book, *La Mort du grand écrivain*, Henri Raczymow maintains there are no longer any "great writers" because democracy and the marketplace are incompatible with the model of the intellectual mentor, as represented by figures like Voltaire, Zola, Gide, or Sartre, and will ultimately prove the death of literature. Although his book refers only to France, it is evident that his conclusions, if they stand, hold true for all modern societies.

Raczymow's argument is coherent. It takes as its starting point a verifiable premise: that in our day there is not a single figure with the stature of a writer like Victor Hugo, who radiated a prestige and authority that transcended his circle of readers as well as solely artistic matters and made him an embodiment of public consciousness, an archetype whose ideas, opinions, way of life, gestures, and obsessions served as the model of behavior for a vast sector of society. What living writer today inspires the fervent devotion that made provincial youths vow to die for Hugo, as reported by Valéry?

According to Raczymow, for a cult like that of the "great writer" to flourish, literature must take on a sacred, magical aura and play the role of religion, something which, he says, began to happen during the Enlightenment, when the iconoclastic philosophers, after dispatching God and the saints, left a void that the republic had to fill with secular heroes. Writers and artists were the prophets, mystics, and supermen of a new society educated in the belief that the arts and letters had the answer to everything and could express, through their best practitioners, the noblest impulses of the human spirit. This atmosphere and these beliefs fostered careers that were like religious crusades, embarked on with devotion, fanaticism, and nearly superhuman ambition. From this would come the literary accomplishments of great creators like Flaubert, Proust, Balzac, and Baudelaire, who, although very different from one another, shared the conviction (also shared by their readers) that they were working for posterity and that if their oeuvre outlived them, it would serve to enrich humanity, or, as Rimbaud said, to "change life," and would justify their existence long after their deaths.

Why are no contemporary writers spurred on as their predecessors were by the promise of immortality? Because all have become convinced that literature isn't eternal but perishable and that books are written, published, read (sometimes), and then vanish forever. This isn't an expression of faith, like the one that made literature a supreme and timeless undertaking and a pantheon of incorruptible titles, but a crude objective reality: today books aren't passports to the eternal but slaves of the present ("Of the here and now," says Raczymow). Those who write them have been ejected from the Olympus where they were enthroned, safe from the contingencies of mediocre life, and *leveled* with the "clotted city masses" of democracy who so revolted the aristocratic Rubens—and also Flaubert, for whom the democratic dream consisted of "elevating the worker to the same level of *bêtise* as the petit bourgeois."

Two mechanisms of democratic society have contributed to the desanctification of literature, making it a purely industrial product. One is sociological and cultural. The leveling out of citizens, the extinction of elites, the establishment of tolerance—the right to "difference and indifference"—and the subsequent development of individualism and narcissism have abolished our interest in the past and our preoccupation with the future, centering our attention on the present and turning the satisfaction of our immediate needs into our primary goal. Victim of this presentism has been the realm of the sacred, an alternate reality that no longer has any reason to exist when a community, whether satisfied or dissatisfied, accepts the world it lives in as the only possible one and renounces the "alterity" of which literary creations are token and sustenance. In a society like this there may be books, but literature is dead.

The other mechanism is economic. "There is no democracy, alas, apart from that of the market," says Raczymow. In other words, the book, stripped of its status as religious or mythical object, becomes a mere good at the mercy of the frenetic ups and downs—the iron law—of supply and demand, according to which "the book is a product and one product eliminates another, even one by the same writer." The effect of the vortex in which no book comes to rest, all passing through and none returning, is the banalization of literature, since it counts now only as a product for immediate consumption, an ephemeral entertainment, or a source of information that expires as soon as it appears.

Of course, the great instrument of democracy is the television, not the book. It diverts and distracts leveled-out society, administering to us the doses of humor, emotion, sex, and sentiment that we require in order not to be bored. The small screen has managed to fulfill the outsize ambition that always burned in the heart of literature and that literature never satisfied: to reach everyone, to make all of society partake of its "creations." In the "kingdom of narcissistic play," books have become entirely dispensable, though that doesn't mean they'll disappear. They'll continue to proliferate, but they will be emptied of their former substance and will enjoy the precarious and fleeting existence of novelties, jumbled together and interchangeable on the chaotic sea where all a work's merits are decided by its publicity campaign or the theatrical talents of its author. Democracy and the marketplace have engineered another twist: now that there is no public opinion but just a public, it is the writer-stars—those who know how to make the most of the audiovisual media, the mediagenic—who give prestige to books, and not vice versa, as was true in the past. As a result, we have reached a level of grim degradation best anticipated by Tocqueville: the era of writers who "prefer success to glory."

Although I don't entirely share Raczymow's pessimistic view of the fate of literature, I read his book with much interest, because it seems to me that he puts his finger on an often overlooked problem: the new role our modern, open society has imposed on the writer. It is true that the mandarin writer no longer has a place in today's world. Figures like Sartre in France or Ortega y Gasset and Unamuno in their time, or Octavio Paz, served as guides and teachers on all the important issues and filled a void that only the "great writer" seemed capable of filling, whether because few others participated in public life, because democracy was nonexistent, or because literature had a mythical prestige. In a free society, the influence that a writer exerts—sometimes profitably—over submissive societies is useless: the complexity and multiplicity of the problems make him talk nonsense if he tries to give his opinion on everything. His opinion and positions may be very well thought out, but not necessarily better thought out than those of anyone else—scientists, professionals, technicians—and in any case, his opinions must be judged on their own merits and not approved merely because they come from someone who writes well. This desanctification of the persona of the writer doesn't seem a bad thing to me; on the contrary, it puts things in their proper place, since, in truth, someone talented at literary creation and capable of writing good novels or beautiful poems isn't necessarily also generally discerning.

Nor do I believe that we should rend our clothes because, as Raczymow says, in modern democratic society the novel must above all "divert" and "entertain" to justify its existence. Haven't the works of literature that we most admire always done exactly that—books like *Don Quixote* or *War and Peace* or *The Human Condition* that we read over and over again and that each time hypnotize us just as they did the first time? It's true that in an open society with multiple mechanisms for the display and debate of the problems and aspirations of social groups, literature must be entertaining above all or it will simply cease to exist. But amusement and entertainment are not incompatible with intellectual rigor, imaginative audacity, the free flight of fantasy, or elegant expression.

Instead of falling into depression and considering himself an obsolete being rejected by modernity, today's writer should feel stimulated by the formidable challenge of creating a literature worthy of our times and able to reach the vast potential public that awaits it, now that, thanks to democracy and the marketplace, so many human beings know how to read and can buy books, something that was never the case in the past when literature was, in effect, a religion and the writer a little god to whom "the immense minorities" rendered tribute and adoration. The curtain has undoubtedly fallen on those pontificating and narcissistic writers; but the show can go on if their successors contrive to be less pretentious and very amusing.

London, November 1994

Trench Town Rock

F aced with the inexorable advance of Cromwell's forces, which invaded Jamaica in 1655, the Spanish colonists freed their fifteen hundred slaves, who disappeared into the wild. In the turbulent centuries to come, they would reappear under the name Maroons (derived from the term *cimarrón*, meaning fugitive slave) and enveloped in an aura of indomitability. From this fierce lineage Marcus Garvey was born in 1887, apostle of negritude and the African-American diaspora. Without Garvey, the cult of Rastafarianism would never have transcended its Jamaican borders; without Garvey's teachings, Bob Marley as we know him would never have existed.

It is to Garvey that the prophetic warning is attributed (though historians dispute it): "Look to Africa for the crowning of a Black king; he shall be the redeemer." Years later, in 1930, Ras Tafari Makonnen was named emperor of Ethiopia and proclaimed negus (king of kings). In Jamaica, on the trees and roofs of villages and on the walls of ghettos, devout reproductions of Haile Selassie's face and the green, red, and gold of the Ethiopian flag began to appear. The faithful of the new religion were of humble origin, and their doctrine was simple: Jah (apocope of Jehovah) would lead his people back to Ethiopia at a secret hour, bringing them out of Babylon (the world dominated by white men, vice, and cruelty). That moment was drawing near, because Jah had been incarnated in the monarch of Addis Ababa. The Rastas spurned alcohol, tobacco, meat, seafood, and salt and obeyed the Levitical injunction (25:5) not to cut their hair, beards, or nails. Their rite of communion and basic ceremony was the smoking of ganja (marijuana), the sacred plant ennobled by King Solomon, from whose tomb it sprang.

The first time that Robert Nesta Marley saw a Rasta was in Nine Miles, a hamlet in the parish of St. Ann, where he was born in 1945. Son of a black woman and a white man, who married her but abandoned her immediately afterward, the mulatto boy listened raptly to the medieval stories of Prester John with which the village wise man, an inspired teller of tales, entertained his listeners. The appearance one day of a man with a nest of snakes on his head and a stormy look in his eye, a man who seemed to float rather than walk, frightened the child, who dreamed of him that night. Marley's conversion to Rastafarianism would come much later.

Nine Miles must not have changed much since then. It is still a very poor village at the summit of a steep mountain range, which one reaches by following an extremely long, winding, and precipitous path. The wooden shack where Bob Marley was born doesn't exist anymore. The faithful are rebuilding it in cement, and they've planted a clump of ganja at the threshold. His tomb is higher up, on another peak that must be scaled on foot and from which, I'm told, on the black day of the burial one could see a winding column of mourners many miles long. Here is the stone where he would sit to meditate and compose, and here, his guitar. A tapestry embroidered by Ethiopians adorns the shrine, which must be entered barefoot and from which hang, like votive offerings, photographs, newspaper clippings, little flags, and even the hood ornament of Marley's car, a BMW, his favorite because its initials united those of his name and that of the Wailers, the musical group with which he rose to fame.

The Rasta acting as our guide is taking communion, and a North American couple who hitched a ride in our van are partaking as well. The visit includes a walk through a large field of sacred plants. Since marijuana is in theory prohibited in Jamaica, I ask the communion-taker whether he has ever had problems with the police. He shrugs his shoulders: "Sometimes they come and pull the plants up. So what? They grow back again. They're natural, right?" The prohibition is a formality. A few days before, at a Reggae Bash, or open-air concert in Ocho Rios, ganja was sold loose or rolled in spliffs in plain sight and vendors hawked it like soda or beer. And I don't think I've ever been in a public place in Jamaica without being offered some or seeing someone—and not just the Rastas—smoking it.

But it's not at Nine Miles, or at the mansion on Hope Road in Kingston, which his producer bought for him at the height of his career and now houses a museum dedicated to his memory, where clues to Bob Marley must be sought. The place to look is the slum neighborhood of Trench Town on the western edge of the Jamaican capital, since it was on its violent and spiritual streets that he spent his childhood and youth, where he became a Rasta and an artist, and where even now the social ferment of his philosophy and music can be breathed. The flies and the mounds of garbage, the motley collection of odds and ends with which the poor have built their tumbledown homes, are the same as those of any Third World slum. The difference is that here, besides seeing filth, hunger, and violence, one catches whiffs everywhere one turns of that "religiosity in a primal state" that Claudel glimpsed in Rimbaud's poetry. It emanates from the bearded face of the Lion of Judaea and from the Abyssinian colors that crop up on planks, gates, and corrugated metal and on the Merovingian caps in which the Rastas gather up their dreadlocks when they play soccer. When he was a boy, before the guru Mortimer Planner converted him and sent him down the mystical path that he would follow to the end, the Bob Marley who made himself known on these streets as a gang member, soccer player, and idler must have been a kind of Rimbaud: angel and demon, charming and coarse, brilliant and crude.

Like the Rastafarian cult, reggae is forged of the sweat and blood of Trench Town: mixed up in it are the atavistic rhythms of the tribes from which the Rastas' ancestors were snatched (the wall around the neighborhood is a reminder of the slave market to which they were brought), the accumulated suffering and rage of centuries of servitude and oppression, a messianic hope born out of a naïve reading of the Bible, nostalgia for a mythical Africa cloaked in sumptuous fantasies of Eden, and a desperate, narcissistic eagerness to find and lose oneself in music.

Bob Marley didn't invent reggae. At the time the Wailers recorded their first albums in the sixties in Kingston's rustic Studio One, it was already being promoted by the Skatalites and other Jamaican bands and had been established as the country's most popular music, despite the resistance of the authorities, who saw in the songs' lyrics an incitement to rebellion and crime. But Marley lent it his unmistakable personal stamp and gave it the dignity of religious rite and political gospel. The poetry with which he infused it moved his compatriots because in it they recognized their torments, the thousand and one injustices of life in Babylon, while also finding in it positive and persuasive reasons to struggle against adversity, to see themselves as Jah's chosen ones, a people about to pass the long test and enter the promised land, a people for whom redemption was imminent.

The music intoxicated them because it was their own traditional music, enriched with modern rhythms from America: rock, jazz, calypso, and hymns. The language Bob Marley spoke to them was the Jamaican patois, indecipherable to unseasoned ears, and his subjects were their quarrels, passions, and feuds, wrapped up in tenderness, mysticism, and pity. The word "authentic" has a dangerous ring when applied to the work of an artist: Is there such a thing as authenticity? Isn't it just a simple technical problem for any creator who knows his craft? For Bob Marley it never was, at least not after 1968, when as a result of his talks with Mortimer Planner he converted definitively to the Rastafarian religion, pouring his vast faith and his mystical *canaille*, his messianic dream and his musical knowledge, his passionate religious zeal and the dense jungle lament of his voice into the songs he composed.

This is why he, out of all the talented composers and artists of the sixties and seventies, was the only one who was not just inspired and original but also entirely authentic. He resisted all temptations, even life, the most beguiling, preferring to die at the age of thirty-six rather than allow the amputation of a cancerous toe, because his religion forbade it. True, he died a very wealthy man—he left thirty million dollars—but he enjoyed very little of his fortune. When one visits the house on Hope Road, the only luxury he permitted himself when his sudden fame made him rich, one notes how meager its luxury is compared with what any half-successful singer can afford today.

In the glory of his last years as well as in the poverty of his early years, his only joy was the dust and debris of Trench Town: kicking a soccer ball around; immersing himself in a mysterious introspection, from which he would return to the world either euphoric or in tears; scrawling a song in a school notebook; exploring a melody as he strummed his guitar; or swallowing the bittersweet smoke of his ganja cigar. He was generous and even prodigal with his friends and enemies, and the happiest day of his life was the day he was able to use his money to help the relatives of the ousted Haile Selassie, the despot he believed was God. When he visited Africa, he discovered that the continent was far from being the land of salvation for blacks that he had exalted in his credo and his songs, and from then on he became less concerned with negritude and more ecumenical, and his pacifist preaching and calls for spirituality were more intense.

One doesn't have to be religious to realize that without religion life would be infinitely emptier and grimmer for the poor and downtrodden and that societies have the religions they require. When I discovered that a son of mine and a group of his friends from school had become practitioners of the faith, I hated the Rastas' picturesque theological syncretisms, their marijuana communions, their horrible dietary laws, and their matted locks. But on the sad streets of Trench Town, or amid the poverty and neglect of the villages of St. Ann, the faith that for my son and his friends was doubtless a passing fad, a fickle extravagance of privileged youth, seemed to me a moving bid for a spiritual life, a bid against moral disintegration and human injustice. I ask forgiveness of the Rastas for what I once thought and wrote about them, and, along with my admiration for his music, I proclaim my respect for the ideas and beliefs of Bob Marley.

Ocho Rios, January 1995

The Prince of Doom

❧ ❧

When a writer's intelligence displays itself with as much brilliance as it does in the essays of Hans Magnus Enzensberger, and chooses its examples so aptly, in support of such a coherently developed and clearly and elegantly styled thesis, it suborns its readers, numbs their critical ability, and makes them accept the most fantastic assertions as undying truths. I'm a confessed victim of this *charme* each time I read Enzensberger, and I do so frequently, since I know of no essayist among my contemporaries who is more stimulating or who has a sharper sense of what is urgent, of the true issues of the day.

A good example of this is two recent essays, "The Great Migration" and "Civil War," collected in *Civil Wars*, which address subjects that will be at the center of international political debate for the immediate future, and possibly for a good part of the next century. Under the spell of his apocalyptic description of the world we live in—a world convulsed by the uprooting of peoples rejected everywhere, and threatened with annihilation by a blind, senseless, molecular, and protoplasmic violence—I experience the kind of "pleasing horror" that Borges says colors his nights when he has been reading fantastic stories. But once the spell of the reading has lifted, I feel the same way I did after I watched David Copperfield rise off the ground and levitate in Earl's Court: I loved it and I clapped, but I'm sure he didn't fly; I know I was taken in by his magic.

Although written separately, the essays refer to flip sides of the same phenomenon. Massive migrations, the cause and effect of a good part of the generalized violence that Enzensberger sees as spreading around the world like an epidemic—a kind of social AIDS—have always existed and, in certain eras, affected a greater percentage of the population than they do today. The difference is that in the past they were welcome—the European colonizers of the United States, Canada, or Australia; the Spanish, Turkish, or Italian guest workers in Germany and Switzerland in the six-ties—and today they inspire panic, a rejection that stirs up racism and xenophobia.

This change in attitude toward the immigrant in modern soci-ety originates in part in so-called structural unemployment, or the permanent disappearance of jobs, which leads the citizens of a country to fear that they will be displaced by foreigners in a shrinking labor market. It also springs in part from their feeling that their cultural identity is threatened when they are obliged to coexist with communities of different languages, customs, and re-ligions that don't want (or aren't permitted) to dissolve into the culture of the host country.

Enzensberger demolishes all the fantasies and myths about "homogeneous societies" (they don't exist) with impeccable argu-ments, and gives as an example German society, which, over the course of its modern history, has received and absorbed innumer-able waves of migration while sending emigrants all around the world. And he correctly points out that the repugnance prosper-ous countries feel for immigrants disappears when those immi-grants are rich. Who would deny a visa to the sultan of Brunei?

Don't Hong Kong bankers obtain British passports with ease? Couldn't a Lebanese, Iranian, or Paraguayan millionaire secure residency in Switzerland?

From all this he concludes that the real problem isn't immigration but poverty and that poverty is also the root and hidden cause of the violence spreading like wildfire around the globe. This far I can follow him. I can also follow his analysis of modern violence, though only up to a point, since I suspect that he exaggerates. According to him, violence no longer requires ideological or religious pretexts to erupt; it is frequently gratuitous and self-destructive, and it is turning the globe into a jungle of opposing tribes, where "all difference has become moral risk" and "a subway car can become a little Bosnia." And yet the nationalist fanaticism seething in the former Yugoslavia or the religious fanaticism that motivated the massacres in Algeria doesn't fit this *identikit*; behind such behavior lies not the mere sleepwalking impulse to kill or die but the conviction—doubtless stupid and criminal—that by acting in such a way one is fighting for a cause that justifies the terror. It is preferable that it should be so, in my opinion, because violence born of an idea or a belief can be combated, while the other, fated kind that supposedly comes metaphysically or genetically programmed in humans is impossible to fight and would inevitably hurtle us toward apocalypse.

Enzensberger's pessimism has as its point of origin the creation of the world market. The triumph of the capitalist system and the fact that today production and commerce can "only" happen on a global scale, within the network of economic interdependence in which businesses and companies function, have created an enormous mass of "structural" poor people (he calls them "the superfluous masses") who, in Third and First World countries (since the Second World has disappeared), live in purgatory, condemned to a marginalized existence from which there is no possibility of

escape. The violence shaking the planet results from the desperation that this tragic situation engenders in a considerable portion
of humanity.

Let's hear it from Enzensberger:

> Few dispute that the world market, now that it is no longer
> a vision of the future but a global reality, produces fewer
> winners and more losers as each year passes. This is not
> confined to the Second and Third Worlds, but applies
> equally in the core capitalist countries. Where, there, whole
> countries, or even whole continents, drop out of the inter-
> national exchange system, here, increasing sections of the
> population can no longer keep up in the competition for
> advantage that gets more brutal by the day . . . The general
> level of violence, you might conclude, is no more than the
> desperate reaction to a hopeless economic situation.

This catastrophism is not supported by events and is grounded in
an erroneous vision of capitalism, which is a much greedier system than Enzensberger supposes. Thanks to its innate voracity,
the system that the market created has been extending itself from
the ancient European cities where it was conceived into every corner of the world and has established a global market that is now,
in effect, an irreversible reality. As a result, poor countries today
can begin to stop being poor and, like Singapore, can develop an
economic structure even more solid than that of Great Britain, or
build up the astronomical financial reserves of Taiwan, or create a
million jobs in five years, as Chile has done.

As I was reading Enzensberger, Philippe de Villiers, the new
leader of the French extreme right, howled in Britain: "One
British worker is worth ninety Filipino workers!" And instead of
being pleased by this good news, he was alarmed and wanted to

use it to justify his theory in favor of protectionist barriers to defend France from such unworthy competition. I can understand that de Villiers, who seems to me a man of another age, might not realize that the cheap production of shirts and pants by Filipino workers also benefits French consumers and that it is very much to the advantage of French industry that the Filipinos, thanks to the markets that their factories are conquering, are raising their living standards and increasing their purchasing power with the result that they can now acquire the products that France is able to produce better than other countries. What I don't understand is how the prince of the European intelligentsia can side with the enemies of economic internationalization, convinced that the wealth of the world is finite, that it has reached its upper limit, and that from now on if one country prospers, another will get poorer.

The truth lies elsewhere. Capitalist countries wouldn't give China the velvet-glove treatment if they feared that its new industries would sink their own (since, as de Villiers would say, one worker from Chicago or Frankfurt is worth two hundred Chinese workers). Those producers are also consumers, and the development of one country provides the businesses of other countries with enormous opportunities. The more the world market grows, quantitatively and qualitatively, the more benefits there will be for those capitalist businesses that realize they must adapt to the rapidly changing conditions of the world market if they do not wish to disappear.

This new reality has profoundly altered the European world and is generating insecurity and fear in those who—correctly—suspect that it will ultimately change institutions, customs, and, especially, privileges that they believed immutable. The idea of nationhood, for example, as well as notions of identity and culture and habits and perspectives in work and human relations will have nothing to do with previous conceptions. A good number of the current conflicts—like those motivated by resurgent nationalism and fundamentalism—are the instinctive reactions of communities and individuals to a revolution that is doing away with tribal culture and creating a world of liberated entities, "free from God or country" but—let us hope—still ruled by law. If the latter also disappears, Enzensberger's nightmare will likely come true, although in ways other than he has foretold.

It is in this globalization of life that one must probe for the source of the collective violence that is, in fact, increasing dramatically. I think it has to do, in good part, with the universalization of communications, which lets the world's poor know, day by day and hour by hour, all that they are lacking and others enjoy. This creates impatience, unrest, frustration, and desperation, and political and religious demagogues know how to cultivate that fertile ground in order to push their demented proposals. But the dissatisfaction of the poor and their disgust with their own poverty are also a formidable energy that, properly channeled, may be converted into an extraordinary force for development. This is what has happened in the countries of Southeast Asia, which, for all the criticism that can be leveled against them—in the realms of political liberties and human rights, for example—have shown that it is possible to create millions of jobs and respectable living conditions in societies that until just yesterday figured among the most backward on earth. The same thing is beginning to happen in Latin America, where Chile is today a model of democratic growth that other countries try to emulate.

This is not naïve optimism but the simple affirmation that there are enough examples in contemporary reality to show that if free enterprise and the market system are adopted with everything that they imply—and they imply much sacrifice and effort, certainly—a country may be lifted out of poverty, even in a relatively short period of time. That few Third World countries have chosen this option is true; but it is also true that it is there, within their reach, waiting for them to decide to select it. It is the first time in history that this has been the case—that countries have been able to choose prosperity or poverty—and even if it were only for that, in defiance of my admired Hans Magnus Enzensberger's portents of doom, I believe that we are both lucky to have been born in this age.

London, March 1995

Under the Skies of Jerusalem

⚜

I must begin with what is most obvious and say how honored I feel to receive a prize that not only rewards a literary work but also recognizes the efforts of an intellectual in the service of freedom. It particularly pleases me that this award is called the Jerusalem Prize and that it is being presented to me in this city and at this moment.

I doubt there is a job in the world today that is as necessary but also as fraught with difficulty as the struggle for freedom. Just a few years ago, in 1989, as metal and stone rained down in the happy tumult of the fall of the Berlin Wall, an optimistic wind swept the planet and our spirits were lifted, because it seemed that particular battle had entered its final phase and soon a new international order based on equitable laws, respect for human rights, and the coexistence of mutually tolerant societies and individuals would reign. At last, the dream of a reconciled humanity living in peace with its diverse ideas, beliefs, and customs and competing in a friendly way for progress and prosperity would come true.

Barely six years later, that hope has been succeeded by a deep-seated pessimism. The reemergence of old demons we believed forever vanquished or at least tamed—like nationalism, religious fundamentalism, border disputes, ethnic and racial conflicts, and the refinement and spread of terrorism, which plague many regions, destroy countries, and litter streets and fields with the corpses of the innocent—is now leading many to despair and to wonder whether it is worth fighting to change a world that is lurching so drunkenly and that, to borrow a few lines from Shakespeare, seems to have been created by a sinister little god, full of sound and fury and signifying nothing.

When I hear such declarations of anthropological masochism or I feel in myself the temptation to succumb to the morbid pleasures of nihilism, I close my eyes and recall my first trip to Israel, in 1977. The recollection grounds me, as others are grounded by prayer or a swallow of whiskey. I was here for the first time seventeen years ago, with the ostensible purpose of giving lectures at the Hebrew University of Jerusalem. What I really came for was to see and learn; to discover what about this controversial country was reality and what myth; to listen, see, read, and touch everything. I was here for only a few weeks, but the lessons I learned have stayed with me for a long time. At the foot of the walls of Jerusalem's Old City, there was a girl with golden hair and a gray cape that flapped in the wind who wanted to fight in every revolution and was against all laws, beginning, as the poet says, with the law of gravity. "My countrymen have bought you," she told me. "You've become a Zionist!"

At the time I had just endured several years of intellectual and political reconstruction, after having renounced the collectivist and statist utopia that I embraced in my youth, and now I was defending democratic pragmatism to this girl as a more realistic and human alternative. I found myself leaning toward liberalism (though I still had many doubts) in the continual polemics that I tend to be drawn into by what appears to be my congenital ineptitude for all forms of political correctness. But I was still living with an uneasy nostalgia for what the revolution always seemed to possess in abundance and democracy to lack: the flurry of action, the release, the ascesis, the devotion, the generosity, the risk—in a word, everything that thrills the young and bores the old. In the history of Israel's creation and its fight for survival I found all of those things, in doses more than sufficient to satisfy my appetite for romantic political sentimentalism—an appetite I have never been able to tame completely—since here I saw that in order to live life like an adventure, to reform society, and to change the course of history, it wasn't necessary to do away with freedoms, ride roughshod over the law, support an abusive power, silence criticism, or jail or kill dissenters. Ever since then, I've said that the biggest surprise of my trip to Israel came when I allowed myself to discover that despite what my adversaries, many of my friends, and even I myself thought, my break with authoritarian messianism hadn't turned me into a fossilized "reactionary"; rather, I was still secretly in touch with the desire for rebellion and reform that usually (and entirely unfairly) is seen as the exclusive patrimony of the left.

Don't think I've come here to sing Israel's praises in return and thanks for the Jerusalem Prize. Not at all. Before and after that 1977 trip, I've disagreed with the politics of different Israeli governments, and I have criticized them—for their stubbornness, for example, in refusing to recognize the Palestinian people's right to independence and for the human rights abuses committed in the repression of terrorism in the occupied territories—but I've always made it clear that these were also criticisms formulated here, by many Israeli citizens and sometimes with blazing virulence, in a climate of the most unrestricted freedom.

This aspect of Israel's history—its always having remained a society open to discussion, criticism, and the regular election of officials, even at the most critical moments and in the throes of war, when its very existence was imperiled—is the most lasting lesson Israel has to offer the rest of the world, especially all those so-called Third World nations, in which internal or external difficulties and problems are often brandished as the excuse for violating freedoms or used to justify the tyrannies that keep so many of them sunk in barbarity and backwardness. What country has confronted more obstacles and problems than tiny Israel? Keeping the flame of freedom alive in its breast hasn't made it weaker or poorer; it has, on the contrary, brought it honor and given more weight to its cause before the nations of the world. This was one lesson of my trip that helped me to clarify many ideas and would lead me always to cite Israel as living proof that there is no better guarantee of progress and survival for a nation than the culture of freedom, no matter what the nation's circumstances or level of development.

The other lesson, which personally delighted me even more, since I am a novelist and I devote my days and nights to the extremely pleasant task of inventing lies that will pass as truths, was to discover that fiction and history don't always repel each other but can in fact mesh in certain cases like two lovers intertwined. Let us not forget: before it was history, Israel was a fantasy that, like the creature from Borges's story "The Circular Ruins," was transferred to the real world from the numinous mists of the human imagination. Literature is full of such magic, of course, but, as far as I am aware, Israel is the only country in the history of the world that can pride itself, like a character from Edgar Allan Poe, Robert Louis Stevenson, or *The Arabian Nights,* on a lineage so explicitly abstract, on having been first longed for, invented, assembled from the subtle subjective matter of which literary and artistic specters are made, and then smuggled into real life by force of daring and willpower.

That this has been possible is, of course, very encouraging for a novelist and, in general, for all of us who have made labors of the imagination the center of our lives: it proves that our vocation is not as gratuitous as one might think, but rather a public necessity, a vaccination against social lethargy and stiffening of the joints. But in addition to boosting the morale of the cloud-dwellers, this realization promises much for those nations—unfortunately, most of the countries of the world—that aspire to climb out of misery, ignorance, despotism, or exploitation. It is possible. Hopes and dreams can come true. It isn't easy, of course. A steely resolve and a capacity for sacrifice and idealism are required, of the kind possessed by the ragged pioneers who made water spring from hostile soil and crops grow where there were stones and who erected shacks in the desert that became towns and then modern cities. History isn't preordained, and no hidden laws, dictated by stern divinity or despotic Nature, govern it. It is written and rewritten by the women and men of this world to the measure of their dreams, effort, and will. This inescapable fact lays a tremendous burden on our shoulders, of course, and prevents us from seeking excuses for our failures. But it also represents the most formidable incentive for nations that feel aggrieved or dispossessed, because it proves that nothing must remain as it is, that history can be what it should be and what we want it to be, and that it depends on us alone.

For this invaluable lesson, which has helped me in my life as a writer and has been the strongest validation of my political convictions so far, I am indebted to Israel. In fact, when seen from the proper angle, what my militant friend at odds with the law of gravity (who, if memory doesn't fail me, outshone the light of day with stockings in seven colors that were brighter than the rays of a Jerusalem sunset) suspected has in a certain way come true: here I contracted an incurable weakness for Zionism, or at least for what there is in it of a quest for a realizable utopia, of a fiction that was incarnated in history and changed the lives of millions of people for the better.

To be perfectly frank, however, there is another side to the Zionist utopia with which I cannot sympathize: the side that legitimizes nationalism, historical homeland borders, and that cataclysmic nineteenth-century conception of the nation-state that has caused as much bloodshed worldwide as the wars of religion. Although I love the Peruvian land where I was born, which furnished me with the memories and nostalgia that fuel my writing, and also Spain, which has enriched my life by granting me a second nationality, let me be quick to say, borrowing a title from an essay by Fernando Savater, that I am "against homelands" and that my ideas on the subject were expressed quite well by Pablo Neruda in those early verses often quoted by Jorge Edwards: "Homeland, / sad word, / like thermometer or elevator." My own political dream is of a world in which borders are allowed to fall into terminal disrepair, passports are moth-eaten, and customs officials take their place alongside pharaohs and alchemists as curiosities of interest only to archaeologists and historians. I know that such an ideal seems a bit distant now, with the frenetic proliferation of new anthems and flags and the escalation of nationalist sentiment, but when I hear my yearning for a world unified under the sign of freedom mocked as a foolish novelist's invention, I am always ready with an irrefutable reply: "And what of the wild fantasies of the Viennese journalist Theodor Herzl? What of the Zionist dream? Didn't they come true?"

At millennium's end it would seem that human history, envious of the kind of Latin American novel dubbed magic realist, has begun all of a sudden to produce such marvels that even the most wildly imaginative novelists are left dazed by the competition. The borders that seemed most unyielding—those separating fiction and reality—seem to have dissolved with events as unexpected as the collapse of the Soviet empire, the reunification of Germany, the disappearance of almost all the dictatorships of Latin America, the peaceful transition of South Africa from a racist and oppressive regime to a pluralist democracy, and so many other happenings that have left us speechless each morning for quite some time now; so why not admit that the gradual integration of the planet, now realized in large part thanks to the internationalization of markets and communications and the globalization of businesses, may keep extending itself into administrative and political realms until the only barriers left standing between people are those that grow and extend themselves freely, that is to say, the fecund barriers of language and culture? The task is difficult, of course, yet not illusory. It is an arduous but worthy undertaking and the only one that can finally bring an end to the custom of slaughter that has accompanied human history like a fateful shadow, from the time of loincloths and clubs up to that of space travel and the information revolution.

The peace accord between Israel and the Palestine Liberation Organization is one of those extraordinary recent occurrences that astonish and move us, one of those events that until not long ago belonged to the beguiling domain of fiction. With so much hostility aroused, so much blood spilled, and so much hatred stored up, it seemed impossible. Nevertheless, it has been signed, and it has survived fanaticism's mad attempts to destroy it. One has to salute the audacity and valor of those who dared to opt for negotiation and peace, to open the door to a future collaboration of two peoples facing each other in a conflict that has already caused so much suffering and loss. And each of us must do the possible and the impossible to support it from where we stand, so that the civilizing clockwork that the accord has put in motion may continue to overcome the suspicions of the disbelievers, win over the pessimists, and inspire the lukewarm until the accord is indestructible and all attempts to turn history into a hell on the part of those seduced by apocalypse are dashed against the will for understanding and harmony that sustains it.

Then the second part of the dream that the Zionist pioneers brought from the four corners of the earth to this barren and vulnerable country, at the time a lost province of the Ottoman Empire, can begin to come true. Those pioneers, let us remember, didn't just want to build a country or create a safe, free, and honorable society for a persecuted people. They also dreamed of working shoulder to shoulder with their Arab neighbors to overcome poverty and of setting out in friendship on a quest for justice and modernity with all the peoples of the land richest in gods, religions, and spiritual life that humanity has ever known. In the turbulence that Israel has weathered since its independence, this aspect of the Zionist dream has disappeared behind dark clouds of confrontation and violence. But now, under the difficult aegis of peace, that noble ambition appears again from behind the mountains of Edom, in the clear sky that so disconcerts the first-time visitor to Jerusalem, who, welcomed by its brightness and bathed in translucent light from above, experiences something strange, like the brush of invisible wings that is felt upon contact with great poetry. Maybe the mention of this promising sign sparkling in the sky over Jerusalem is a good place to end these ramblings of a novelist who offers you once again his joy and gratitude.

Jerusalem, March 15, 1995

French Identity

❧ ❧

*L*a *Nouvelle Revue Française* recently circulated a little survey to writers around the world: "Apart from the trio great wines/high fashion/perfume, do you think that any perceptible symbols of French identity still exist? Do you agree with the idea that the decline of French literature abroad began with the *nouveau roman*? What do you expect from France in all fields?" I can't resist the temptation to respond publicly.

Any concerns about the "identity" of a human group make my hair stand on end, because I've become convinced that behind them always lurks a conspiracy against individual freedom. Of course I don't deny the obvious fact that a group of people who speak the same language, were born and live in the same region, face the same problems, and observe the same religion or customs have certain things in common, but I do deny that this common denominator defines each of them fully, abolishing or relegating to an insignificant second place what each member of the group calls specifically his own, the collection of qualities or personal traits that sets him apart from everyone else.

The concept of identity, when it is not used on an exclusively individual scale and is intended to represent a conglomerate, is reductive and dehumanizing, a magic ideological filter that extracts all original and creative human traits, anything that hasn't been imposed by inheritance or geographic location or social pressure but has come out of the ability to resist those influences and counteract them with free acts, independently conceived.

It is perhaps possible that cultures still survive in remote corners of the Amazon, Borneo, or Africa that are so isolated and primitive and so anchored in the prehistoric-era ritual repetition of daily acts that the individual hasn't properly been born and the social group exists as a self-absorbed, compact, and undifferentiated whole, allowing the tribe to survive when threatened by wild beasts, thunder, and the world's many magic forces. The only traits that really count are those that are shared, and they overwhelmingly prevail over the minimal differences of each tribe member. In this little humanity of clone-like beings, the notion of collective identity—a dangerous invention that is the foundation of nationalism—would possibly have reason to exist.

But even this hypothesis seems doubtful to me. The testimony of ethnologists and anthropologists who have studied the most isolated and archaic communities is generally conclusive: as necessary and important as common customs and beliefs are for the defense of the group, the margin of initiative and creativity its members maintain in order to distinguish themselves from the whole is great, and individual differences prevail when they are examined in their own terms and not as mere epiphenomena of the collective.

When one speaks of "French identity," clearly one is referring not to an archaic and isolated community, a superstitious tribal kingdom that neither trades nor mixes with the rest of the world and relies on elemental survival tactics—the only domain in which "the social" may be considered historical reality and not an ideological trap—but to a highly civilized and modern society upon which language, tradition, institutions, ideas, rites, beliefs, and practices may have imprinted a collective personality, a sensibility and idiosyncrasy borne uniquely and nontransferably by every French woman and man, a kind of metaphysical substance that unites all of them in an exclusive and exclusionary way and is subtly expressed in their deeds, dreams, greatest undertakings, and smallest pranks, which because of their origin are all indelibly stamped as "French."

Surveying my own surroundings, I compare the French women and men I know, admire, love, or hate; I consult my memory as an inveterate snoop, my nearly seven years of life in Paris, my vast readings in French, and my ravenous curiosity about everything good and bad happening in France, and I swear that I don't get even a hint of the "identity" that is supposedly capable of transubstantiating Flaubert and the Maid of Orléans, Chrétien de Troyes and Louis-Ferdinand Céline, the chef Paul Bocuse and Father Charles de Foucauld, Paul Claudel and Jean Genet, Pascal and the Marquis de Sade, the liberal essays of Jean-François Revel and the racist demagoguery of Le Pen, the wine-sodden clochards of the Place Maubert-Mutualité and the witty little nonagenarian countess of the *16ème* who once asked Jorge Edwards, "Chilien? Et c'est grave ça?" into a single being or an indissoluble ontological entity.

All of them speak French (though fairly different kinds of French), of course, but aside from this obvious linguistic likeness, an extremely long list of differences and contradictions could be drawn up that would make clear the artificial nature of any reductionist effort to see them as interchangeable, their well-defined and irreducible individual personalities dissolved into a single social entity that represents all of them and of which they are at the same time offshoots and mouthpieces. It is clear, too, that it wouldn't be difficult to find a lineage or dynasty of kindred spirits for each of them that crosses the boundaries of Frenchness and stretches into the most far-flung and diverse regions of the world. Then it would become clear that each one of them, while still being French—and precisely because his or her native culture stimulated a capacity for individual emancipation from the flock—was capable of constructing an individual identity over the course of a lifetime of grandeur or infamy, hard work or luck, intuition or knowledge, secret appetites and inclinations; in other words, a lifetime of being many other things than what he or she was as a result of the most precarious and miserable of circumstances, birthplace.

For simplicity's sake, we can say that France has probably contributed more than any other European culture to the emancipation of the individual from sheep-like servitude, to breaking the ties that bind the primitive to the social whole; in other words, to developing the freedom that allows human beings to stop being cogs in a social mechanism and to become sovereign entities, able to make decisions and set about inventing themselves as free and autonomous beings, creators of themselves, more various and richer than anything social coordinates or collectivist labels—religion, nation, culture, profession, ideology, and so on—could suggest about their "identity." This was brilliantly demonstrated by Sartre in *The Family Idiot*, his oceanic study of Flaubert, in his attempt to discover "what, at this point in time, can we know about a man?" At the end of the third volume, all that is clear from the inconclusive inquiry is that the Norman scribbler, who lived such a seemingly routine and stable life, was really a bottomless pit, a dizzying abyss of complex cultural, psychological, social, and family histories, a tangle of personal choices that eluded all generic classification. If this process of individualist differentiation was already so advanced a human condition in Flaubert's time, by now the elective reality by which individuals are shaped is probably stronger than it has ever been: although we keep referring to things as French—or Spanish or English or German—in order to understand each other, and primarily out of mental laziness and ideological cowardice, these abstractions are becoming ever more useless and confusing. They are references that tell us nothing about concrete individuals, except in the bureaucratic and administrative sphere, and this sphere de-individualizes and dehumanizes the human being, turning him into a specimen and voiding everything specific and particular about him.

That France has contributed more than any other culture to the creation of the sovereign individual is probably true, and exposing the collectivist fallacy that expressions like "cultural identity" obscure, thereby demonstrating why many of us love and admire French culture, is valid, but only if we also acknowledge that France is represented not just by the formidable libertarian, universalist, and democratic tradition encompassing the Declaration of the Rights of Man, Montesquieu and Tocqueville, the nineteenth-century utopists, the *poètes maudits*, surrealism, and Raymond Aron but by obscurantist, fanatic, nationalist, and racist traditions as well, which may also be claimed by Francophiles around the world, along with the panoply of writers and thinkers notable for championing them (from Gobineau to Céline, Gustave Le Bon to Charles Maurras, Robespierre to Drieu La Rochelle, and Joseph de Maistre—who wrote in French, although he wasn't born in France—to Robert Brasillach). Like all great cultures, French culture has no accompanying identity, or, rather, it has many contradictory ones; it is a crowded marketplace with fruits and vegetables for all tastes: the revolutionary, the reactionary, the agnostic, the Catholic, the liberal, the conservative, the anarchist, and the fascist.

The anguish about a supposed decadence of French literature seems alarming to me, not because it signals a real problem but because I detect in it symptoms of nationalism, of which one of the worst aspects is cultural. True, in the last twenty or thirty years no novels or poems seem to have been written in France comparable to those by its greatest creators, but in the field of the social sciences—the historical, philosophical, anthropological, or political essay—important books have appeared that have been read and discussed by half the world, like the recent ones by François Furet, Jean-François Revel, Alain Besançon, Claude Lévi-Strauss, and a good number of others. And isn't France's cultural pride sufficiently nourished by the Olympian and undisputed reign of the terrible trinity—Lacan, Foucault, and Derrida—over almost all the liberal arts colleges of the United States and a good part of Europe and the Third World?

In fact, what might seem to justify alarm is not the state of letters and thought in France—they are flourishing—but the country's cultural politics, which for some time has been showing marked signs of provincialism, not to say *bêtise*. Although the French government's recent posturing and campaigns (on both the left and the right, let us not forget) in support of the "cultural exception" intended to protect French film and television industries from *Jurassic* contamination, and the warlike administrative tirades against anglicisms that might erode the beautiful language of Racine, could without doubt be said to derive from a native tradition, they have seemed shameful to many of us because they recall not Molière or Descartes or Baudelaire but Monsieur Homais's idea of culture or the clowning of the Grand Guignol. But not even this should worry us too much, because it is evident that what there is of truly universal and lasting value in the language and letters of France will survive the worst efforts of functionaries who believe that cultures are defended with censorship, obligatory quotas, customs regulations, and bans and that languages must be shut up in concentration camps and guarded by *flics* and *mouchards* disguised as lexicographers.

London, July 1995

The Sign of the Cross

No one in Germany paid much attention to a suit brought before the Federal Constitutional Court by two disciples of the humanist Rudolf Steiner from a remote village in Bavaria, alleging that their three small children had been "traumatized" by being regularly obliged to see the spectacle of Christ on the cross on the walls of the public school they attended.

But every last family in the country knew—and a good many of them were left openmouthed in astonishment to learn it—that the high court charged with ensuring that the principles of the constitution are justly upheld in the political, economic, and administrative life of Germany, and that admits no appeals, had found in favor of the plaintiffs. As announced by its president, the eminent jurist Johann Friedrich Henschel, the court's eight magistrates ruled that the Bavarian school's offer to replace the crucifixes on its walls with plain crosses—in the hopes that this simplification would "detraumatize" the plaintiffs' children—was insufficient, and they ordered the state of Bavaria to remove all crosses and crucifixes from classrooms since "the state must be neutral in religious matters." The Court then proceeded to stipulate that a school could keep the Christian symbol in its classrooms only by the unanimous agreement of parents, teachers, and students. The shock waves from the scandal have reached even the peaceful lake in the Austrian woods where I've come seeking refuge from the heat and dryness of London.

The state of Bavaria is not just a paradise of cholesterol and triglycerides, though the world's best beer and sausages may be had there. It is also a stronghold of political conservatism and a place where the Catholic Church is solidly rooted (I'm not suggesting that the one is related to the other): more than 90 percent of the 850,000 Bavarian schoolchildren come from practicing Catholic families. The Christian Social Union, the local variant and ally of Chancellor Helmut Kohl's Christian Democratic party, exerts undisputed political control over the region. The leader of the CSU, Theo Waigel, was the first to protest the Court's decision, in an article in the party organ, *Bayernkurier*. "Because of the Court's ostentatious efforts to protect minorities and progressively relegate the needs of the majority to a distant second place, our established values and constitutional patriotism are in jeopardy," he wrote.

A measured response, if we compare it with that of His Excellency the Archbishop of Munich, Friedrich Cardinal Wetter, who was brought to the verge of apoplexy and—even more serious from the democratic point of view—civic mutiny by the affair. "Not even the Nazis removed the crosses from our schools," exclaimed Wetter. "Are we going to allow a democratic state governed by the rule of law to do something even a dictatorship couldn't?" Of course not! The cardinal has urged civil disobedience—all schools must defy the Court's ruling—and plans to convene an open-air service, on September 23, that will surely attract the papist masses. The act will be celebrated to the belligerent eurythmics of a slogan coined by this same prince of the Church: "The cross is here, and it's here to stay!"

If the poll takers have done their work well, a healthy majority of Germans support the rebellious cardinal Wetter: 58 percent condemn the Court's decision, and only 37 percent approve of it. Seizing the moment, Chancellor Kohl has hurried to reprove the magistrates for a decision that seems "contrary to our Christian tradition" and "incomprehensible from the point of view of the content and the consequences that it may have."

But perhaps even more damaging still for the cause that the Constitutional Court is championing is that the only politicians who have thus far come out in its defense have been that handful of shabby and vegetarian parliamentarians, lovers of chlorophyll and fasting—the Greens—whom nobody in this country of dedicated sausage and steak eaters takes very seriously. Werner Schulz, their parliamentary leader in Bonn, has proclaimed the state's duty to maintain a rigorous neutrality in religious affairs, "especially now, when, because of the actions of Muslim fundamentalists and other sects, the freedom of worship is threatened."

He has asked that the state stop collecting the tax that subsidizes the Church and that it replace the classes on Christianity taught in the public schools with teaching on ethics and beliefs in general, without privileging any specific religion.

From the refreshing cold waters of Lake Fuschl, I'd like to raise my hoarse voice in support of the Constitutional Court of Germany and applaud its clear-thinking judges for a ruling that, in my opinion, furthers the steady process of democratization that the country has been embarked on since the end of the Second World War. This ruling is the single most important development in recent history insofar as the future of western Europe is concerned. I say this not because I have the slightest aesthetic objection to crucifixes and crosses or because I harbor the slightest aversion for Christians and Catholics. On the contrary: although I'm not a believer, I'm convinced that a society cannot achieve a sophisticated democratic culture—in other words, it cannot be fully free or lawful—if it isn't profoundly suffused with spiritual and moral life, which, for the immense majority of human beings, is indissociable from religion. That is the opinion of Paul Johnson, who for at least twenty years has been documenting in his prolific studies the primordial role that faith and Christian religious practices played in the appearance of a democratic culture in the midst of the fog of arbitrariness and despotism in which the human race was stumbling.

But unlike Johnson, I'm also convinced that if the state doesn't preserve its secular character, and gives in, for example, to quantitative considerations like those being brandished by the adversaries of the German Constitutional Court (why shouldn't the state be Christian if the great majority of its citizens are?), and identifies with a specific church, democracy is lost, in the short or the long term. Lost for one very simple reason: no church is democratic. All churches postulate a truth that is overwhelmingly backed up by the transcendence and wand-waving omnipotence of a divine being; against this omnipotence all rational arguments must dash themselves and be shattered. Churches would negate themselves—they would cease to exist—if they were flexible and tolerant and prepared to accept the basic principles of democratic life, like pluralism, relativism, the coexistence of contradictory truths, the constant mutual concessions required to arrive at a social consensus. How long would Catholicism survive if, let us say, the dogma of the Immaculate Conception were put to the vote of believers?

The dogmatic and intransigent nature of religion becomes evident in the case of Islam, because the societies where Islam has put down roots have not undergone the secularization that, in the West, separated religion from the state and privatized it (made it an individual right rather than a public duty), obliging religion to adapt to its new circumstances, or rather, to confine itself to activities that were ever more private and less public. But it is supremely naïve to conclude from this that if the Church were to recover the temporal powers it has lost in modern democratic societies, those societies would still be as free and open as they are now. I invite optimists who believe such a thing, like my esteemed Paul Johnson, to have a look at those Third World societies where the Catholic Church still has the power to sway the making of laws and the government of society, and see what is happening there vis-à-vis film censorship, divorce, and birth control, so that they understand that when Catholicism is in the position to impose its truths, it doesn't hesitate to do so any way it can, and not only on the faithful but also on all the nonbelievers within its reach.

That is why a democratic society, if it wants to continue as such, not only must guarantee freedom of worship and nourish in its bosom an intense religious life but also must take care that the Church—any church—not transgress the bounds of its proper sphere, which is the private. It must also be kept from infiltrating the state and imposing its particular convictions on the whole of society, something that can only be done by violating the freedom of nonbelievers. The presence of a cross or crucifix in a public school is as abusive toward those who aren't Christian as the imposition of the Islamic veil would be in a class where there are Christian and Buddhist children as well as Muslim ones, or the Jewish *kippah* in a Mormon seminary. Since there is no way to observe everyone's beliefs at once, the state's policy can only be neutrality. The judges of the Constitutional Court of Karlsruhe have done what they should, and their ruling does them honor.

Fuschl, August 1995

Ceausescu's House

⊰ ⊱

I f all Romania's institutions had made the transition from
Nicolae Ceausescu's Stalinist dictatorship to Ion Iliescu's wobbly democracy as smoothly as the Writers' Union, life on that
island of Latin culture in the Slavic heart of Europe once known
as Dacia would be very different. When the Romanian writers be-
longing to the union lost their state subsidies after the dictatorship's collapse in 1989, they demonstrated a pragmatism generally
not associated with their colleagues around the world and rented
part of their headquarters to a casino—one of the few profitable
businesses in the new Romania. With the rent they've been able to
fund their journals, vacation camps, and home for the elderly.

"Being self-sufficient guarantees us absolute independence
from political power," the president explained as he led me
around the belle epoque building and its incredibly ornate salons,
full of columns, velvet, and chandeliers. "Our two thousand members represent every political faction in the country." (That is
undoubtedly true, but over the four talk-filled days I spent in
Bucharest, I never met a writer with anything good to say about
the government.) The union's lectures and intellectual debates
aren't disturbed by the presence of the gamblers—mafiosi, smug-

glers, nouveaux riches, foreigners of mysterious occupation—who play roulette and chemin de fer on the upper floors, because the Romanian millionaire who built this fin de siècle palace gave it impenetrable, soundproof walls, as if taking advance precautions to facilitate the unusual cohabitation of gambling and culture.

This was not the only surprise of my trip. Just as startling was the religious furor and monarchist nostalgia that have seized a good portion of the intelligentsia ever since the fall of Communism. It was something I'd read many reports of in recent years: the rebirth of churches and the resurgence of popular faith in countries where the sudden disappearance of a system perfectly calibrated to paralyze all initiative and individual responsibility and provide prefabricated answers to every question left a spiritual void felt by many of the world's orphans and lost souls. But in Romania the phenomenon was something I could see and touch. I can't remember ever having heard so much talk in intellectual circles about transcendence and faith as in Bucharest, or having been asked so many times whether I believed in God or was planning to convert. A fine ex-dissident poet who had been persecuted confessed to me that "in times as confusing as these, if I hadn't returned to the fold, I would have had to kill myself." And on a weekend trip to the Carpathians, the Hispanist and film critic Manuela Cernat, an old friend of mine, disconcerted me by devotedly kissing all the icons in the monasteries and all the talismans, scapulars, and rings of the (innumerable) Orthodox monks we met along the way.

According to polls, the idea of a return to monarchy doesn't seem to have the great support of the electorate (barely 10 percent), but to judge by what I saw, read, and heard among the people I met, if the vote were broken down and everything depended on the intellectuals, the exiled king Michael would be escorted down a red carpet back to his old throne. Many people spoke to me of the explosion of popular enthusiasm that greeted him the last time the government allowed him to visit Romania, and in the prestigious opposition newspaper, *România Libera*, articles continually appear presenting the monarchist option as a cure for all the country's ills. King Juan Carlos's role in democratizing and modernizing Spain is one of the arguments most frequently voiced by the defenders of this option, who see in a constitutional monarchy the only safeguard against slips back into dictatorship; others believe that the half century that has passed since the king's forced abdication makes his return impossible now. "It's the illusion of a few dreamers," a university professor assured me.

I'm not in a position to know, of course, nor was I able to come to much of a conclusion about the future of Romania based on the opinions and copious and contradictory information I was regaled with everywhere on my lightning trip. People expressed themselves without fear and even phrased their criticisms bluntly, but their points of view differed so widely, and were sometimes so wild and unlikely, that I often felt I was traveling in a world of make-believe. Right and left I was informed that the 1989 revolution, which ended with Ceausescu's ignominious fall, had been "stolen" by crafty apparatchik Communists, who, disguised now as champions of democracy, continue in power under Iliescu. But when I asked how Iliescu (whom some even accuse of having worked for the Soviet KGB) was able to win elections, no one could give me a convincing explanation. And I got even more confused when I heard some of his most bitter opponents mutter under their breath that he'd probably win the next election too, since the leader of the opposing coalition, Bucharest University rector Emil Constantinescu, isn't well known and lacks charisma, though he is universally repected for his integrity and intellectual powers.

What confuses me is this: The immense majority of Romanians hate what Ceausescu's regime stood for; on that point no one seems to have any doubts. If that is the case, someone like Iliescu, who was organically linked to the regime, should win elections only if they are rigged, not free. But I haven't heard anyone claim that the previous elections were sullied by electoral fraud, or predict that the upcoming ones will be. What does that mean? It means that Iliescu's victories have undoubtedly had much more to do with the opposition's ineptitude than with his own merits. The opposition's internal battles, its dissolution into groups and loosely defined factions, and its inability to put together a clear and attractive alternative blueprint for government must have hurt it even more than Professor Constantinescu's lack of charisma (Iliescu doesn't seem particularly charismatic, either). On the other hand, a good part of Romanian society still seems seized by paranoia, a malady common in countries under the sway of dictatorship. It is understandable that people accustomed to living under constraint and having all their actions and movements systematically monitored—as was the case under Ceausescu—should come to see life as a mechanism regulated by all-powerful and fateful forces, in the face of which they are impotent. In a democracy, that kind of attitude condemns a citizen (or a party) to total political shutdown and leads him to conceal his ineptitude behind an absurd victim complex and seek out scapegoats for his own failures. I say this because over my four days in Romania, I heard statements made by intellectuals—yes, intellectuals—that turned my stomach. For example: That Romania won't get ahead unless it shakes off (the way a dog shakes off fleas, they meant) its millions of Gypsies, who are responsible for all the country's crimes, smuggling, and indecency and whose mafias support Iliescu, who, besides, is tainted with "Gypsy blood" himself. And how does one distinguish this human misfit, the Gypsy, from a pure-blooded Romanian? Very simple: by pulling down his pants and taking a look at his member, since if you're a Gypsy, "it's as black as coal."

I don't know how many anti-Iliescu Romanians think this way, but even if there are only a few of them, they deserve to lose so long as they persist. And I don't know whether Iliescu has contracted the xenophobia virus that afflicts some of his compatriots, but even if he has, he certainly wouldn't let it show: he's too clever to reveal such unsightly prejudices. He invited me to lunch, and showed me around the ancient monastery that is now the Cotroceni Palace, residence of the president. Ceausescu added on a wing of sumptuous rooms, where marble and traditionally crafted precious woods proliferate. The current president is cold, calculating, pleasant, big, and burly. He has a clever answer for every question, especially the uncomfortable ones: yes, he was a Communist, secretary of the Communist Youth, government minister, and member of the Central Committee. But in 1971, when he accompanied Ceausescu to the People's Republic of China and North Korea and the Romanian dictator became enthused with the systems established by Mao and Kim Il Sung, he distanced himself from him. "Were you purged?" I ask him. "Sidelined," he corrects me. In other words, sent to the provinces and assigned administrative duties of secondary importance, and then dropped even lower in the hierarchy, put at the head of a technical publishing house. He left his office the night of December 22, 1989, to join the people of Bucharest, who were pouring out into the streets to battle tyranny. Fate, prudence, composure, a constructive attitude, and organizational talents—in his own words—raised him very rapidly to the heights of power, where he is now securely ensconced and determined to remain a while longer. It seems he hasn't changed much, except, of course, insofar as his ideology is concerned, since he is now fully committed to democracy.

Ion Iliescu, trained as an engineer, and the Dominican poet

Joaquín Balaguer are like two peas in a pod. Both prospered thanks to the rare ability they share of knowing how to make themselves useful without seeming to pose a threat to the dictators they served—Nicolae Ceausescu and Generalissimo Trujillo—and by maintaining just the right distance from them until democracy arrived, when they could boast that they had always secretly believed in democracy (without suffering any punishment or hardship as a result). And both continued to prosper when their newly democratic countries, submerged in chaos and plagued by the civic inexperience that is one legacy of dictatorship, needed capable managers who could impose some kind of order and direction on societies adrift. Both are living proof that certain regimes take much longer to die than the petty tyrants who preside over them.

The Ceausescus have already been eaten by worms, but it will take the Romanian people time, work, and imagination to bury the inheritance they were left by that notorious pair. In Bucharest I declined an offer to visit the dictator's most famous construction project, the horrendous monument to megalomania and reinforced concrete that is the People's House, a Babylonian building into which Ceausescu poured astronomical sums and that now flaunts its tremendous ugliness and uselessness in what was once the Old City of Bucharest. But although I managed to forgo that visit, I couldn't escape the former dictator's mania for construction. In the Carpathians, on the outskirts of Olanesti, in an arcadian landscape of wooded slopes bronzed by the autumn sun, there suddenly appeared a massive, pretentious, intrusive, absurd edifice, constructed from tons of cement, full of rugs and crystal chandeliers, vast halls and shining mirrors, silky drapes and slabs of marble—the last thing he built. All of Romania is littered with houses like this, at which Ceausescu would appear unexpectedly to sleep. This was the last in the series. He planned to spend

Christmas 1989 here, the holiday the Romanians ruined for him by overthrowing him. The house was left waiting, its climate-controlled pool, heliport, and billiards room ready for his arrival. Just maintaining this white elephant must cost the Romanian taxpayer dearly. What to do with it? Sell it? Who would buy it? It wouldn't be any good as a hotel, because, although it's gigantic, it has only five bedrooms. And it wouldn't work as a country retreat, either, unless Citizen Kane comes back to life and decides he wants to nurse his delusions of grandeur in the solitude of the border region between Valachia and Transylvania. What to do, then, with this last gift of Ceausescu to the new Romanian society in the making? The friendly worker who showed it to me thought I was joking when I said that in my opinion it should be blown up tomorrow with everything in it and that trees should be planted again in the earth it had sullied.

Bucharest, October 1995

The Joys of Necrophilia

⋞ ⋟

Argentina is probably the only country in the world with sufficient reserves of heroism, masochism, or foolishness to allow its citizens to go to the theater in the middle of the summer, with temperatures reaching Saharan heights, and broil themselves alive listening to lectures on liberalism. I know this because I was the madman giving the lectures, bathed in sweat and staving off tachycardia and dizzy spells in Rosario, Buenos Aires, Tucumán, and Mendoza over the course of this unreal past week as the newspapers announced record-breaking temperatures (113 degrees in the shade) with a baffling air of triumph.

I was accompanied by the tireless Gerardo Bongiovanni, an idealist from Rosario who was determined that no effort be spared in spreading the gospel of freedom, even if it required us to brave brazier, grill, and pyre, images insufficient to convey the blaze of that southern summer. Besides arranging conferences, roundtable discussions, seminars, and dialogues, he managed to organize lavish barbecues that would have horrified a vegetarian but that resuscitated me, an inveterate carnivore, and made up for the glare of the sun. One afternoon, as we were traveling down the broad

Paraná River, he suggested that instead of repeating the line "take the bull by the horns" in my lectures, I should eliminate either the animal or the verb, since in Argentinean Spanish the allegory was technically absurd and grotesquely indecent (in Argentina, *coger* [to take] means to fornicate). My instinct tells me that Gerardo and his sense of humor had something to do with the gentlemen who, as we left those hot auditoriums, would ask in a seemingly guileless manner if I, too, believed, like Pedro Camacho in *Aunt Julia and the Scriptwriter*, "that Argentineans have an irrepressible proclivity for infanticide and cannibalism."

But perhaps nothing contributed so much to the sensation of unreality that suffused those seven days as the novel I was reading along the way, snatching every spare minute as I traveled by car and plane, changed hotels and cities, and swung between bloating and dehydration: *Santa Evita*, by Tomás Eloy Martínez. I beseech readers to plunge into it without a moment's delay and discover, as I did, the (literary) pleasures of necrophilia.

I met its author on my first trip to Buenos Aires, in the mid-sixties, when he was the star reporter of the weekly *Primera Plana*. He spoke with the pleasant lilt of Tucumán, drawling his *r*'s; he had kissed the hand of Joseph Jean Lanza del Vasto in public; and despite his youth, it was said that he was "married every so often," as Neruda once put it, and always to incredibly beautiful models. Since then, I've run into him frequently—in Venezuela, where he lived in exile from Argentina's military regime, in Paris during the unrest of 1968, in swinging London—and most recently in the ugliest city of the ugliest state of the United States—New Brunswick, New Jersey—where he was teaching at Rutgers University and editing, by fax from his house in a neighborhood of ultra-Orthodox Jews, the literary supplement of the Buenos Aires newspaper *Clarín*. With such credentials, it should come as no surprise that Tomás Eloy Martínez is capable of anything, including the feat of composing a master-piece.

Since anything can be a novel, *Santa Evita* is one too, but it is also a biography, a sociopolitical mural, an inquiry, a historical document, a hysterical fantasy, a surrealist slapstick, and a tender and moving radio play. It has the deicidal ambition that drives great narrative projects, and in it resides, beneath the displays of imagination and flights of lyricism, a painstaking labor, an investigation carried out with sleuth-like tenacity and the consummate dexterity required to fit the author's very rich material into a structure that milks the story for all it's worth. As is the case with successful fictions, the book is not what it seems to be at first, and it is doubtless something other than its author intended.

What it seems to be is the story of the cadaver of Eva Perón, from the moment that Eva's illustrious husband delivers her still-warm body into the hands of a Spanish embalmer—Dr. Ara—for her to be eternalized, until, after roaming two continents and several countries and playing the leading role in bizarre, mean-dering adventures (she is copied, worshipped, mutilated, deified, caressed, profaned, hidden in ambulances, cinemas, attics, military bunkers, the bilges of ships), she is finally buried more than two decades later, like a character out of García Márquez, in the Reco-leta Cemetery of Buenos Aires, under more tons of steel and rein-forced concrete than a bomb shelter.

Interwoven with this story is another, that of the live Evita, from her provincial and illegitimate birth in Junín to her political epiphany and glorious death thirty-three years later, with half Ar-gentina at her feet, after a lurid and difficult life as a repertory ac-tress in second-class radio shows and theaters, a creature of the night protected by wealthy impresarios. After she meets Perón, at a critical juncture in his political career, her life changes course, ballooning until it is a central element and symbol of the blessing or historical catastrophe (depending on one's perspective) called Peronism, in which Argentina is still mired. That history has been chronicled many times, with admiration or disdain, by Evita's political devotees and adversaries, but in the novel it seems different, fresh, because of the shadings and ambiguities lent it by the stories surrounding it.

Besides the ones I've mentioned—those dealing with live Eva Perón and dead Eva Perón—two more stories are told in this multifaceted book: the story of the handful of Army Intelligence Service officers charged by the military regime that overthrew Perón with keeping Evita's embalmed cadaver safe from the Peronist masses who want to rescue it, and the story of the author himself (a character camouflaged under the apocryphal pseudonym Tomás Eloy Martínez) in the process of writing *Santa Evita*. To these two last stories the novel owes its most imaginative and unusual pages and its best character, a neurotic figure worthy of the anarchist stories of Joseph Conrad or the Catholic-political-spy-thriller novels of Graham Greene: Colonel Carlos Eugenio de Moori Koenig, security theorist and practitioner, gossip strategist and pillar of the state, and victim and executioner of Evita's unburied body, which makes him an alcoholic, a sinister paranoiac, a fetishist, a necrophiliac lover, a bit of human filth, and a madman.

Not the least of *Santa Evita*'s wiles is its ability to make us believe that this character existed, or rather, that the de Moori Koenig who did exist was the way the novel paints him. This is as false, of course, as imagining that the flesh-and-blood Eva Perón, or the embalmed one, or the excessively excitable and extravagantly depressed writer called Tomás Eloy Martínez who insinuates himself into the story in order to show himself writing it, is a transcription, a reflection, a truth. No: each is a trick, a lie, a fiction. They all have been subtly stripped of their reality, manipulated with the same ghoulish dexterity with which Dr.

Ara—another marvel of invention—plucks Evita's body from the impure realm of corrosion and transfers it into the pure one of fantasy; they have been transformed into literary characters, that is to say, ghosts, myths, counterfeit figures, and conjured beings that transcend their real-life models and inhabit the independent universe of fiction, the opposite of History.

The power of persuasion of the kind of novel producing these sleights of hand resides in the practical details of its construction and the ability of its prose to cast a spell over the reader. The structure of *Santa Evita* is asymmetrical, labyrinthine, and extremely effective; its language—a domain in which the author has risked much and several times comes close to cracking his skull—is, too. The abyss he skirts in choosing the language of his story and giving it rhythm and harmony is the seductive and thoroughly treacherous one of preciousness. In the novel musicians don't perform but "muddy" Vivaldi's "Summer" and "murder" Schubert's "Ave Maria"; patients don't undergo surgery but "face consecutive operations"; and a scriptwriter describes the noise of a crowd with these rhetorical effusions: "The uncontrollable *now* spreads its wings of a bat, of a butterfly, of a forget-me-not. The *nows* of cattle and waving spears of grain buzz; nothing can put a stop to their frenzy, their lance thrust, their fiery echo." And to describe a dark cold day, the narrator coins this bit of futurist madness: "The sheep of the mist stretched their legs in the deserted streets, and you could hear them bleating down inside your bones" (in a less pastoral allegory, D'Annunzio calls Marinetti "Idiot poet with flashes of imbecility").

Though taken out of context these and similar sentences make the reader cringe, in context they are indispensable and work perfectly, as is the case with certain exceptionally precious bits of works by García Márquez or Manuel Puig. I have no doubt that if this grotesque and terrible story had been narrated in more sober,

less pyrotechnic prose, without the mawkish excesses, the melo-
dramatic affronts, the modernist metaphors, and the sentimental
blackmailing of the reader, it would be impossible to believe, and
page after page would be annihilated by the reader's critical de-
fenses. It is credible—moving and unsettling, in fact—by virtue of
the defiant molding of form to content: the author has discovered
the exact degree of verbal and aesthetic distortion required to re-
late a series of adventures that, although encompassing extremes
of ridiculousness, absurdity, extravagance, and stupidity, exude a
profound humanity.

The magic of a good novel deludes its readers, makes them
swallow the wildest stories whole, and corrupts them at will. I
confess that this one had its way with me, and in such matters I'm
a seasoned expert, someone who doesn't succumb easily to the
tricks of fiction. *Santa Evita* conquered me: from the very first
page, I believed, I was enthralled, I suffered, I enjoyed, and in the
course of my reading I contracted hideous vices and betrayed the
liberal principles I hold most dear, the same ones I was expound-
ing all week, amid the fire and boiling lava of summer, to my
friends in Rosario, Buenos Aires, Tucumán, and Mendoza. I, who
hate tyrants and despots with all my soul and despise their follow-
ers and the sheep-like masses they mesmerize even more, suddenly found myself, on a sizzling morning in my room with its
Doric columns—yes, Doric columns—at the Tucumán Grand
Hotel, wanting Evita to come back to life and return to the Pink
House to lead the Peronist revolution once again, giving away
houses, wedding dresses, and false teeth. And in Mendoza, in the
shadows of the Plaza Hotel with its facade like a Masonic temple,
I found myself dreamily wondering—horror of horrors!—why
an exquisite cadaver—after being eternally preserved, made
beautiful, and purified by the arts of Dr. Ara, bridegroom of
death—shouldn't, indeed, be desirable. When a book is capable of

inducing such excesses in a being of firm principles and frugal habits, the conclusion is inevitable: it must be prohibited (as all novels were during the Inquisition, since the genre was considered a public hazard) or read immediately.

Mendoza, December 1995

The Old Man with the Bunions

❦ ❦

To catch the bus in Lima, I had to walk a few blocks down Porta Street, in the heart of Miraflores. It was a little tree-lined street, along which—this was the mid-1950s—wooden one-story houses still stood, with banisters and pillars painted green, window grates, and gardens of laurels, pansies, geraniums, and climbing vines; homes built at the beginning of the century, when the neighborhood was still a country retreat separated from the capital by small farms and open fields.

At one of those toy houses, a little old man was always on the porch, rocking in a rocking chair as ancient as he was, shrunken and bundled up in blankets against the cold, his feet stuffed into a pair of slippers misshapen by his bunions. There was something mysterious and otherworldly about him: maybe his solitude, his unknown origin, or the memories into which he seemed to with-draw morning and evening, staring into space from his fading garden. He intrigued me so much that I progressed from saying hello as I passed his house, to stopping and making small talk with him over the gate and giving him magazines I had read, to becoming his friend. We spoke several times, I sitting on the steps of the porch of worm-eaten planks and my singular neighbor rocking in his chronometer of a rocking chair, propelled by the push of his deformed feet, which barely brushed the ground.

I don't remember his name or whether he lived with anyone besides the Indian maid to whom he communicated in gestures and who in the evenings would bring us a cup of steaming tea and the spongy cakes called *chancay*. His Spanish was labored, barely comprehensible, and one of his eyes was always weeping. I learned a few things about him: that he had a small fur shop in a garage on La Paz—which at that time was a street of artisans, loan sharks, junk dealers, and resalers—that he had come to Peru from Poland, and that he was the survivor of a concentration camp, possibly Auschwitz. I was afforded this last piece of information as if by chance, in an impromptu remark that gave me a brief glimpse into his personal history, the secrets of which he guarded stubbornly, brusquely cutting me off each time I asked him about his life, as if my questions were an unpardonable impertinence. This was the era of *Life* in Spanish, and I had brought him the most recent issue of the magazine and was showing him, with horrified commentary, the picture of a jumble of human forms—skin and bone, shaved heads, eyes bulging from hunger or fear—half naked, one on top of the other, knit and curled together to make a Dantesque pyramid, beings on the verge of annihilation who were saved by the arrival of the Allied troops. "There's nothing horrifying about it," he corrected me, the little light in his eye seeming almost melancholy. "We crowded together that way so we wouldn't freeze to death, to keep warm. It was the only good moment of the day." I don't think he told me anything else or that I asked anything. I must have left soon after, uncomfortable and sorry to have stirred up unawares the atrocious depths of my neighbor's memory.

This anecdote, and the image of the little old gnome of a Pole brought to the other side of the world, to peaceful Miraflores, by the torments of the Second World War, have dogged me as I've read, with disgust and fascination, Pierre Drieu La Rochelle's *Journal, 1939–1945*, published in France—after anguished doubts and legitimate scruples—by Gallimard. Drieu isn't a writer I know well or like—the only works of his that I've read with any enthusiasm are *The Fire Within* and a collection of literary essays—but I've been intrigued by the cult that has been forming around his person over the last few decades, the mythology that emanates from him, his aura of writer *maudit*, whose suicide at the end of the war, when he was about to be arrested for collaborating with the Nazis, put an end to his tumultuous life as inveterate rebel, intellectual agitator, impenitent Don Juan (one of his lovers was Victoria Ocampo, whom he accuses in the *Journal* of having procured money from him by shameful means), and a man with a Nietzschean propensity for the excesses of intense life and early death. Many studies, theses, biographies, and issues of magazines have been devoted to him and his novels, which are frequently reissued and have a loyal following.

Although *Journal, 1939–1945* is nauseating and endlessly repugnant, it isn't a bad thing that it's been published, even if only as a historical document and as proof, through the exposition of a paradigmatic case, that intelligence, knowledge, and high culture can coexist with extreme forms of inhumanity, political blindness, and ethical confusion. The *Journal* should be read especially by those who have helped denature the idea of fascism by applying the word "fascist" without rhyme or reason to their political adversaries, until the word has taken on a frivolous face value that dilutes its visceral relationship with one of the worst slaughters in the history of humankind. Drieu La Rochelle was a real fascist. Like the great existential philosopher Martin Heidegger, but more explicitly and concretely, he celebrated Adolf Hitler's rise to power as the beginning of a new era in which human history

would progress toward a world purged of dross, thanks to the
leadership of a superman and the heroism of a higher people and
race. Drieu La Rochelle bitterly bemoans his unfitness, because of
his hemorrhoids and varicose veins, to wear the black uniform,
the steel helmet, the high boots, and the armbands with swastikas
and lightning bolts of the SS man, the blond giant of Hitler's
shock troops, symbol and personification of the "new man,"
whom Drieu regularly anoints with erotic ejaculations of admiration, calling him idealistic, brave, generous, virile, beautiful, and
Nordic (in his lexicon these last three are aesthetic and moral attributes).

Hitler is the great revolutionary and historic purifier, charged
with the task of dissolving borders and saving Europe from the
double menace that threatens it: the merchants of Wall Street and
the hordes of the Kremlin. Hitler will unify Europe under the
aegis of a vertical power and restore its medieval grandeur by
rooting out the cancers that have precipitated its decadence: par-
liaments, parties, politicking, miscegenation, expatriated capital,
inferior races, and, above all, Jews.

The recurrent and obsessive anti-Semitism that impregnates
the pages of the *Journal* lingers like a noxious miasma in the
reader's memory, like the stink of cheap brothels, the smell of
sharp tobacco, dirty feet, and rue-water that cannot be washed
away or masked with dousings of cologne. The Jews are, to Drieu
La Rochelle, an excrescence that humanity must do away with for
prophylactic reasons. Everything about them repels him: their appearance, their attire, their habits, their way of speaking, their historical rootlessness, their cosmopolitanism, their mercantile spirit,
and their eternal conspiracy to destroy from within the societies
that they have infiltrated and that sustain them. They are responsible, simultaneously, for both capitalism and Communism.
Drieu, whose first wife was Jewish—as he confesses in the *Journal*,

he used up her fortune in order to be able to write in comfort, and it allowed him to live the last year of his life in hiding—rails against his own friends because of their "race" and trusts that Hitler, after overthrowing England, won't soften under the pressure of the "democrats" who have infiltrated his inner circle and will scour the world of its plague, imprisoning all the Jews on an island (Madagascar, for example), where they'll live cloistered for all eternity.

The redesign of Europe, to which he devotes extensive reflection, has as its crux the racial criterion (ethnic cleansing). Aryan, Nordic, white, and blond Europe will erect impassable barriers separating itself from societies corrupted by the contamination of Arab, African, or Gypsy blood. Southern Italy, Spain, Portugal, and Greece are disqualified, of course, from being part of this glaucous and pristine European enclave that will rule the world; but even the south of France will be ethnically excluded because of its impurities and racial mixing. Drieu relegates it to the assembly of second-class nations.

The person who scrawled these idiocies in the tranquillity of his library in occupied France wasn't an imbecile. He had associated since his youth with the most distinguished intellectuals of his day, and he was considered one of them. Friend of André Malraux, Jean Paulhan, Saint-John Perse, and André Gide, he founded with them the magazine that presided over cultural life in France—*La Nouvelle Revue Française*, which he edited for a few years—and his novels, plays, and essays were read, followed, and discussed by a demanding public. In this very *Journal*, when he isn't spewing hatred of the Jews or raving about physical heroism and the aesthetics of war, he reflects subtly on Eastern religions, compares Buddhism with Christianity, analyzes Saint Thomas Aquinas and Saint Augustine, and displays a vast knowledge of Zen. His literary judgments are arbitrary but penetrating, and his prose, despite being rushed, has a vigorous dash not devoid of charm.

How to reconcile the two? How to understand that the same person who is awed by the millenarian wisdom of Sanskrit texts and so delicately dismantles the metaphors of Baudelaire could also be a supplier of the ideas, arguments, reasoning, and myths that set in motion the machinery of the Holocaust and the transportation of millions of human beings from every corner of Europe to the crematoriums? I don't know. It's possible that there is no acceptable answer to that momentous question. But it is necessary to ask it, over and over again, because ideas—words—are not devoid of responsibility, or gratuitous. They generate action, shape behavior, and direct from afar the movements of those who engineer cataclysms. There is a thread running straight from the bloody racist fantasies that Drieu La Rochelle's rapacious mind elaborated in his study to the tragedy bitterly pondered by my friend and neighbor in his emigrant old age, the Porta Street furrier with outsize bunions.

Madrid, March 1996

A Bourgeois Paradise

❧ ❧

Although the word "civilization" is out of fashion and the idea it represents has become politically incorrect, each time fate has brought me to the Netherlands in recent years, that has been the notion that immediately springs to mind: a civilized country. Or, more accurately perhaps, a country committed to civilizing itself, to expanding its citizens' spaces for freedom, culture, choice, and human rights.

Except in the civic promotion of women, in which Norway has left it behind, the Netherlands is facing the great challenges of our times with more audacity than any other society in the world. Whether the issue is drugs, abortion, euthanasia, sexual minorities, the social and political integration of immigrants, religion and churches, or aid to the Third World, the Netherlands has gone further than any other country in enacting permissive and tolerant policies intended to guarantee, in the whirlwind of contemporary Europe, the democratic ideals par excellence of individual sovereignty and coexistence in diversity. That some initiatives undertaken in these matters haven't produced the expected results (as seems to be the case with the legalization of so-called soft drugs) or are still the object of ferocious controversy (like homosexual marriage or the decriminalization of assisted suicide) doesn't tarnish but rather underscores the bravery of the institutions and people who, instead of burying their heads in the sand, honestly and valiantly confront a complex set of problems that, for the first time in history, are emerging from underground to occupy center stage in current affairs.

All this is done without fanfare or intellectual grandstanding, without lectures to the rest of the world, and even with an attempt to avoid provoking antagonism and controversy among those governments, churches, and media outlets that criticize the reforms from outside and occasionally present them as portents of the apocalypse. This discretion is an aspect of the Netherlands' cultural heritage, which, despite being incredibly rich, is one of the least heralded that I know. Almost all its great figures—from Rembrandt to van Gogh—have been recognized only posthumously by the rest of Europe after having lived and worked, diligently and without fuss, in the diffident half-light of bourgeois anonymity that seems to have been the preferred circumstance of its thinkers and creators and something like a national tendency (although I know very well that there is no such thing).

It was, in any case, the condition of the mysterious gentleman who is the reason for my being here on this cheerful, sunny weekend, with spring exploding at last and the gardens of The Hague and Delft greeting the dawn bright with tulips. There was never a more inconspicuous, routine, or provincial life than that lived by Johannes Vermeer (1632–1675), teacher and art dealer, who was born and died in Delft and whose biography can be summed up in five words: he painted and he procreated. These are the only facts about which his biographers may be utterly certain: in his forty-three years of life, he worked a lot but painted very little—only forty-four paintings are documented as his, of which thirty-six have survived—and he was a very attentive husband, as proved by the fifteen children he had with his wife, Catharina Bolnes, four of whom died soon after birth.

It is almost certain that he was ushered into the world and spent his early years at The Flying Fox, an inn run by his father. Innkeeper was a very respectable profession in seventeenth-century Delft, where beer, along with pottery and woolen cloth, was a principal source of wealth. At the age of twenty, despite the opposition of both families, he married a girl from Delft's Catholic minority (he had been raised Protestant and converted to the "papist faith," as it was called then). That same year he was admitted to the Guild of Saint Luke, which gave him the right to sell his own paintings and to deal in other painters' work. He never attained the prosperity of the affluent families of the city of twenty-five thousand inhabitants, but neither did he know poverty. He lived more or less well, although with occasional lean periods, assisted by his mother-in-law and from time to time selling Italian fabrics to make ends meet, until the terrible recession of 1675, which ruined him (it is suspected that the shock killed him). He was so meticulous and exacting in his work that the birth of each of his oils was like a geologic event: his average production was a couple of paintings a year at most. Although he was respected as an artist in his small city, he was not known in his lifetime outside it, even in Holland. Glory was a few centuries in coming.

Now it has reached its pinnacle, with an exhibition in the Mauritshuis of The Hague that brings together twenty-three of his paintings and the complementary (and magnificent) show in the Prinsenhof of his native city, called *Delft Masters: Vermeer's Contemporaries.* At both, cosmopolitan and devoted crowds squeeze in—I've overheard every language imaginable—who have come from many miles away. They pack the galleries, and the visitor must crane his neck to see over the heads and shoulders of so many museum-goers. No matter. To inhabit for a few hours the world invented by Vermeer is one of those experiences that momentarily fill us to overflowing with joy and a zest for life, because it gives us the illusion of having touched the crucial center of existence, of understanding what we are here for and why.

The associations that this world immediately elicits are: placidity, calm, order, domestic life, bourgeois families and habits, the prosperity of hardworking shopkeepers. Urban and secular, it is a world of routine and efficiency, without heroism or mysticism, in which there is no place for eros and its excesses; a world distrustful of strong emotions and lacking in imagination, although well educated, well groomed, and immaculate. Faith seems assimilated into material life, and the spirit endowed with powerful earthly roots, not vying with the body but in friendly harmony with it. Of the two paintings on religious subjects, one, *Christ in the House of Martha and Mary*, has been rendered bourgeois and secularized to the extent that, without the timid halo over the head of the male figure, one could take it for an amiable gathering of three friends about to have a bite to eat. The other, *Allegory of Faith*, contrary to what it intends to portray—the apotheosis of true religion, incarnated in a beautiful matron who straddles the globe and at whose feet a serpent bleeds from the mouth—is glacially precious, the fanatic precision and polish of each object keeping all sentiment at arm's length and precluding emotion.

This world is extremely simple and predictable, immersed in the everyday and enemy of the exceptional. Its motifs are few and recurrent: women and girls in elegant middle-class interiors, spotless black-and-white checkerboard floors, landscapes and still lifes on the walls, and big windows of translucent glass that flawlessly let in the light. Music is performed, and reading a common pastime, since books appear among the brocades and on the sturdy pieces of furniture, and musical instruments abound—clavichords, virginals, mandolins, and flutes—with which the ladies while away their leisure time. Women's love of fabrics and jewelry is exhibited without the least shame, with the clear conscience that success in business gave the industrious merchants of Delft (the Dutch East India Company's ships left each week for the Orient loaded with cloth and pottery and full of barrels of foamy beer for the long crossing). But even more than the sumptuous dresses of silk, satin, or velvet and the fine lace, pearls are the delight of these well-to-do bourgeois ladies. They are everywhere, sparkling in the pale little ears of girls of marriageable age, wound around the necks of married women, and in every adornment ever designed by clever jewelers to flatter feminine vanity: in brooches, tiaras, rings, and pins and on strings that spill out of dressing tables.

This prosperity, however, is never excessive, is somehow contained at the exact limit where elegance becomes affectation and luxury becomes exhibitionism and frivolity. Everything seems so moderate, and people and their possessions seem so well suited to each other that it is impossible not to accept one and the other as linked by a secret and intimate bond, by a kind of necessity. It is a world that one could call educated, respectful of science, curious about what lies on the other side of the sea (among Vermeer's subjects is a geographer surrounded by maps and armed with a compass), and convinced that the arts—painting and music, above all—enrich life.

And yet to describe the world of Vermeer as I have just described it is an exercise in futility. It was conceived and realized in forms and colors, not in words, and upon being translated into conceptual discourse, it loses what makes it inimitable and unique: its perfection. It isn't easy to define perfection, since definitions are by nature imperfect. Most of the paintings by the master of Delft deserve this high and mysterious classification, because nothing is superfluous and nothing lacking in them; no element is out of place, and all the elements together complete the whole. The inhabitants of these canvases—the soldiers with broadswords and plumed hats, the alabaster damsels, the bits of stale bread, or the minute flaws in a wall—are united by something that seems to underlie their strictly plastic qualities. The beauty they exude is more than artistic. Besides dazzling us, it unsettles us, because it seems to give meaning and reality to the lovely and incomprehensible vocabulary of religion: grace, spirit, miracle, transcendence, soul.

When a creator reaches the heights of a Vermeer, we discover how insufficient the explications that critics, philosophers, and psychologists give us of artistic genius still are, despite everything we know. The brushes of this ordinary and methodical bourgeois transformed the small world in which he lived and was inspired—a world of mediocre appetites and boring habits, devoid of flights of fancy, impetuous sentiments, or desires—into a sovereign reality, without defects or mistakes or unnecessary or harmful ingredients, a country of inherent grandeur and aesthetic self-sufficiency brimming with coherence and pleased with itself, where everything celebrates and justifies what is. I don't know whether heaven exists, but if it does it may well resemble the bourgeois paradise of Johannes Vermeer.

The Hague, May 1996

Cassandra's Prophecies

⚜ ⚜

S ince *Language and Silence* fell into my hands thirty years ago, I've considered Professor George Steiner one of the most stimulating critical minds of our day. I've continued to read what he writes, and book after book my high opinion is confirmed, even when I disagree with his conclusions. But for a while now, I've suspected he was beginning to succumb to the temptation to which great talents often fall prey, that of frivolous facility, or the propensity to prove anything, even some mistaken views, with elegant prose and what appears to be solid learning.

Professor Steiner has just announced both the death of literature and the existence of a secret book he has written, to be published posthumously, on languages and the act of love: "One makes love very differently in German than in English or Italian," he has explained, with a certainty that Don Juan de Mañara would envy. Very well. This announcement is at least more original and, insofar as readers are concerned, more optimistic than the first.

The culture of the near future, according to Steiner, will do away with literature because of two factors that already exert a decisive influence on contemporary life. The first is technology. The novel as a genre is in no shape to compete with the so-called virtual reality produced by computers, a universe of fantasy and creativity that, though still in its infancy, already surpasses what lies between the covers of the best works of fiction. The First World War was the death knell of the novel, and its swan song was James Joyce's *Finnegans Wake*. Poetry will survive, but at a distance from the evanescent book, as an oral art subordinate to music and the pastimes that have replaced literature as magnets for the best modern intelligence: television, film, dance, and advertising.

According to the statistical artillery Steiner deploys in support of his thesis, the humanities now only attract mediocrities and the dregs of the university, while talented young people flock to study the sciences. And the proof of this is that the entrance requirements for humanities departments in the best academic centers of England and the United States have dropped to unseemly levels. Meanwhile, at Cambridge, Princeton, and MIT, the requirements for the first year of mathematics or physics are "what, less than fifteen years ago, would have been postdoctoral research." While humanistic studies stagnate, slip backward, or are degraded, scientific and technological studies reach the speed of light.

Professor Steiner explains in detail, with his usual intellectual flair, a supposed historical law according to which every age's limited quota of creative talent is concentrated, for mysterious reasons, in a specific area of human activity, which as a result enjoys a period of extraordinary flowering and achievement. So just as painting flourished in the Florentine Quattrocento and the novel stepped into the breach in nineteenth-century Europe, now the creative genius of the species has abandoned arts and letters and nourishes and enriches science and technology and the genres that most benefit from their accomplishments and inventions: in other words, the audiovisual. Not without a certain cheek, Steiner assures us that in our day "the difference between poetry and advertising jingles is very difficult to distinguish" and that it isn't uncommon to find "one-liners of which Restoration comedy would have been proud" in radio or television advertisements for commercial products.

To speak of beauty in a world where ad agency copywriters are our Dantes and Petrarchs, and where soap operas and reality shows take the place of *Don Quixote* and *War and Peace*, will always be possible, but clearly the meaning of the word will have been essentially altered. Although we may have trouble comprehending it, the children around us have already understood it and act accordingly. Steiner explains what scientists have explained to him: that any child who has mastered the use of the computer chooses among three or four possible solutions to all the problems posed by the holographic screen, not on the basis of their truth—since all are true—but on the basis of their "beauty," or their form, coherence, and the perfectness of their technical configuration, which corresponds to what is classically considered artistic value. The child establishes this hierarchy with the certainty with which previous generations distinguished between a beautiful and an ugly painting. This development seems to Steiner the inevitable consequence of the evolution of art after the genre has hit bottom, as supposedly happened to the novel after Joyce. Now there is nothing left but the Hegelian qualitative leap: How could the traditional idea of beauty in the visual arts have survived the productions of Marcel Duchamp, who could sign a urinal, or the self-destructing and ephemeral machines of Jean Tinguely?

It's been a while since an essay irritated me as much as the one I'm discussing here. What annoys me (I promise) is not that, given my job, its thesis turns me into a modern counterpart of the dinosaurs and pterodactyls when they were on the verge of extinction. Rather, it's the superior and mocking air with which Professor Steiner assumes the role of a cultural Cassandra, announcing, with cheerful masochism—and, for full sarcastic effect, in a public lecture before the Publishers Association of Great Britain, which, upon the occasion of its centenary, had invited him to give a talk about the book—the end of one civilization and the dawning of another, ontologically different and purged of the printed page.

As far as the thesis itself is concerned, it is probably true in its broader strokes, though doubtless exaggerated and presented with unnecessary dramatics. There is no question that in fields like electronics and computer science, technology has made astounding strides, or that the audiovisual media siphon off more and more potential readers of literature. Coming from someone more qualified than anyone else to know better, however, the claim that advertising and the small screen are already producing masterpieces on the same level as literary ones seems a wild provocation. In any event, that is not yet the case, and those of us who try to combine our love for books with more or less regular exposure to television and film are made aware on a daily basis that it will be a long time before that fantasy comes true, if it ever does.

And besides, the prospect that the book may be relegated to a minority activity and nearly driven underground in the society of the future is not something that should demoralize lovers of literature. On the contrary, many good things may come of that marginalization. This, in my opinion, is the Achilles' heel of Steiner's argument: to have forgotten that fiction and poetry were enjoyed by a majority and truly popular only when they were oral, spoken and sung in squares and on the road. Since these arts were put into writing, their public has been reduced to a negligible minority, an educated elite, which, of course, grew somewhat with the invention of the printing press. But literature has never been a genre for "the masses," not even today, when the artistic and creative book reaches an important sector of the population (though never a majority in the strict sense) in a very few modern and prosperous countries. I highly doubt, for example, that the readers of novels and poems in Spain could fill the stands of the Real Madrid soccer stadium. And I'm afraid that in Peru they would fit into a cinema, with room left over.

On the other hand, the most notorious consequence of the great expansion of the audience for literary books—the forging of those large minorities in countries like France, England, and the United States—has been, paradoxically, not the massive dissemination of the best literature but the plummeting of intellectual and artistic standards for literary novels. This expansion has given rise to a subculture—that of the best-seller—which, instead of facilitating the enjoyment and appreciation by a vast public of the greatest literary creations in prose or verse, has caused new readers almost exclusively to read manufactured products that are, in the best of cases, only bad and, in the worst, of a dizzying stupidity that almost certainly corrupts its consumers and vaccinates them definitively against real literature.

By way of illustration I'd like to mention two examples that have just come to me out of the blue. I read in the *Times* this morning that since President Bill Clinton invited her to read a poem at his inauguration, Maya Angelou, an American poet of the second or even the third rank, is the most widely read poet of all time in the English language. Just this year, Angelou, who often addresses the theme of poverty in her poetry, earned royalties of four and a half million dollars. How much must the beautiful long-legged model Naomi Campbell have earned when, some time ago, she published a novel launched with a barrage of radio and television ads? Naturally, I'm not against models writing novels. But therein lies the problem. Miss Campbell didn't write the book: she only appears as its author.

Why should we shed tears for the disappearance of this circus of posing, confusion, and vanity? If this is what will vanish under the steamrolling onslaught of audiovisual culture, so be it. The book won't die, of course. It will return to its former position, kept alive by a minority enclave who will demand the rigor, good prose, inventiveness, ideas, persuasive illusions, freedom, and audacities that are notable for their absence in the great majority of the books that now usurp the title of literature. In that future fraternity of catechists of the book, Professor Steiner will be read and discussed, without his needing to play—at his age—the *enfant terrible*.

London, May 1996

The Immigrants

Some friends invited me to spend the weekend at a country house in La Mancha, and there they introduced me to the Peruvian couple who cleaned and cared for the place. The man and woman were very young, from Lambayeque, and they described to me the series of adventures that had brought them to Spain. In the Spanish consulate in Lima they were denied a visa, but an agency specializing in cases like theirs got them a visa for Italy (whether real or forged they didn't know) that cost them one thousand dollars. Another agency took charge of them in Genoa; it helped them to secretly traverse the Côte d'Azur and cross the Pyrenees on foot, along goat paths in freezing-cold weather, for the relatively affordable price of two thousand dollars. They had now been living for a few months in the land of Quixote, and they were beginning to get used to their new country.

A year and a half later I saw them again, in the same place. They were much better adjusted and not just because of the time that had passed; eleven members of their Lambayeque family had followed in their footsteps and were now settled in Spain. All had work, as domestics. This story reminded me of another, almost identical tale that I heard a few years ago from a Peruvian in New

York, an illegal immigrant who cleaned the cafeteria at the Museum of Modern Art. She had survived a true odyssey, traveling by bus from Lima to Mexico and crossing the Rio Grande with the "coyotes," and she was delighted by the way times had changed: her mother, instead of enduring such torment to get into the United States through the back door, had come in recently by the main entrance. In other words, she had gotten on a plane in Lima and disembarked at Kennedy Airport, with papers efficiently forged in Peru.

These people, and the millions like them who come from anywhere there is hunger, unemployment, oppression, and violence and who clandestinely cross the borders of countries that are prosperous, peaceful, and rich in opportunity, are certainly breaking the law, but they are exercising a natural and moral right which no legal norm or regulation should try to eliminate: the right to life, to survival, to escape the infernal existence they are condemned to by the barbarous regimes entrenched on half the earth's surface. If ethical considerations had any persuasive effect at all, the women and men who brave the Straits of Gibraltar or the Florida Keys or the electric fences of Tijuana or the docks of Marseille in search of work, freedom, and a future should be received with open arms. But since arguments appealing to human solidarity move no one, maybe this practical one will be more effective: better to accept immigration, even if reluctantly, because, welcome or unwelcome, as the two examples I began this article with go to show, there's no way to stop it.

If you don't believe me, ask the most powerful country on earth. Let the United States tell how much it spends trying to bar the doors of golden California and sweltering Texas to Mexicans, Guatemalans, Salvadorans, and Hondurans, and to protect the emerald coastline of Florida from Cubans, Haitians, Colombians, and Peruvians; ask how many each day stream in, blithely evading all the land, sea, and air patrols, passing over or under the barbed-wire fences built at exorbitant cost and also, most notable, under the noses of highly trained immigration officers. They arrive thanks to an industrial infrastructure more effective than all the useless filtering devices installed out of a panicky fear of the immigrant, who in recent years has become a universal scapegoat, blamed for every calamity.

Anti-immigration policies are doomed to fail because they'll never manage to halt the influx. In the meantime, they have the perverse effect of undermining the democratic institutions of those countries that enact them, giving a veneer of legitimacy to xenophobia and racism and paving the way to authoritarianism. A few years ago, a fascist party like Le Pen's National Front in France, established exclusively on the basis of the demonization of the immigrant, was a paltry blemish on the face of democracy; today it is a "respectable" political force that controls almost a fifth of the electorate. And in Spain we witnessed, not long ago, the embarrassing spectacle of some poor illegal Africans who were drugged by the police in order to facilitate their expulsion from the country. So it begins, and it could end with the notorious hunts for undesirable foreigners that punctuate the universal history of wrongdoing, like the purging of Armenians in Turkey, Haitians in the Dominican Republic, or Jews in Germany.

Immigrants cannot be stopped by police measures for a very simple reason: in their home countries, the incentives for them to leave are more powerful than the obstacles put in their path to dissuade them from coming. In other words, there is work for them where they are headed. If there weren't, they wouldn't come. Immigrants are destitute but not stupid. They don't flee from hunger, at the cost of infinite hardship, in order to die of starvation abroad. They come, like my countrymen from Lambayeque settled in La Mancha, because there are jobs available that no

Spaniard (read North American, Frenchman, Englishman) would take for the pay and conditions that these people accept; the same was true of the hundreds of thousands of Spaniards who invaded Germany, France, Switzerland, and the Low Countries in the sixties, bringing with them an energy and man power that contributed enormously to the tremendous industrial takeoff of the host countries (and helped Spain itself, with the flow of funds it entailed).

This is the first law of immigration, which has been obscured by the prevailing demonization: the immigrant doesn't usurp jobs, he creates them, and he is always a factor of progress, never of decline. The historian A. J. P. Taylor explained that the Industrial Revolution that made England great would never have been possible if Great Britain hadn't been a country without borders at the time, a place where anyone could settle anywhere (the only requirement being to obey the laws), invest or withdraw money, open or close businesses, and hire employees or seek employment oneself. The astounding development of the United States in the nineteenth century, and of Argentina, Canada, and Venezuela in the 1930s and 1940s, coincided with open-door immigration policies. This was recalled by Steve Forbes in the U.S. Republican presidential primaries this year, when he dared to propose the reestablishment of open borders, pure and simple, as instituted by the United States in its proudest moments. Senator Jack Kemp, who had the courage to support this proposal of thoroughly liberal derivation, is now a candidate for the vice presidency alongside Senator Bob Dole, and if he is consistent, he should defend it in the campaign for the White House.

Is there no way, then, to block or stem the migratory tide that sweeps the developed world from every corner of the Third World? Beyond dropping atomic bombs on the four-fifths of the planet that lives in poverty, there is not. It is entirely useless to spend the money of much-abused taxpayers to design ever more costly plans to seal the borders, because there is not one successful case to prove the efficacy of repressive policies. On the other hand, one hundred cases prove that borders turn into sieves when the societies they pretend to protect exert a magnetic pull on the disinherited. Immigration will slow when the countries that attract it are in crisis or saturated and thus become less attractive, or when the countries that generate it are able to offer their citizens work and opportunities for improvement. Galicians stay in Galicia today and Murcians stay in Murcia because they can live decently, as they couldn't forty or fifty years ago, and offer their children a better future than they could by breaking their backs on the pampas of Argentina or picking grapes in the French Midi. The same is true of the Irish, which is why they no longer emigrate with dreams of becoming policemen in Manhattan; the Italians stay in Italy because they can support themselves better at home than by making pizzas in Chicago.

There are kind souls who, in order to moderate immigration, propose that the governments of modern countries institute a generous policy of economic aid to the Third World. In principle, this seems very altruistic. If this help is understood as help to Third World governments, however, such a policy will aggravate the problem rather than attack its root causes. The aid that goes to gangsters like Mobutu in Zaire or the military regime of Nigeria or any of the other African dictatorships only serves to further swell the private bank accounts those despots keep in Switzerland; in other words, it increases corruption without benefiting the victims in the least. If aid is to be given, it must be carefully channeled to the private sector and monitored in every instance so that it does what it is intended to do, which is to create employment and develop resources, far from state gangrene.

In reality, the most effective way for democratic countries to help poor countries is by opening trade borders, purchasing their products, stimulating exchange, and instituting an energetic policy of incentives and sanctions to further their democratization, since, just as in Latin America, despotism and political authoritarianism are today the major obstacles keeping the African continent from overcoming the systematic impoverishment that has been its fate since decolonization.

This may seem a very gloomy essay to those who believe that immigration—especially black-, mulatto-, yellow-, or copper-skinned immigration—heralds an uncertain future for Western democracies. That is not the case for those who, like myself, are convinced that immigration of any color or flavor represents an injection of life, energy, and culture and that countries everywhere should consider it a blessing.

London, August 1996

The Devil's Advocate

⨏ ⨎

G eorge Soros became famous in September 1992, when he "broke" the Bank of England in a daring speculation against the pound sterling, bumping the pound outside the oscillation margins fixed for European currencies and making two billion dollars in one night.

There is another reason, however, besides his substantial earnings in the world's financial markets, for which Soros—a Hungarian Jew who suffered under first Nazism, then Communism, in his country, and at the age of seventeen fled to England, where he studied with Karl Popper and Friedrich Hayek at the London School of Economics before debuting as a financier on Wall Street—deserves to be known: the foundation that bears his name has spent and continues to spend a good portion of his immense business profits promoting democracy and human rights in countries ruled by dictatorships or recently freed from them, like those of central Europe.

Now this prince of capitalism has just added another feather to his cap: a long essay in *The Atlantic Monthly* harshly attacking the capitalist system and declaring that the free market and the philosophy of laissez-faire are the most serious threats existing today to open societies, world peace, and democratic culture. I hasten to add that although Soros isn't exactly an original thinker or a great stylist of the English language, he is far from being—as is often true of successful businessmen—a boring mediocrity when he isn't discussing what he knows, which is making money. He is well educated, he has ideas, and he is, for example, capable of quoting Popper (whose disciple he considers himself) from memory.

His long essay, nevertheless, is much more notable for the identity of its author than for what is expressed in it. Its theses only endorse, with some shadings of their own and without contributing fresh arguments, the criticisms of the free market or "untamed capitalism" advanced by those on the left, contending that without cautious state regulation and sophisticated policies for the redistribution of wealth, the market brutally polarizes society between those few who are rich and the very many who are poor, fosters an atmosphere of high tension and social violence, destroys consensus, and generates a climate favorable to the rebirth of antidemocratic ideologies (on the right and on the left).

"Although I have made a fortune in the financial markets," explains Soros, "I now fear that the untrammeled intensification of laissez-faire capitalism and the spread of market values into all areas of life is endangering our open and democratic society." This danger manifests itself in many different ways. A new, intransigent dogmatism has replaced the Marxist dogmas of class struggle and surplus value: the concept of the market as panacea, intelligent allocator of resources, and essential instrument of the prosperity of nations.

The new orthodoxy is false, however, since market freedom, or the free play of supply and demand, is usually an illusion. This is true of financial markets, for example, where the factors that determine the rise or fall of prices aren't always objective but often psychological variables of expectation or confidence which cause prices to soar or plummet. Then, too, in our postmodern era, publicity and marketing, not free competition, cause the public to desire certain products and force out others, thus upsetting a central assumption of market theory: the consumer's ability to make rational choices.

Even more troubling than the uncontrolled and unchecked rule of the market is the social Darwinism that results from it. Since the laissez-faire dogmatists have made taboo the very idea of state intervention in economic life to correct abuses or imbalances, "wealth does accumulate in the hands of its owners, and if there is no mechanism for redistribution, the inequities can become intolerable." At the national level, this leads to tensions, social crises, and a lack of civic support for institutions. In the international arena, the failure of rich countries to offer support to poor ones, and of democratic nations to offer support to those just testing their freedom, may lead to total collapse and a reversal of what seemed, with the fall of the Berlin Wall in 1989, the emergence of a new world order defined by the values of democracy.

Instead of seeing the planet sown with the open societies that were expected as a result of the Soviet empire's disappearance, we are witness to a horrible spectacle: the establishment, in the name of laissez-faire, of a robber-baron capitalism in the former Communist countries, with its most outrageous and atrocious expression in Russia. How long will that grotesque system of "free competition" survive, in which bands of gangsters wrestle for control of every market, corruption is the air the citizens breathe, and success only smiles on the most soulless and conniving? It is surprising, in fact, that the enemies of democracy haven't attracted more adherents in the former Communist countries, despite the terrible frustration of most people's hopes.

Soros recalls that when Adam Smith developed his theory of

the "invisible hand," he was convinced that it was undergirded by very solid moral philosophy, and that all the great liberal thinkers, even Popper, always believed that the market and the economic success it ensured were a means, a path toward the realization of higher ethical ideals of social solidarity, cultural progress, and the individual pursuit of perfection. In the version of capitalism triumphant today, he says, that has changed radically. Economic success has become the supreme value. Money is the determining criterion of the rightness or wrongness of any endeavor, the sole indicator of the respect or disdain deserved by businesses, people, or even countries. "The cult of success has replaced a belief in principles. Society has lost its anchor."

Only in this last part of his critique does it seem to me that Soros puts his finger on a painful problem, for which no one (himself included) has yet discovered an effective remedy. It is true that the freer the market and the more wealth it produces in a society, the more it dehumanizes and impoverishes personal relationships, since it considerably depletes spiritual and religious life, weakens the family, and turns existence into a suffocating routine governed by competition. But the great liberal thinkers were always aware of this, and from Smith to Ludwig von Mises they emphasized that if civilization was to be upheld, the free market must have as its indispensable complement an intense cultural and religious life. None of them could have foreseen that the development of technology, science, and the economy would provoke the collapse of religious culture and lead to such a radical transformation of culture in general. All open societies face this challenge, and none has yet found a creative response that might serve as a model for the rest.

In any case, getting to the crux of Soros's critique, I ask myself what society or country he could have in mind when he castigates unbridled capitalism for preventing the state from intervening in the economy, from putting into practice the kind of wealth re-distribution that would give capitalism a human face. Not the United States, certainly, where the state rechannels 35 percent of the national revenue into social programs, much less Europe, where Great Britain, the least redistributive country, devotes 40 percent of the national wealth to the welfare state. The odd thing is that, exactly contrary to his thesis, the developed capitalist countries with the most liberal economies (or, to be more exact, the least interventionist, since there has never been a contemporary economic society completely given over to laissez-faire except possibly Hong Kong—unfortunately, not for much longer) are the ones with the most advanced systems of social security and the ones that invest most in "correcting" inequalities.

The market doesn't just require free competition; it also demands the existence of a clear and equitable legal system that guarantees respect for contracts and defends citizens and businesses against abuse and injustice. This doesn't exist in Russia or many of the former Soviet republics, and this lack explains why a twisted and criminal version of the production and distribution of wealth has been established in those countries—as well as in much of the underdeveloped world—that is as far from the kind of liberal capitalism prevailing in societies with democratic institutions as Communism used to be. It's not an overblown market economy that encourages the proliferation of mafias in Russia, but the lack of a legal structure, a state worthy of the name, and honest and efficient judges.

Soros's remedy for capitalism's excesses is state intervention: higher taxes, regulations and rules, and also, I suspect, although he doesn't say so, a substantial public sector parallel to the private one. Considering all the horrific disasters that such practices have engendered in the Third World, it makes my hair stand on end to think that they are being promoted by one of Wall Street's most successful billionaires as the best way to protect open society and democratic culture. Soros doesn't realize, it seems, that the history of Latin America is practically a mathematical illustration of what happens to countries whose governments, in an attempt to correct the excesses of "untamed capitalism," intervene and regulate all of economic life as he recommends. The result isn't—alas!—a blend of social justice and well-being but rampant corruption fostered by mafioso alliances between governments and influential "capitalists," who substitute monopolies and captive markets for free competition, stifle the generation of wealth, massively spread poverty, and always end up establishing authoritarian systems sooner or later, sometimes openly and sometimes in disguise.

In order for a theory to be taken seriously in the fields of politics and economics, it must concur with current living reality (as opposed to the way things work in the arts, where theories may be justified by their intrinsic beauty). Put to this test, Soros's theory doesn't pass. The kind of unbridled capitalism he attacks, with its unregulated markets and governments shackled by the sacred taboo of laissez-faire, is a poetic fiction, something that has never existed and probably never will. The rift that in his view has opened up between open society and capitalist systems is not based on proof: a glance around is enough to show that in open societies, in the sense Popper gave the term, the free market is liveliest and most effective, and in more authoritarian and oppressive societies, the economy is most dependent on state control.

In other words, George Soros is much more successful as a practicing capitalist than he is at reflecting on and judging the system to which he owes his billions.

London, January 1997

A Defense of Sects

❦

In 1983 I attended a conference on the media in Cartagena, Colombia, presided over by the respected intellectuals Germán Arciniegas and Jacques Soustelle. There were at this conference, besides journalists from all over the world, some tireless young people endowed with the fixed and smoldering gaze of those who believe themselves to be in full possession of the truth. At a given moment, the Reverend Sun Myung Moon, head of the Unification Church, the organization that was sponsoring the congress through a front, made his appearance, causing a huge commotion among the youths. A little later, I realized that the progressive mafia had added to my roster of sins that of having sold out to a sinister sect, the Moonies.

Ever since I lost my faith, I've been in search of another to replace it, so I rushed with great excitement to see if the one espoused by that round and smiling Korean with his mangled English might be up to the task. This led me to read the magnificent book on the Unification Church by Eileen Barker, a professor at the London School of Economics who has probably studied the phenomenon of the proliferation of religious sects at the end of the millennium more seriously and responsibly than anyone else (I met her at that conference in Cartagena). From her I learned, among many other things, that the Reverend Moon not only considers himself assigned by the Creator to the trifling task of uniting Judaism, Christianity, and Buddhism in a single church but also believes himself to be a hypostasis of Buddha and Jesus Christ. This, naturally, utterly disqualifies me from joining his ranks: if, despite the excellent credentials that two thousand years of history have conferred on him, I am totally incapable of believing in the divinity of Christ, it would be hard for me to accept him in the form of a North Korean evangelist who couldn't even beat the U.S. Internal Revenue Service (which sent him to jail for a year for tax evasion).

However, if the Moonies (and the sixteen hundred other religious groups and factions registered by INFORM, which is headed by Professor Barker) leave me skeptical, I feel the same way about those who for some time have devoted themselves to harassing these groups and petitioning governments to outlaw them, arguing that they corrupt youth, destabilize families, swindle their own members, and infiltrate state institutions. What is happening these days in Germany with the Church of Scientology gives this subject a troubling immediacy. The authorities of some states of the Federal Republic—Bavaria, especially—intend to exclude Scientologists from administrative posts, and they have organized boycotts of films featuring John Travolta and Tom Cruise because they belong to the Church of Scientology, and have banned Chick Corea from giving a concert in Baden-Württemberg for the same reason.

Although it is an absurd exaggeration to compare this harassment to the persecution suffered by the Jews under Nazism, as was done in a declaration signed by thirty-four Hollywood personalities in a paid advertisement in *The New York Times* protesting the German initiatives against Scientology, such acts do constitute a flagrant violation of the democratic principles of tolerance and pluralism and set a dangerous precedent. It's fine to accuse Tom Cruise and his beautiful wife, Nicole Kidman, of impoverished sensibilities and terrible literary taste if they prefer reading the scientific-theological productions of L. Ron Hubbard, who founded the Church of Scientology four decades ago, to the Gospels. But in a country whose constitution guarantees its citizens the right to believe in whatever they like, or not to believe in anything at all, why should the authorities feel that they may stick their noses into the matter?

The only serious argument for prohibiting or discriminating against religious sects lies outside the reach of democratic regimes; it is viable in those societies where religious power and political power are one and the same and where, as in Saudi Arabia or Sudan, the state determines which is the true religion, thereby assuming the right to prohibit false ones and to punish heretics, heterodoxy, sacrilege, and enemies of the faith. In an open society, this isn't possible: the state must respect individual beliefs, as wild as they may seem, and must not identify itself with any church, since if it does it will inevitably end up riding roughshod over the beliefs (or lack of beliefs) of a large number of its citizens. We have seen this recently in Chile, one of the most modern states in Latin America but nevertheless little better than the Stone Age in some respects, since it still hasn't passed a divorce law, owing to the opposition of the influential Catholic Church.

The contentions wielded against sects are often correct. Their converts are frequently fanatics, their methods of proselytizing are intrusive (one Jehovah's Witness besieged me for a long year in Paris, trying to convince me to take the redemptive plunge and driving me into a frenzy of exasperation), and many of them literally empty their members' pockets. Couldn't one say exactly the same thing, though, about many extremely respectable offshoots of traditional religions? Are the ultra-Orthodox Jews of Mea Shearim in Jerusalem, who come out on Saturdays to stone cars driving through their neighborhood, a model of flexibility? Is Opus Dei by any chance less demanding in the commitment it requires from its full-fledged members than the most intransigent evangelical operations? These are examples selected at random, out of many others, which prove many times over that all religions—from those validated by the patina of centuries and millennia, a rich literature, and the blood of martyrs, to the most incredibly flamboyant, based in Brooklyn, Salt Lake City, or Tokyo and promoted on the Internet—are potentially intolerant and by nature monopolistic and that the justifications for limiting or prohibiting the functioning of some of them are just as valid when applied to any other. In other words, one is left with two options: either all are prohibited without exception, as has been attempted by some naïve regimes—the French Revolution, Lenin, Mao, Castro—or all are authorized, with the sole stipulation that they obey the law.

It hardly bears saying that I am a firm believer in this second option. And not just because the ability to practice a religion without facing discrimination or persecution is a basic human right. For the vast majority of human beings, religion is the only path leading to a spiritual life and an ethical conscience. Without religions there would be no such thing as human coexistence or respect for the law or any of the essential covenants that sustain civilized life. One very great mistake, repeated many times over in the course of history, has been the belief that knowledge, science, and culture would eventually liberate man from the "superstitions" of religion, until progress made religion obsolete. Secularization has not replaced our gods with the ideas, knowledge, or convictions that might have taken their place. It has left a spiritual void that human beings fill as best they can, sometimes with grotesque substitutes or multiple forms of neurosis or by heeding the call of those sects which, precisely because of their welcoming and tight-knit nature and their meticulous plan for all the instants of physical and spiritual life, offer balance and order to those who feel confused, lonely, or lost in today's world.

In this sense they are useful and should be not only respected but encouraged. Certainly not, however, with subsidies or taxpayers' money. The democratic state, which is and may only be secular or neutral in matters of religion, gives up that neutrality if it exempts one religion from paying taxes and allows it other privileges which are not extended to minority faiths by arguing that the majority or a considerable percentage of the country's citizens profess the same faith. This is a dangerous policy, because it discriminates in the subjective sphere of beliefs and promotes institutional corruption.

The furthest one should go in this regard is to do what Brazil did when it built Brasília, its new capital: donate a stretch of land along an ad hoc avenue and allow any church in the world to build a house of worship on it if it likes. Several dozen stand there, if my memory doesn't deceive me: big, ostentatious buildings, pluralistic and idiosyncratic in design, among which thunders, proud and bristling with cupolas and indecipherable symbols, the Rosicrucian Cathedral.

Santo Domingo, February 1997

A Walk through Hebron

U p on a roof on Shalala Street, the main street of Hebron,
a swarm of Palestinian children play their favorite game.
They are eight, ten, twelve years old, and they throw
stones or shoot them with slings over a crumbling ledge, from
which they gather their ammunition. Half a dozen policemen in
black uniforms try halfheartedly and unsuccessfully to restrain
them: the children—impossible not to think of Gavroche and *Les
Misérables*—wriggle out of their grasp, and sometimes throw peb-
bles or stones as they are dragged into the street. Below, a crowd
of adult men (seeded with a few clumps of women) watch what is
happening with anger and frustration from behind the police bar-
ricade—of officers and armored cars—that keeps them from getting close to the Israeli soldiers, whose helmets, rifles, and green
uniforms may be spotted thirty or forty meters ahead.

The no-man's-land that separates them is sown with objects,
some so huge—rocks, slabs of pavement, iron rods, chunks of
metal—that it seems they must have been launched by catapults,
not human arms. As we cross it, pressed against the wall since the
hail of stones continues though it is slackening now, I see the
Palestinian policemen struggling to pull away more children,

who are trying to sneak up on the enemy from unlikely hiding places—the hollows of windows, the eaves and gutters of roofs, the mouths of drainpipes. I see some of them from very close up, and I am shaken by the precocious, unbridled, incommensurable hatred I see stamped on their features.

Hebron is one of the eight cities on the west bank of the Jordan River that was returned to the Palestinian Authority by Israel as a result of the Oslo Accords. One hundred twenty thousand Palestinians and 450 Israelis live here, these last concentrated in the settlements of Beit Hadassah and Avraham Avinu, not far from where I am. At ten this morning, two students from one of the settlements' religious schools shot and killed a young Palestinian who, they said, had tried to attack them. In the demonstrations that have convulsed the area since then, two more Palestinians have been killed, and one hundred people wounded, by the rubber bullets that the Israeli army uses to deal with street unrest. We heard the shooting when we arrived in the city, half an hour ago. The no-man's-land I am crossing is littered with these bullets, some round and some cylindrical; I put one in my pocket to keep as a souvenir.

The Israeli soldiers on guard at the other end of the no-man's-land are also very young, and although in theory they can't be under eighteen, the age at which they begin their three-year military service, some seem to be sixteen or even fifteen. They shield themselves from the stones around corners and behind jutting walls; they wear helmets, visors, bulletproof vests, clusters of grenades, and rifles; and one of them, overcome by the heat or nervous strain, has just collapsed and is on the ground choking and vomiting. His companions urge us to leave the area, since stones are still raining down from time to time.

We continue on, and less than half a block away is the settlement of Beit Hadassah, surrounded by barbed wire, floodlights, and sandbags and guarded by soldiers and Israeli police. It is a single multistoried building with two side wings, which we are allowed to enter after we show our identification papers. I spot two settlers carrying buckets of cement with Uzi machine guns over their shoulders, but what perplexes me is a small group of children who, in the midst of the turmoil, play on a slide, swing, and build sand castles. There is a brutal counterpoint between this idyllic childhood scene and what is happening around us just a few feet away on the streets of Hebron; what has happened and will continue to happen around this defiant enclave and those like it that dot the West Bank, so long as Palestinian-Israeli violence persists and until the two nations settle on some form of coexistence.

When I was in Israel two years ago, the miracle seemed possible and already on its way to being accomplished. The climate of optimism was rousing and contagious. I heard Shimon Peres say, "There will be peace. The accords are irreversible," and I believed him wholeheartedly. Then came the assassination of Yitzhak Rabin, Peres's defeat in the elections, and the rise to power of the Likud and Bibi Netanyahu, and the forward motion was halted abruptly. Now pessimism reigns everywhere, and not a single one of my Israeli friends holds out much hope that the tendency will be reversed in the near future. Some of them, like the writer Amos Elon, even believe that the Oslo Accords are already dead and buried and that only the merest simulation of them has been retained, for appearance' sake. In other words, they believe that once again the little flame of apocalypse has begun to flutter on the horizon of the Middle East.

This prospect doesn't at all seem to trouble the only Beit Hadassah settler with whom I manage to exchange a few words. He is thin, blond, and blue-eyed, with two delicate earlocks that the wind brushes against his cheeks, and, like most Jewish settlers, he is soberly dressed. He has the look of those who are secure in their beliefs and knowledge, who never doubt. When I say to him, motioning toward the children playing, that it is terrible for them to live like this, in confinement and under duress, among weapons, stone throwing, explosions, and uncertainty, that it will leave permanent scars, he looks at me with pity, not scorn. "They are very happy," he assures me. "I wish I had been lucky enough to live here as a child, the way they live. Excuse me now, I must make lunch for my daughter."

That 450 people with a different language, customs, and religion should live in a city of 120,000 Arabs doesn't seem terrible. Under normal circumstances, it could even be healthy. But as things stand, it is a provocation and a major obstacle to peaceful coexistence. The settlers know this very well, and it is what makes them dig themselves in here, forming these enclaves in Palestinian territory. Once they are established, the Israeli state is obliged to protect them, which means maintaining military patrols around the settlement. And to do that, it must build a barracks and a headquarters. This infrastructure has an impoverishing and paralyzing effect on the surrounding area, which is then prone to the kind of incidents and violence that we witnessed this morning. The Arab market that separates the colonies of Beit Hadassah and Avraham Avinu, which we later cross, is deserted except for a few cats sunning themselves among the garbage piles, and the doors and windows of some of the businesses are boarded up, as if they have been permanently closed.

At the entrance to the Avraham Avinu settlement is an enormous poster that says, in Hebrew and English: "This market was built on a synagogue taken by the Arabs in the year 1929." The text alludes to a small Jewish community established since time immemorial in Hebron, which was massacred by the Arabs during the 1929 rebellion. Very close by rises one of the most revered holy places of Jews and Muslims alike: the former call it the Tomb of the Patriarchs, and the latter the Abraham Mosque.

In fact, the synagogue and the mosque are a single building, divided by a wall reinforced with sheets of steel and equipped with widely separated entrances for the faithful of each religion. Now, in order to enter the mosque, one must pass through a metal detector and submit to careful questioning by the Israeli patrol stationed at the door. These precautions have been tightened since, two years ago, a settler from a Jewish settlement on the outskirts of Hebron, the doctor Baruch Goldstein, entered this vast and carpeted space at prayer time and, become a killing machine, raked the crowd with machine-gun fire, leaving 29 dead and 125 wounded, and thus letting the world know that fanatic and homicidal madness is not the exclusive patrimony of Hamas or Islamic Jihad but a bloody excrescence that also afflicts Jewish extremist groups.

Walking around downtown Hebron on a morning like this, escorted by Juan Carlos Gumucio (of *El País*) and his wife, Marie Colvin (a *Sunday Times* correspondent whose nose was broken by a stone not long ago), is a practical illustration of Isaiah Berlin's theory of contradictory truths. It is a mistake, Berlin explains, to believe that one truth always eliminates its opposite, that it is not possible for two clashing truths to coexist. In the realm of politics and history, such a situation may arise, as it has in the conflict that so often bloodies Palestinians and Israelis. To any tolerant observer who judges the matter rationally, the accusations that each levels against the other are equally persuasive.

No one can deny the Israelis their right to a land that is tied to their history, culture, and faith, or their right to a country that they've created by investing an incredible amount of heroism, sacrifice, and imagination—a country, it is also worth remembering, that is the only working democracy in the Middle East, a region of limitless despotism. And who could deny the Palestinian people, after the exile, war, dispersion, persecution, and discrimination they have suffered—which makes them so closely resemble the Jewish people—the right to finally have what they never had in the past, an independent and sovereign state?

That two truths are "contradictory" doesn't mean they can't exist side by side. The concepts of justice and freedom secretly repel each other, but democratic society and the culture of freedom have managed to keep these embattled siblings from destroying each other; on the contrary, coexisting in tense harmony under the rule of law, they make possible the advance of civilization. Israelis and Palestinians must learn to live alongside each other for the simple reason that, despite what the fanatics believe, there is no other alternative—except apocalypse, which is not a solution, since no social problem is resolved by collective suicide. The Oslo peace accords, signed by Rabin, Peres, and Arafat, and the steps taken in the following months to put them into effect, finally ended the stalemate and proved that what had seemed impossible was possible.

Until Oslo, the major obstacle to negotiation came from the Palestinian side, from its extremely violent methods and its senseless refusal to recognize Israel's right to exist; it seemed politically under the sway of intransigent extremism. The accords demonstrated that there was a flexible and pragmatic contingent willing to make the indispensable concessions to achieve peace and that it wielded sufficient power to resist the partisans of all or nothing. In Israel such a force has always existed, but, unfortunately, until Oslo it hadn't found a partner in its Palestinian adversary. Today, the main obstacle to enacting the accords is Netanyahu's government and his arrogant initiatives and brusque gestures, which have once again fraught with distrust and hostility a relationship that was beginning to grow easier. The West, especially the

United States, with which Israel maintains very close relations, has the obligation to pressure the Israeli government to respect the spirit and letter of the Oslo Accords, which, for the first time since its birth, have opened up for Israel the possibility of peace and collaboration with the whole Arab world.

Jerusalem, April 1997

Seven Years, Seven Days

☙ ❧

Fom my desk across the bay, I can clearly make out the two islands—San Lorenzo and El Frontón—and the spur of La Punta cleaving the waters of the Pacific. It is a glorious day, unusual in the middle of May, by which time Lima is usually already draped in the white veil that made Melville call it a "ghostly city." Beneath the midday sun, the sea blazes, bombarded by seagulls who let themselves fall from on high, wings folded, in pursuit of submarine delicacies.

At a naval base near those whitish isles, Abimael Guzmán and Víctor Polay languish under tight lockup in underground cells. Their crimes as the top leaders of the Shining Path and the Túpac Amaru Revolutionary Movement (MRTA), respectively, and the insecurity and indignation they aroused among Peruvians were decisive factors in the crumbling of democracy and in providing justification for the regime that has governed Peru since April 5, 1992.

The MRTA's seizure of the Japanese embassy made the outside world believe terrorism was on the rise. The attack was, rather, its swan song. Leaderless and hit hard by government repression, the Shining Path and the MRTA, although they show sporadic signs of life, no longer figure significantly in Peruvian daily existence. In the seven days I've spent here, not a single person has mentioned them to me. The violence everyone talks about is criminal, not political: houses robbed, watches and bracelets snatched from drivers, people kidnapped as they go about their daily business. Where terrorism is concerned, and especially after the successful rescue of the hostages at the Japanese embassy, the regime may pride itself on its achievements.

And the economic successes it boasts of? In 1990, when I left for Europe, Peru seemed to be falling apart, worn down by terrorism and the populist politics of Alan García. Hyperinflation, a sharp drop in salaries, one bankruptcy after another, the disappearance of savings and any kind of investment, the country quarantined by the international financial community, an enormous, inefficient, and corrupt public sector consuming the meager resources of the state: the outlook was grim. All that is now in the past, and to my astonishment its lessons seem to have been well learned. This week, I haven't seen the smallest sign that anyone misses García's politics, which impoverished the country more than all the wars in its history. The newspaper *La República*, spearhead of the opposition, denounces human rights abuses, the constant violations of the law, and corruption, but it takes care not to request a return to statism and interventionism.

In this realm, too, the changes are unmistakable. The economy has righted itself, and a minority segment of the population is plainly benefiting from privatization, the opening of borders, and the creation of markets. There is an explosion in the construction of apartment buildings for the upper classes, and Lima is full of supermarkets, department stores, malls, North American fast-food chains (McDonald's, Pizza Hut, Burger King, Kentucky Fried Chicken), video stores, modern movie theaters, and restaurants; under the auspices of the brand-new Telefónica, new users get telephone service in just a few days (I had to wait nine years for mine). One hundred television channels reach the homes of those able to pay for cable, and several grand luxury hotels have been built. At the one where the model Claudia Schiffer recently stayed, the suite she occupied cost fifteen hundred dollars a day (this was related to me with patriotic pride). These hotels have a large and cosmopolitan clientele, since every week more Spanish, Canadian, American, Japanese, and Korean investors arrive in search of projects: "Peru," I am assured by a credible friend, "has become a very attractive country for international capitalism." Congratulations: I always said it was possible, when few believed it was and our government did its best to keep it from being so.

Modernization has also come, though more uncertainly, to some pockets in the interior. On the pampas of Ica, there has been a proliferation of small and medium-size businesses that employ drip irrigation and other up-to-the-minute technologies to grow tomatoes, asparagus, flowers, and other products for export; mining investments in the central and northern Andes are considerable.

All of this is wonderful, of course, but to deduce from these signs that Peru is caught up in a process of sustained and unstoppable development, like Chile's, would be a mistake. The truth is, the economic developments still only affect a tiny fraction of the population, the top sliver of society, while the sacrifices demanded of the majority are enormous. The opening of borders raised prices to international heights, while salaries remain at underdevelopment levels, and hundreds of thousands of families go hungry or barely get by. The rates of infant mortality, malnutrition, tuberculosis, illiteracy, and delinquency are still horrifying. And practically nothing has changed for the poorest of the poor—the peasants of the Sierra—who are still the "nation apart" of which José María Arguedas spoke. This deep fissure between the sector of society that is becoming steadily more prosperous and the majority, for whom modernization comes in dribs and drabs if at all, is not, as the new ideological mantra repeats, the inevitable result of "neoliberalism." On the contrary, the problem is that many of the reforms were scarcely liberal or not liberal at all. A good example is the privatization process, which only transferred state monopolies into private hands and did not take advantage of its mandate to massively increase the number of landowners among the poor, as was done in England or is being done now in Poland, the Czech Republic, and other central European countries.

In any case, defective and insufficient as they may be, the economic reforms instituted by Fujimori's authoritarian regime are a step in the right direction, and the democratic government that will someday replace Fujimori should extend and perfect them, certainly not retreat. It is a notable sign of progress that the state has unburdened itself of useless public businesses, that the country has entered world markets, and that the responsibility for creating wealth falls increasingly on civil society and not on the bureaucrats. There is no other way to escape underdevelopment.

These economic advances, however, contrast ominously with what is happening in the country's political life. Instead of making progress toward a freer and more democratic society, Peru has retreated into its most sinister past. Contrary to what I supposed, the regime is barely keeping up appearances, instead shamelessly flaunting its authoritarian character and an arrogance based on military force. The Congress is laughable: its obsequiousness and corruption surpass even those displayed under Manuel Odría's dictatorship. The desperate efforts of the small minority of members of the opposition—whose courage and good intentions I don't doubt—only serve to make their impotence more pathetic in the face of a regimented majority which unquestioningly and unswervingly (as one is taught in the army) obeys its sad duty to lend a veneer of legality to all the excesses, and sometimes crimes, of the regime. Over the course of these seven days, it has been preparing to unseat the Constitutional Court, because four of its magistrates have dared to oppose reelecting Fujimori in the year 2000.

If Congress is a farce, the Ministry of Justice is a debilitated and mistreated institution that has lost a good deal of its power to the boundless jurisdiction of the military, in whose tribunals (secret, elusive, and masked) the true law is laid down. Not just "subversives" are claimed by the army judiciary, but also those involved in cases in which the state's interests and secrets are at stake. For example, the assassins and torturers of the Colina Group, the regime's death squad, which has been credited with deeds like the massacre at Barrios Altos, the assassination of students and professors at La Cantuta University, and the very recent dismembering of one National Intelligence Service agent and the torturing of another in the cellars of the General Headquarters (both had talked too much). Drug traffickers who inconvenience the government may also be pulled out of the civil justice system and turned over to the Supreme Counsel of Military Justice, as happened to "Vaticano," a mafia leader who revealed that for years he had had high military officials on his payroll receiving bribes, among them the notorious Vladimiro Montesinos, presidential adviser, CIA lackey, and strongman of the dictatorship, who (it has just been revealed) last year mysteriously made more than a million dollars.

The absolute (and barely disguised) preponderance of the military over the civilian in public life is the main obstacle Peru must overcome if it is to restore democracy one day. The military is now the backbone of power, and civil institutions are frills, to be reconceived and refashioned at will. The National Intelligence Service—the eyes, ears, and muscle of the regime, born out of the coup it planned itself and executed on April 5, 1992—makes all the important decisions, manipulates and misinforms the public, and hatches plans to discredit (and sometimes financially ruin or even liquidate) dissidents and members of the opposition. Purged of its most professional and principled officers, who have been dismissed or removed from any important posts, the armed forces, under the direction of Montesinos and General Nicolás de Bari Hermosa, have once more become, as in the era of the dictators Juan Velasco and Odría, the ruling party, the supreme arbiters of national political life, although for the moment it retains a civilian puppet as president in order to placate international opinion, which no longer accepts gorillas in berets and gold braid at the helms of Latin American governments.

To reverse this state of affairs it is not enough for Fujimori to lose ground in the polls or for more and more Peruvians to confess in whispers to trusted confidants (heaven forbid the government should send them to SUNAT for an investigation of their tax statements) that they are embarrassed and concerned about the future because they've realized that no matter how solid it seems now, in the long run nothing creates more instability and chaos than dictatorship. It would require a multiparty and popular mobilization like the one that confronted Pinochet's regime in Chile, a mobilization capable of resisting the authorities' infinite forms of intimidation and blackmail, to rally national and international public opinion to the cause of democracy, stripping away the blindfolds that still prevent the nation and the world from glimpsing the true face of the Peruvian regime. This mobilization is nowhere near taking place. As hardworking and idealistic as it may be (and this week I've witnessed how thoroughly hardworking and idealistic it is), the democratic opposition—in Congress, the limited free press, and the small civil spaces where public expression is possible—is still very weak and fragmented. It lacks leadership and any alternative proposal that can persuade most Peruvians of the advantages of freedom and legality over brute force and deception and, at the same time, guarantee that the needed process of democratization will in no way signify the smallest backward step away from what has already been gained through modernization and the establishment of economic order.

So long as this mobilization fails to occur—and in the joy of these seven days spent among friends, many of whom I was seeing for the first time in seven years, the only melancholy note has been the realization that the failure persists—Fujimori, Montesinos, Bari Hermosa, and the army of soldiers and civilians at their command will live as calmly and unconcernedly as the blithe white seagulls which, just a few meters from my desk, fish this morning in the Pacific in the pearly light of day.

Lima, May 1997

Nudes in a Classical Garden

uring the sixties, much of which I spent living in Paris, I
heard many jokes about the Belgians. They were as bad
as the jokes the Spanish tell about the natives of Lepe, or
the Peruvians tell about people from Huacho, jokes in which the
French got their laughs from an ontological silliness that their
neighbors bore the brunt of all their lives. The jokes described the
Belgians as dull, predictable, good-hearted, cautious, bovine, and,
most of all, devoid of imagination.

Since then the Belgians have several times managed to make
front-page news (proving—to themselves as well—the fallacious-
ness of such national stereotypes), whether for the fierce linguistic
quarrels between the Walloons and the Flemish, who have more
than once been on the verge of splitting their country apart, or, recently, for the macabre joint sport of murder and pedophilia practiced by some of the country's citizens, which has filled the streets
of Brussels with furious demonstrators protesting the complicity
and neglect of the police and the justice system in these horrible
cases. Each time, those jokes have tended to crop up in my memory, followed by a pang of guilt.

Unimaginative, the natives of this low-lying country, whose

mountains are, as Jacques Brel sang, the spires of their cathedrals? So far as politics and crime are concerned, for the moment they have proved themselves as extravagant, outrageous, and fierce as anyone. And in painting? Three of Belgium's artists—René Magritte, James Ensor, and Paul Delvaux—alone have fantasized and dreamed more than whole communities of painters from the most creative countries of the century now drawing to a close.

The work of the first two I knew well; that of Delvaux, however, I had seen only in bits and pieces, in small shows or in reproductions that never gave a full sense of the originals. Now, thanks to the retrospective organized by the Royal Museums of Fine Arts in Brussels to celebrate the centenary of Paul Delvaux (1897–1994), which brings together a quarter of his oeuvre (including drawings, engravings, and nearly fifty notebooks), I know why, if I had to single out one of the great trio, my choice would be Delvaux. He was the most driven of the three, the one who most tenaciously and loyally heeded his demons, the one who best managed to orchestrate the unnatural alliance between academic formalism and thematic delirium that is the common denominator of the trio and of so many symbolists and surrealists.

Reading the biography of this peaceable scion of the Belgian bourgeoisie, no one would suspect that the son and brother of lawyers who appears in childhood photographs escorted by uniformed nursemaids and sporting the kind of hoods adorned with pom-poms that spoiled children wear, with the same stunned face that the nudes among the Greek temples in his paintings would later display, was endowed with such a remarkable oneiric talent, or such a quiet but persistent irreverence for the crippling conformist values and principles of the environment into which he was born. When his parents told him that Miss Anne-Marie "Tam" de Martelaere, with whom he had fallen in love, wasn't right for him, he obeyed them. (But he kept loving her, and a quarter century later, upon meeting her again, he married her.) And he didn't dare to enroll in the art academy until his family had resigned itself to his becoming an artist—once he had shown unmistakable proof of his unfitness for law and architecture.

All Delvaux's life—a long, monotonous, and minimalist life in everything that did not concern painting—is marked by this exterior respect for form and convention, a submission to conformity and authority that was only eclipsed when he took up his pencil or brush, the magic act, one might say, that freed him against his will from his family, social circle, and country and deposited him bound hand and foot into a more rebellious and creative servitude: that of his obsessions.

These were few and they are well documented, in his painting and his life. Only a handful of interesting things happened to Delvaux, but he certainly took full advantage of them. He was dazzled by the Jules Verne stories he read as a child, and half a century later he was still recalling the geologist Otto Lidenbrock from *Journey to the Center of the Earth* and the astronomer Palmyrin Rosette from *Off on a Comet*. The memory of the human skeletons that danced in the windows of his primary school in St.-Gilles never left him, and they served as models for the beautiful series *Crucifixions* (and for the innumerable skeletons that roam his paintings), presented at the Venice Biennale in 1954. They caused such a scandal that Angelo Giuseppe Cardinal Roncalli (the future Pope John XXIII) censored the exhibition.

Around 1929, at a fair near the Gare du Midi in Brussels, Delvaux happened upon a stall pompously calling itself the Spitzner Museum, which exhibited, among various human deformities, a Venus made of wax. Powered by an ingenious mechanism, it seemed to breathe. I won't say that he fell in love with her, because the idea of such a proper gentleman indulging in the kind of mad acts favored by the characters in Luis García Berlanga's films is inconceivable, but her image did stir and torment him for the rest of his life; he conjured her up time and again over the years, in the same half-sullen, half-mysterious pose in which she appears in his loveliest paintings, sometimes bathed in burning, sensual sunlight and sometimes half hidden in the subtle bluish glow of the moon. The Spitzner Museum had shown him (he said when he was very old) "that a 'drama' could be expressed in painting without giving up its plastic qualities."

All the decisive events and images that gave rise to the recurrent motifs of his mythology appear in his notebooks and letters: train stations, classical architecture, symmetrical gardens, and, of course, the 1934 *Minotaure* exhibition in Belgium, where he saw for the first time eight "metaphysical" landscapes by Giorgio De Chirico. The impression they made on him caused him to retreat to Spy, a Walloon village, where he remained until he had succeeded in painting spaces like the Italian's, terribly empty but full of something menacing and invisible, captured by the brush an instant before it materialized.

But probably the most important experience of Delvaux's life—and I would swear that it came just as belatedly as his discovery that he was a painter—was his realization that, beneath the bulky clothes that covered them, women had hips, thighs, and breasts, a body better than any other being or object for representing the thing that the surrealists tried to capture with exalted nouns: the marvelous, the poetic, the intriguing, the disturbing, the fantastic. They searched for it; he found it. No contemporary painter has paid homage with such devotion, delicacy, and imagination to the female body, that miracle which Delvaux never tired of extolling and which he would continue to portray, with the same childlike astonishment, when he was past ninety, though with wobbly strokes. His first nudes, dating from the late twenties, reveal traces of the influence of psychology. Later, they are purged of emotion, sentiment, and specific traits, and they merge into a single form, which, though generic, is always intense and carnal. Usually blond, with big eyes lit by some vision, a rather opulent shape, and never a smile relieving the intense concentration of the face, Delvaux's women seem to imitate statues, whether in his airless gardens, at the foot of Greek columns, or in deserted stations. One look is enough to tell you that each is unattainable and untouchable, a sacred being, capable of awakening desire in others but incapable of feeling it herself, even on those few occasions in which another silhouette—masculine or feminine—reaches to caress her. Only when she changes into a tree, fish, flower, or skeleton does she seem at ease. This is a world without men, since when men appear, they immediately realize they are out of place. André Breton said it best: "Delvaux has made the universe the realm of woman, and always the same woman . . ." He's right. But Delvaux also made the universe a place astoundingly different from the one we know and inhabit, rich in insinuations and suggestions of every sort. It moves us and it unsettles us, because, while it is naïve, fragile, and surprising, it also seems to hide something malignant and to be at the point of disappearing at any moment, like the landscapes we visit in dreams.

Around the Royal Museums of Brussels is the neighborhood of Sablon, crowded with antiques shops, art galleries, and cafés and restaurants whose terraces spill onto the sidewalks and all the way to the cobbled streets. It is a radiantly sunny Sunday, the sky a deep blue, a wonderful day for eating outside (a *carbonnade*, of course) and for drinking beer on tap, which the natives of this country make thick and foamy. At the tables around me, families of Walloons and Flemings do everything possible to resemble the characters in the bad French jokes about Belgians, to make me believe that they are careful, polite, well dressed, so proper they're nearly invisible. But appearances don't deceive me. After having spent three hours with Paul Delvaux? Never again. Now I know that behind the prim and proper facades lurk deeds of inconceivable daring and wicked monsters and that all those mad dreamers like Ghelderode, Maeterlinck, Ensor, Magritte, and Delvaux employed the same strategy, the better to hide themselves, pretending to be good neighbors, placid members of the bourgeoisie taking the dog out for a stroll every morning with religious punctuality.

Brussels, May 1997

Epitaph for a Library

❧ ❧

Yesterday I got incontrovertible proof that my cozy and beloved London refuge was about to be snatched from me. I entered the Reading Room of the library, in the heart of the British Museum, and instead of being embraced by the usual warmth, I was faced with a bleak spectacle: half of the countless shelves that ring the space had been emptied, and in place of the elegant rows of thousands of bound books were stretches of faded wood, scattered with spots that looked like spiderwebs. I don't think I've had such a feeling of betrayal and loneliness since I was five years old, when my mother took me to the La Salle School, in Cochabamba, and left me in Brother Justiniano's classroom.

I first came to this place thirty-two years ago, when I had just arrived in London, in order to read the books of Edmund Wilson, whose essay on the evolution of the idea of socialism—*To the Finland Station*—had captivated me. Before I even noticed the wealth of the collection—some nine million volumes—I was dazzled by the beauty of the central Reading Room, sheltered by those shelves smelling of leather and paper and bathed in a bluish light falling discreetly from the incredible cupola built by Sydney Smirke in

1857, the biggest in the world after the Pantheon in Rome, which bests it by barely two feet in diameter. Used to working in impersonal and uncomfortable libraries, like the Bibliothèque Nationale in Paris, which was always so crowded that at exam time it was necessary to line up in the Place de la Bourse for an hour before it opened in order to get in, I couldn't believe that this one, besides being so beautiful, was so comfortable, so silent and hospitable, with soft seats and long tables where you could spread out your notebooks, index cards, and tall piles of books without disturbing your neighbors. Old Marx spent a good part of his life here, according to Edmund Wilson, and in the sixties his desk was still on view to the right of the entrance, though it disappeared with all its fellows when that row was given over to computers in the mid-eighties.

Without exaggerating, I can say that I've spent four or five afternoons a week of all my time in London over three decades in the Reading Room of the British Library and that here I've been immensely happy, happier than any other place in the world. Here, lulled by the whisper of the little carts that go around from reader to reader delivering requests, and soothed by the absolute certainty that no telephone or doorbell would ring, or any visitor appear, I prepared my literature classes when I taught at Queen Mary's College and at King's College; here I've written letters, articles, essays, plays, and half a dozen novels. And here I've read hundreds of books, thanks to which I've learned almost everything I know. But mainly in this room I've fantasized and dreamed alongside the great poets, the illustrious weavers of spells, the masters of fiction.

I grew accustomed to working in libraries when I was a university student, and everywhere I've lived I've tried to continue the practice, so much so that my recollections of countries and cities are in good part determined by the images and anecdotes I retain of their libraries. The one in the old mansion of San Marcos in Lima had a dense and colonial atmosphere, and the books exhaled little puffs of dust that made you sneeze. In the National Library, on Abancay Avenue, the students made a hellish noise and the proctors who shushed them (emulated them, rather) with piercing whistles were even worse. In the library of the National Club, where I worked, I read the whole erotic collection *Les Maîtres de l'amour*, edited, introduced, and translated by Guillaume Apollinaire. In the freezing National Library of Madrid in the late fifties you had to wear a coat so as not to catch cold, but I went there every afternoon to read novels of chivalry. The discomfort of the one in Paris surpassed all the others: if you absentmindedly moved your arm away from your body, you would dig your elbow into your neighbor's ribs. There, one afternoon, I lifted my eyes from a crazy book about crazy people, *Children of Clay*, by Raymond Queneau, and found myself face-to-face with Simone de Beauvoir, who was sitting across from me, writing furiously.

My biggest surprise on the subject of libraries came from a learned Chilean charged with acquiring Latin American books at the Library of Congress in Washington, D.C. When I asked him in 1965 how he chose what to buy, he responded: "Very easy. I buy every book that is published." This was also the millionaire policy of the great Harvard University library, where you had to look for books yourself, following a complicated path indicated by the computer that served as receptionist. In the semester I spent there, I never managed to orient myself in that labyrinth, which meant I could never read what I wanted to read, but only what I stumbled upon in my wanderings in the belly of that bibliographic beast. I can't complain, however, since I made marvelous discoveries, like the memoirs of Aleksandr Herzen—a Russian liberal, no less!—and *The Octopus* by Frank Norris.

In the Princeton University library one snowy afternoon, taking advantage of my neighbor's inattention, I sneaked a glance at the book he was reading and happened upon a quote concerning the cult of Dionysus in ancient Greece which caused me to alter entirely the novel I was writing and to attempt in it a modern Andean re-creation of the classical myth about irrational forces and divine inebriation. The New York Public Library was the most efficient of all—no subscription card was required, and the books you requested were brought out in minutes—but it had the hardest seats, so it was impossible to work there for more than a few hours unless you brought a cushion to protect your coccyx.

Of all these libraries and of some others I have pleasant memories, but none of them, separately or together, has helped me, stimulated me, or served me so well as the Reading Room. Of the innumerable episodes with which I could illustrate this statement I choose this one: finding in its catalogue the tiny magazine published in the Amazon half a century ago by the Dominican fathers serving in that remote region, which constitutes one of the few records of the Machiguengas and their myths, legends, customs, and language. I had asked friends in Lima to find it and photocopy it, to no avail—I needed the material for a novel—and it turned out that the whole collection was here, in the British Library, at my disposal.

In 1978, when the Labour government then in power announced that because of overcrowding a new library would be built and that the Reading Room would be returned to the British Museum, a shiver ran down my spine. But given the abysmal state of the British economy then, I calculated that the costly project would probably take more years to complete than I had left to live. Nevertheless, after the eighties, things began to look up in the United Kingdom, and the new building, to be erected in St. Pancras, a neighborhood most famous for its pimps and prostitutes, began to grow and reveal its horrendous face of bricks and jail-house bars. The historian Hugh Thomas formed a committee to try to convince the authorities that even though the British Library was moving to a new location, the Reading Room at the British Museum should be preserved. I was a member of the committee, and I wrote letters and signed petitions, but they did no good, because the British Museum was determined to recover what by law belonged to it and its influence and arguments prevailed over ours.

Now everything is lost. The books have already been taken to St. Pancras, and although in theory the Reading Room will be open until the middle of October and a month later the Humanities Reading Room that is to replace it will open, it has already begun to die, little by little, ever since its books, which were its soul, were torn out and it was left an empty shell. Some few of us sentimentalists will keep coming until the last day, as we accompany those who are very dear in their final agonies in order to be by their side as they draw their final breath, but nothing will be the same these months, not the old silent bustle or the comfortable feeling with which one read, researched, took notes, and wrote there, plunged into a curious state of being, that of having escaped the march of time, of having touched in that concave space of blue light the atemporality of life as it is lived through books and through the ideas and admirable fantasies incarnated in them.

Of course, in the almost twenty years that have passed since construction began, the St. Pancras library has already become too small and won't be able to house all the stock, which will be dispersed in warehouses scattered around London. The defects and deficiencies that apparently afflict it have made the *Times Literary Supplement* describe it as "the British Library or the Great Disaster." I, of course, haven't been inside, and when I pass by it I look at the contrived flourishes of its courtyard, not at its stony blood-red walls, which make one think of banks, barracks, or power stations rather than intellectual labors. I, of course, won't set foot there until I no longer have any choice, and I'll keep proclaiming until my death that in replacing that much-loved place with this monstrosity, a shameful crime has been committed, and one that is easy to explain besides, since aren't these the same people who sent poor Oscar Wilde to jail and outlawed *Ulysses* and *Lady Chatterley's Lover?*

London, June 1997

The Hour of the Charlatans

❧ ❧

On the afternoon of Jean Baudrillard's lecture, I arrived at the Institute of Contemporary Arts half an hour early to look around its bookstore, which, though tiny, I've always considered a model of its kind. But a surprise was in store for me, because since my last visit the little place had undergone a classificatory revolution. The old-fashioned sections of earlier days—literature, philosophy, art, film, criticism—had been replaced with postmodern ones like cultural theory, class and gender, race and culture, and a shelf labeled "The Sexual Subject," which gave me a brief moment of hope but turned out to have nothing to do with eroticism, only philological patristics and linguistic machismo.

Poetry, the novel, and theater had been eradicated; a few screenplays were the only creative form on display. Occupying a place of honor was a book by Deleuze and Guattari titled *Nomadology* and another book, apparently extremely important, by a group of psychoanalysts, jurists, and sociologists on the deconstruction of justice. Not a single one of the titles most prominently displayed (like *Rethinking Feminist Identification*, *The Material Queer*, *Ideology and Cultural Identity*, and *The Lesbian Idol*) appealed to me, so I left without buying anything, something that rarely happens to me in a bookstore.

I had come to hear Baudrillard speak because the French sociologist and philosopher, one of the heroes of postmodernism, bears much responsibility for what is happening these days in our cultural life (if that term still has a reason to exist alongside phenomenons like the one under way at the London ICA bookstore). And also because I wanted to see him face-to-face, after so many years. In the late sixties both of us attended the third-cycle courses given at the Sorbonne by Lucien Goldmann and Roland Barthes, and we both lent a helping hand to Algeria's FLN through the aid networks created in France by the philosopher Francis Jeanson. At that time, everyone already knew that Baudrillard had a brilliant intellectual career ahead of him.

He was extremely intelligent and expressed himself with admirable eloquence. Back then, he seemed very serious, and it wouldn't have offended him to be described as a modern humanist. I remember hearing him, in a St. Michel bistro, savagely and amusingly tear apart Foucault's thesis on the nonexistence of man in *The Order of Things*, which had just appeared. He had excellent literary taste, and he was one of the first in France to note the genius of Italo Calvino, in a splendid essay on Calvino that Sartre published in *Les Temps Modernes*. Later, at the end of the sixties, he wrote two dense, stimulating, long-winded, and sophisticated books that would cement his reputation, *The System of Objects* and *The Consumer Society*. From that point on, and as his influence spread around the world, setting down particularly strong roots in Anglo-Saxon countries—proof: the packed auditorium at the ICA and the hundreds of people outside who couldn't get tickets—his talent, following what seems to be the fated course of the best French thinkers of our day, has become more and more focused on an ambitious undertaking: the demolition of what is, and its replacement with a ver-bose unreality.

His lecture—which he began by citing *Jurassic Park*—more than confirmed this for me. The compatriots who preceded him in this labor of attack and demolition were more cautious. According to Foucault, man doesn't exist, but at least his inexistence has presence, occupying reality with its versatile void. Barthes believed that real substance could be found only in style, the inflection that each animate life is capable of im-printing on the river of words in which the self appears and dis-appears like a will-o'-the-wisp. For Derrida, real life is the life of texts, a universe of self-sufficient forms that modify and refer back to one another without ever coming close to addressing inessential human experience, that remote and pallid shadow of the word.

Baudrillard's sleight of hand is even more categorical. True re-ality doesn't exist anymore; it has been replaced by virtual reality, the product of advertising and the media. What used to be called "information" actually does the complete opposite of informing us about what is happening around us. It supplants and nullifies the real world of deeds and objective actions: they are cloned versions of what we see on television, selected and prepared by media pro-fessionals (or conjurers), and they substitute for what was once known as historical reality, the objective knowledge of what is go-ing on in the world.

Real-world events can no longer be objective. Their truth and ontological consistency are undermined from the start by the corrosive process of their projection as the manipulated and falsified images of virtual reality; these are the only images admissible and comprehensible to a humanity tamed by the media fantasy world we are born into and in which we live and die (no more and no less than Spielberg's dinosaurs). Besides abolishing history, television "news" also vanquishes time, since it eliminates all critical perspective on what is happening: the broadcasts occur at the same time as the events they are supposedly reporting on, and these events last no longer than the fleeting instant in which they are enunciated, then disappear, swept away by others which in turn are annihilated by new ones. This vertiginous denaturalization of the actual world has resulted, purely and simply, in its evaporation and in its replacement by the truth of media-created fiction, the only true reality of our age: the age—says Baudrillard—of "simulacra."

That we live in an era of large-scale representations of reality that make it difficult to understand the real world seems to me an unassailable truth. But isn't it clear that nothing, not even media mumbo jumbo, has muddied our understanding of what is really going on in the world more than certain intellectual theories, which, like the wise men from one of Borges's lovely fantasies, pretend to embed speculative play and the dreams of fiction in real life?

In the essay he wrote proving that the Gulf War "did not take place"—since all that business involving Saddam Hussein, Kuwait, and the allied forces was no more than television playacting—Baudrillard stated: "What is scandalous, in our day, is not attacks on moral values, but on the principle of reality." I wholly agree. At the same time, this seems to me an involuntary and harsh self-criticism from someone who, for many years now, has invested his dialectic shrewdness and the persuasive power of his intelligence in proving to us that audiovisual technology and the communications revolution have abolished the human ability to tell the difference between truth and lies or history and fiction, and have made us, bipeds of flesh and blood strayed into the media labyrinth of our time, mere ghostly automatons, pieces of machinery stripped of freedom and knowledge and condemned to expire without ever having lived.

At the end of the lecture, I didn't go up to say hello or to remind him of the bygone days of our youth, when ideas and books excited us and he still believed we existed.

Fuschl, August 1997

Elephant Dung

༄ ༅

In England, believe it or not, art scandals are still possible. The very respectable Royal Academy of Arts, a private institution founded in 1768 that often presents, in its Mayfair gallery, retrospectives of great classic artists or of modern artists anointed by the critics, is these days at the center of one that is delighting the press and the philistines who don't waste their time at exhibitions. But they'll turn out in force for this one, thanks to the scandal, thus permitting—every cloud has a silver lining—the poor Royal Academy to weather its chronic economic crises a little longer.

Was it with this end in mind that the academy organized its *Sensation* show of works by young British painters and sculptors from the collection of the advertising magnate Charles Saatchi? If so, it was a great success. Though they may hold their noses, the masses will certainly come to have a look at the works of young Chris Ofili—twenty-nine years old, student of the Royal College of Art, and star of his generation, according to one critic—who mounts his works on bases of hardened elephant dung. It isn't for this peculiarity, however, that Ofili has made tabloid headlines, but for his blasphemous piece *The Holy Virgin Mary*, in which the mother of Jesus appears surrounded by pornographic photographs.

But it isn't this painting that has provoked most comment. That prize goes to the portrait of a famous child murderer, Myra Hindley, composed of children's handprints by the shrewd artist. Another of the show's innovative works is a collaboration by Jake and Dinos Chapman; it is called *Zygotic Acceleration*, and—as its title implies?—it unfurls a fan of androgynous children whose faces are really erect phalluses. It goes without saying that accusations of pedophilia have been raised against the inspired authors. If the exhibition is truly representative of what inspires and concerns young artists in Great Britain, one has to conclude that genital obsession is at the top of the list. For example, Mat Collishaw has produced a work showing, gigantic in the foreground, the impact of a bullet on the human brain; but what the spectator really sees is a vagina and a vulva. And what to say about the daring creator who has crammed his glass boxes with human bones and, apparently, the remains of a fetus?

What is notable about the affair isn't that products of this sort slip into top galleries but that people are still surprised by it. As far as I'm concerned, I noticed that something was rotten in the art world exactly thirty-seven years ago, in Paris, when a good friend, a Cuban sculptor fed up with the galleries' refusal to show the splendid wood carvings that I watched him labor over from morning to night in his *chambre de bonne*, decided that the surest route to success in art was to do something attention catching. Immediately he produced some "sculptures" that consisted of pieces of rotten meat in glass boxes, with live flies flying around inside. A few speakers made the buzz of the flies echo throughout the place, like a terrific threat. Sure enough, he triumphed; even Jean-Marie Drot, star of French television and radio, devoted a program to him.

The most unexpected and disturbing consequence of the evolution of modern art and the myriad experiments feeding it is that there are no longer any objective criteria that make it possible to qualify or disqualify something as a work of art or situate it within a hierarchy. The possibility began to disappear with the cubist revolution and disappeared entirely with abstract art. Today, "anything" can be art and "nothing" is, depending on the sovereign whim of the spectator, who has been elevated, since the demise of all aesthetic guidelines, to the level of arbiter and judge, a position once held solely by certain critics. The only more or less generalized gauge for works of art today has nothing to do with art; it is imposed by a market controlled and manipulated by gallery cartels and dealers. Rather than reflecting tastes and aesthetic sensibilities, it revolves around publicity and public-relations campaigns and, in many cases, simple scams.

About a month ago, I attended the Venice Biennale for the fourth time in my life. (It will be the last.) I was there for a few hours, I think, and as I left I realized I would not welcome into my house a single one of all the paintings, sculptures, and objects I had seen in the twenty or so pavilions I had visited. The spectacle was as boring, farcical, and bleak as the show at the Royal Academy but one hundred times bigger, with dozens of countries represented in the pathetic display. Under the guise of modernity, the experiment—the search for "new means of expression"—in reality documented the terrible dearth of ideas, artistic culture, dexterous craftsmanship, and authenticity and integrity that marks a good portion of the artistic work of our times. There are exceptions, of course. But it is extremely difficult to locate them, because, contrary to the way things happen in the field of literature—where the aesthetic codes that permit the identification of originality, novelty, talent, and mastery, or crudity and fraud, have not yet collapsed completely and where publishing houses still exist (for how much longer?) that maintain coherent and exacting standards—in the case of painting the system is rotten to the core. Often the most talented artists have no way of reaching an audience, whether because they refuse to be corrupted or because they are simply no good at doing battle in the dishonest jungle where artistic successes and failures are decided.

A few blocks from the Royal Academy, at Trafalgar Square, in the modern wing of the National Gallery, there is a small exhibition that should be obligatory viewing for every young person today who aspires to paint, sculpt, compose, write, or make films. It is called *Seurat and the Bathers*, and it is devoted to the painting *Bathers at Asnières*, one of the artist's two most famous pieces (the other is *A Sunday on La Grande Jatte*), painted between 1883 and 1884. Although he worked on this extraordinary canvas for two years, over the course of which (as one realizes at the show) he made innumerable sketches and studies of the details and entirety of the painting, the exhibition reveals that the whole of Seurat's life was a slow, stubborn, tireless, and fanatic preparation to reach the formal perfection he achieved in his two masterworks.

In *Bathers at Asnières*, that perfection astonishes and, in a way, overwhelms us: the repose of the figures sunning themselves, bathing in the river, or contemplating the scenery, beneath a midday sun that seems to dissolve the distant bridge, the locomotive crossing it, and the chimneys of Passy into the dazzle of a mirage. This tranquillity, this balance, and this secret harmony between man and water, cloud and sailboat, costume and oars are certainly manifestations of a total command of the medium, the sureness of line, and the use of color, all achieved by dint of effort; but they also represent an elevated and noble conception of the art of painting as a means of spiritual fulfillment and a source of pleasure in and of itself, in which painting is understood as its own best reward, a métier in the practice of which one finds meaning and joy.

When he finished this painting, Seurat was barely twenty-four, the average age, in other words, of those strident young *Sensation* artists at the Royal Academy; he lived only six more years. His tiny oeuvre is one of the artistic beacons of the nineteenth century. The admiration it arouses in us derives from more than technical skill and meticulous craftsmanship. Beyond all that, and somehow supporting and fostering it, is an attitude, an ethic, a manner of surrendering oneself to the service of an ideal, which a creator must embrace in order to transcend and extend the limits of a tradition, as Seurat did. This way of "choosing to be an artist" seems lost forever to today's impatient and cynical youth, who dream of seizing glory any way they can, even if to reach it they must climb a mountain of pachydermatous shit.

London, September 1997

A Maiden

⫸ ⫷

She is the same age as Shakespeare's Juliet—fourteen—and, like Juliet's, hers is a tragic and romantic story. She is beautiful, especially when seen in profile. Her long, exotic face, with its high cheekbones and big, slightly almond-shaped eyes, suggests a remote Oriental heritage. Her mouth is open, as if to defy the world with the whiteness of her perfect teeth, which protrude slightly, lifting her upper lip in a coquettish pout. Her very long black hair, gathered in two swaths, frames her face like a bride's cap, and is then plaited into a braid that falls to her waist and circles it. She is silent and still, like a character from the Japanese theater, in her raiment of fine alpaca. Her name is Juanita. She was born more than five hundred years ago, somewhere in the Andes, and now she lives in a glass box (which is, in fact, a computer in disguise), in a glacial cold of nineteen degrees below zero, protected from the touch of humans and decay.

I hate mummies, and every one I've seen, in museums, tombs, or private collections, has seemed utterly repellent to me. I've never felt the emotions aroused in so many human beings—not just archaeologists—by those trepanned skulls riddled with holes, their eye sockets empty and the bone calcified, bearing witness to past civilizations. What they mostly remind me of is our mortality and the horrid matter into which we are converted if we don't choose to be cremated.

I agreed to visit Juanita at the small museum constructed especially for her by the Catholic University of Arequipa because my painter friend Fernando de Szyszlo, who is fascinated by pre-Columbian history, was eager to make the trip. But I was convinced that the sight of her ancient child's body would turn my stomach. I was wrong. As soon as I saw her, I was moved, and enchanted by her beauty; if it hadn't been for fear of what the neighbors might think, I would've stolen her and set her up in my house as mistress and life companion.

Her story is as exotic as her delicate features and ambiguous pose, which could be that of a submissive slave or a despotic empress. On September 18, 1995, the anthropologist Johan Reinhard, accompanied by the Andean guide Miguel Zárate, was scaling the summit of the volcano Ampato (20,702 feet high), in southern Peru. They weren't looking for prehistoric remains but were trying to get a close-up view of the neighboring volcano, snowy Sabancaya, which was erupting just then. Clouds of smoldering white ash were falling on Ampato and had melted the permanent snow cover at its summit, which Reinhard and Zárate had nearly reached. All of a sudden Zárate spotted a blaze of color in the snow among the rocks: it was the feathers of an Inca cap or headdress. After searching the site a little longer, they found the rest: a funeral bundle which, because of the erosion of the ice at the summit, had surfaced and slid two hundred feet from the place where it had been buried five centuries before. The fall hadn't hurt Juanita (so christened after Reinhard, his first name being Johan); it had merely torn the top blanket she was wrapped in. In twenty-three years of climbing mountains—eight in the Himalayas, fifteen in the Andes—in search of traces of the past, Johan Reinhard had never felt anything like what he felt that morning, at 20,702 feet above sea level, beneath a blazing sun, when he held the Inca girl in his arms. Johan, an amiable gringo, told me the whole story of the adventure with an archaeological glee that (for the first time in my life) I found completely justified.

Convinced that if they left Juanita exposed on the mountaintop until they came back for her with an expedition they ran the risk that she might be stolen by grave robbers or swept away in a flood, they decided to take her with them. The detailed account of the three days it took them to descend Ampato carrying Juanita —the eighty-pound bundle well lashed to the anthropologist's backpack—has all the color and excitement of a good film, which it will doubtless become sooner or later.

In the slightly more than two years that have passed since then, the lovely Juanita has become an international celebrity. Under the auspices of the National Geographic Society, she traveled to the United States, where she was visited by a quarter of a million people, among them President Clinton. A famous dental surgeon wrote: "If only North American girls had teeth as white, healthy, and complete as this Peruvian young lady."

Juanita has been surveyed by all kinds of high-tech machines at Johns Hopkins University; examined, probed, and puzzled over by armies of experts and technicians; and finally returned to Arequipa in the coffin-computer specially built for her. All these examinations have made it possible to reconstruct, with a precision that borders on science fiction, almost her whole story.

The girl was sacrificed to Apu (the Inca word for god) Ampato, on the very summit of the volcano, to pacify his rage and to ensure prosperity for the Indian settlements of the region. Exactly six hours before her execution, she was given a vegetable stew to eat. The recipe for this dish is being reconstructed by a team of biologists. Her throat was not cut, nor was she strangled. Her death was the result of a precise blow to her right temple. "So perfectly executed that she must not have felt any pain at all," I was assured by Dr. José Antonio Chávez, who co-directed with Reinhard a new expedition to the area's volcanoes, where they found the tombs of two more children, also sacrificed to the voracity of the Andean Apus.

It is likely that after being chosen as a sacrificial victim, Juanita was venerated and paraded around the Andes—possibly taken to Cuzco and presented to the Inca emperor—before climbing from the Colca valley in a ritual procession, followed by bejeweled llamas, musicians, dancers, and hundreds of worshippers, up the steep slopes of Ampato to the edge of the crater, where the sacrificial platform stood. Did Juanita feel fear, panic, in those final moments? To judge by the absolute serenity stamped on her delicate features, and by the calm arrogance with which she receives the stares of her countless visitors, one would say that she didn't, that perhaps she accepted her fate with resignation and maybe even rejoiced at the brief, brutal procedure that would transport her to the world of the Andean gods, transformed into a goddess herself.

She was buried in a sumptuous robe, her head covered with a rainbow of braided feathers, her body wrapped in three layers of dresses finely woven of alpaca wool, her feet laced into a pair of light leather sandals. Silver brooches, engraved vessels, a bowl of *chicha* (an alcoholic drink made from fermented maize), a plate of corn, a little metal llama, and other sacred or domestic objects—all recovered intact—accompanied her in her centuries-long rest at the mouth of the volcano, until the chance warming of Ampato's icy cap melted the walls that protected her slumber and practically delivered her into the arms of Johan Reinhard and Miguel Zárate.

There she is now, in a little middle-class house in the quiet city where I was born, embarked on a new stage in her life, which will last maybe another five hundred years. In her computerized coffin, preserved from extinction by its polar cold, she testifies—depending on how you look at it—to the ceremonial riches and the mysterious beliefs of a lost civilization, or to the infinitely cruel ways in which human stupidity once exorcised its fears, and often still does.

Arequipa, November 1997

Mandela's Island

కఠ ఈ

When, in the winter of 1964, Nelson Mandela landed on Robben Island to serve a life sentence of forced labor, the island had known more than three centuries of horror. First the Dutch and then the British had banished blacks resistant to colonial rule there, simultaneously using it as a leper colony, madhouse, and jail for common criminals. Treacherous currents and sharks took care of the foolhardy who tried to escape by swimming. When the Republic of South Africa was established, the government stopped sending madmen and lepers to Robben Island; from then on it was solely a prison for outlaws and political rebels.

Until a few years before Mandela was sent there, the apartheid government, inaugurated in 1948 with the electoral victory of Hendrik Verwoerd's National Party, kept the common and political prisoners mixed, so that the former would torment the latter. This policy was discontinued when the authorities realized that cohabitation allowed for the indoctrination of many thieves, assassins, and vagrants, who soon swelled the ranks of the two principal resistance forces: the African National Congress and the Pan Africanist Congress. Though the common criminals and political prisoners were separated, the latter were also rigidly divided among themselves when Mandela arrived; leaders who were considered highly dangerous, as he was, were sent to Section B, where the security was tighter, and to their many sufferings was added that of living in almost constant isolation.

His cell, Number Five, which he occupied for the eighteen years he was on the island—out of the twenty-seven in all he spent in prison—is six and a half feet across, seven and a half feet long, and ten feet high: it looks like a closet, the den of a beast, rather than a human dwelling. The thick cement walls make it an oven in summer and an icebox in winter. Through the single small barred window, one can see a courtyard surrounded by a wall, which was patrolled by armed guards in Mandela's time. They were all white, and the immense majority were Afrikaners, just as the inmates of Robben Island were all black. The white prisoners had separate prisons, as did those of mixed Indian or Asian origin, dubbed "Coloured" by the system.

Apartheid went much deeper than racial segregation. It dictated a complex ranking of people by levels of humanity, with whites at the top, blacks at the bottom, and hybrids higher or lower on the scale depending on the percentage of whiteness possessed by the individual. In 1964, the South African prison system rigorously applied this philosophy, which had been championed by Verwoerd—more an intellectual than a politician—from his sociology chair at the University of Stellenbosch before the majority of the white South African establishment embraced it in 1948. It determined different regimens of food, clothing, work, and punishments for the inmate depending on the color of his skin. This meant that while mulattoes or Hindus had the right to Diet D, which included bread, vegetables, and coffee; blacks, allotted Diet F, were allowed nothing of the kind and had to nourish themselves solely on maize porridge. Discrimination was inflexible even when it came to the portions of food they all received:

Coloured inmates got two and a half ounces of sugar a day and blacks barely two. Those of mixed race slept on mattresses, and the Africans on straw mats; the former got three blankets, the latter, two.

Mandela accepted these distinctions without protesting about the food and bedding, but in the respectful manner he always affected, and which he never tired of recommending that his companions adopt in their dealings with prison authorities, he announced that he wouldn't wear the shorts that the regime assigned to black prisoners (with the intention of humiliating them, since this was the uniform worn by black servants in white households). Threats, brutal reprisals, solitary confinement, and other savage punishments, like the "box," which required the inmate to stand inside a small rectangle for hours and hours without moving until he lost consciousness (one of the methods of torture responsible for most suicides among the prison population), were all in vain. In the end, the political prisoners of Robben Island were issued the long pants that until then could be worn only by whites and prisoners of mixed race.

The day began at five-thirty in the morning. The prisoner had the right to leave his cell for a few minutes to empty his bucket of excrement and to wash in a common sink; although it was forbidden to speak to one's fellow prisoners, rapid exchanges with the other inmates of Section B were sometimes possible in these shared early-morning moments, or at least a silent physical and visual communication that lifted the spirits. After the first maize porridge of the day, the prisoners were led into the courtyard. There, sitting on the floor in silence and widely separated from one another, they broke up loads of limestone with pick and hammer. At mid-morning and at mid-afternoon, they were allowed a half-hour break, during which they could walk around the courtyard and stretch their legs. They received two more helpings of porridge, one at noon and the other at four in the afternoon, after which they were locked in their cells until the next morning. The lightbulb in each cell burned twenty-four hours a day.

The political prisoners had the right to receive a half-hour visit every six months, so long as they weren't being punished. The visit took place in a room where prisoners and visitors were separated by a glass wall with small openings in it, in the presence of two armed guards who were required to interrupt the conversation the instant it departed from family matters and touched on current events or political affairs. Twice a year, they could write and receive letters, which were subjected to rigorous censorship: any sentences that seemed suspicious or as if they might be hiding some political message would be crossed out.

This maddening routine, intended to destroy the prisoner's humanity, desensitize him, and deprive him of his vital reflexes, including hope in its most basic form, failed to achieve its objective in Nelson Mandela's case. The testimony of his ANC friends and PAC adversaries is conclusive: when this regimen was relaxed and he, after nine years of submitting to it, was at last able to study (he received a law degree by correspondence from the University of London), plant a little garden, and interact with the other political prisoners on the island (during the hours of common work in the limestone quarry half a mile from the prison and during breaks), he had achieved a new serenity and profundity. He had also acquired a political knowledge and clarity that were crucial in permitting him to impose his authority first on his Robben Island companions, then on the African National Congress, and finally on the whole country, to an almost comical extent, so that today in South Africa one hears whites (of Afrikaner, English, or other European descent) everywhere lamenting Mandela's decision not to run in the next elections and his decision to cede the ANC presidency to Thabo Mbeki. In the end, what is most extraordinary about Mandela's first decade on Robben Island and his passage through that infernal system isn't that he didn't lose his mind, or his will to live, or his political ideals. It is that in all those years of terror, rather than becoming filled with hatred and resentment, he came to the conclusion that the only sensible way of resolving South Africa's problem was through peaceful negotiation with the racist apartheid government. This strategy was aimed at persuading the country's white community—the 12 percent of the population that had been mercilessly exploiting and discriminating against the remaining 88 percent for centuries—that ending discrimination and embarking on political democratization would lead not to chaos and reprisals, as they feared, but to the beginning of an era of harmony and cooperation among South Africans of all races and cultures.

This generous idea had guided the ANC in its early days, when it was just a group of black leaders determined to do everything possible to show the white racists that people of color were not the barbarians they were believed to be. But at the beginning of the sixties, when the ferocity of government repression reached dizzying extremes, the idea of violent action won over even the moderate trio heading the African National Congress: Mandela, Walter Sisulu, and Oliver Tambo. Although they always rejected the PAC's program, with its calls of "Africa for the Africans" and "Throw the whites into the sea," they created an activist group within the ANC (Umkhonto we Siswe) to handle sabotage and armed action, and they sent young Africans to receive guerrilla training in Cuba, the People's Republic of China, North Korea, and East Germany. When Mandela arrived on Robben Island as Inmate 466/64, the idea that apartheid would only be ended by force, never by dialogue and persuasion, was firmly rooted in African public opinion. And with the National Party at the height of its power and its racist policies in full swing, who would have dared to contradict it?

Nelson Mandela dared, and he did so from the terrible solitude of the cave where he was sentenced to spend the rest of his days. In the second decade of his imprisonment, he developed prodigious tactical abilities, first convincing his own party members, the Communists, and the liberals. By his third decade in prison, when conditions had improved, he was able to communicate with the outside world and even Afrikaner government officials, exhorting them to initiate a dialogue and to come to an agreement that would ensure a free and multiracial future for South Africa. It took him twenty years of struggle and steel-willed confrontation of unspeakable obstacles, but in the end he succeeded, and—while still serving his life sentence—found himself having a civilized cup of tea with the last two apartheid presidents, P. W. Botha and F. W. de Klerk. Now, universally respected by whites, blacks, Indians, and mulattoes, he is the president-elect of the most prosperous and democratic country that the African continent has known in its long and very sad history.

That is why, if you come to this country, you shouldn't content yourself with exploring the pristine South African cities, which seem to have just been scrubbed and polished, or its spectacular beaches, elegant vineyards, or great forests, where lions, elephants, leopards, and giraffes walk free. Nor should you limit yourself to visiting—in order to see all the injustices that still remain to be remedied—the black townships, like Soweto, which sizzle with energy and creativity despite their poverty. Go, first of all, to Robben Island, the scrap of land, dun-colored and hazy in the middle of the sea, that may be spied from the Cape Town waterfront at sunset. One of the most phenomenal and hope-inspiring historical events of the late twentieth century was conceived there, in a cell unfit for man, thanks to the intelligence and greatness of spirit of the most admirable politician alive today.

Cape Town, January 1998

The Other Side of Paradise

⚜ ❧

In his essay on Gandhi, George Orwell ridiculed pacifism, explaining that the method Gandhi used to achieve independence for India could only succeed against a country like Great Britain, which was obliged by democracy to act within certain limits. Would it have worked against someone like Hitler or Stalin, whom nothing prevented from committing genocide? Turning the other cheek may mean a moral triumph, but it is completely useless when confronting totalitarian regimes. In certain circumstances, the only way to defend freedom and human dignity, or to survive at all, is by meeting violence with violence.

Was this the case in Mexico on January 1, 1994, when Subcomandante Marcos rose up in arms with his Zapatista Army for National Liberation (EZLN) and occupied several Chiapas villages? The corrupt dictatorship of the PRI, which since 1929 had enjoyed an all but absolute reign, had begun to lose ground; as the result of growing internal pressure for democratic reform, the dictatorship had ceded some of its power to opposition forces and begun slowly but surely to open up. To some of us it seemed that this process would be seriously hindered by the guerrilla actions and that, rather than aiding the Indians of Chiapas, these actions favored the PRI regime, giving it a welcome excuse to present itself as the guardian of peace and order to a middle class doubtless anxious for democracy but allergic to the idea of a Mexico devastated by civil war, in which the situation of Guatemala or El Salvador during the eighties might be reprised.

No one could have suspected then the peculiar evolution of the "first postmodern revolution," as Carlos Fuentes dubbed it, or the transformation of the masked *subcomandante*, with his pipe and two watches, one on each wrist, into an international star, courtesy of the sensationalistic frenzy of a media eager for exoticism and the irresponsible frivolity of a certain brand of Western progressive. This story should be told in great detail sometime, as testament to the delirious heights of alienation to which ideological *parti pris* can lead and the ease with which a Third World clown can compete with Madonna and the Spice Girls in seducing multitudes, so long as he has mastered the techniques of publicity and the political fashions of the day.

One has to thank the journalists Bertrand de La Grange, of *Le Monde*, and Maite Rico, of *El País*, for having contributed the most serious work written until now on this subject, with their book *Marcos: La genial impostura* (Marcos: The Brilliant Hoax; Aguilar, 1998), in which they patiently and bravely try to untangle the myths and lies surrounding the events in Chiapas. Both have covered these doings on the ground for their respective newspapers, both have firsthand knowledge of the devilish complexity of Mexican political life, and both display—I take my hat off to them—an independence of judgment not common among press correspondents reporting from Latin America. Their account paints a pitiless picture of the situation of the Chiapas Indians from colonial times and describes the terrible marginalization and exploitation they still suffer today under the current economic and political system. But it also proves unequivocally that the Zapatista uprising has not improved the condition of the native communities at all; rather—the other side of paradise—it has made things worse for them, socially and economically, creating great rifts in Chiapas's indigenous society and raising the level of violence that oppresses the Chiapans.

The first myth this investigation explodes is the idea that the Zapatista movement is indigenous and peasant-led. In reality, since the era of the National Liberation Forces, which gave birth to the EZLN, the EZLN has been led—like all its Latin American counterparts—by whites or mestizos of urban origin, strongly influenced by Marxist-Leninist ideology and seduced by volunteer work in the service of the Cuban revolution. This was the case of the university student Rafael Guillén Vicente, the future Subcomandante Marcos, who trained in Cuba. There, rather than focusing on military matters, he assiduously collected information about the life and personal habits of Che Guevara, out of which he later constructed a cloned persona for himself, although with the added trait of a mania for publicity, something the sober Argentinean revolutionary always disdained. In the Zapatista movement, the Indians are tools to be manipulated—"simply guinea pigs," say Rico and La Grange—window decoration, troops supplying the inevitable dead, and sometimes the executioners of other Indians. But never the protagonists; or, better said, the protagonist, because that is always Marcos, especially when he confesses, with effusive rhetorical self-criticism, that he has put himself forward too much and promises to surrender the stage to his "brother and sister Zapatistas" (he has yet to do so).

The second myth to be dismantled is the supposed "nonviolent" character of the Zapatista movement. True, military actions ceased two weeks after the uprising, when President Carlos Salinas, in a typical instance of fine-tuned PRI political Machiavellianism, decreed a "cease-fire" and began a dialogue with the

Zapatistas that his successor, Ernesto Zedillo, has continued. This dialogue has primarily revealed that the rebels lack a minimal program of reforms, a lack for which they have compensated with vague and confused claims in support of an indigenous "identity." These claims have made multiculturalists from North American and European universities delirious with enthusiasm but do nothing to alleviate in the slightest the miserable living conditions of the Chiapas peasants. A distinguished Mexican anthropologist, Roger Bartra, has explained that indigenous fundamentalism and the Church's return to the political arena—two consequences of the Zapatista movement—represent "a setback of the first order." A setback in Mexico's progress toward democratization, no doubt. But the events in Chiapas have been of great assistance to the PRI regime, as this book demonstrates, which means that the EZLN has become, despite itself, the "principal validator" of the system. For now, raising the specter of imminent danger, the Mexican army has obtained a "substantial increase" in budget and troops— it has made frequent purchases of light arms and armored vehicles from the United States, Russia, and France in recent years—and the military has come to play a central role in political life, a typically Latin American tragedy which Mexico had been spared until now.

Though news of the crimes against Zapatistas, like the savage assassination of forty-five Tzotil Indians, almost all women and children, in Acteal on December 22 last year, has been broadcast around the world and roused just indignation, another kind of violence in Chiapas has been deliberately silenced, because to condemn it would be politically incorrect: that committed by the Zapatistas against Indians resistant or hostile to Subcomandante Marcos. The most dramatic pages in the book by Maite Rico and Bertrand de La Grange are those reproducing some of the hundreds (possibly thousands) of letters sent by Indians from various

Chiapas communities to parish priests, NGOs, and local authorities, denouncing—in rudimentary and sometimes barely comprehensible language, which betrays the humble origins of the sender—the thefts and plundering, the expropriations, the physical maltreatment, and the blackmail to which the Chiapas Indians who refused to submit to the designs of the masked Marcos were subjected. More than thirty thousand peasants—almost half the population of Las Cañadas, say the authors—have been forced to flee their places of birth because of the "political cleansing" operations ordered by the individual the distinguished French sociologist Alain Touraine has called—with not a quiver in his voice—"the armed democrat."

It is understandable that Touraine, and Régis Debray, another Marcos champion (in his euphoria he has called Marcos "the best Latin American writer of our times"), and the tireless widow of François Mitterrand should still have their heads in the clouds after a visit to Chiapas as tourists and that they should confuse their desires with reality. What is not comprehensible, however, is the conduct of the slippery Samuel Ruiz, bishop of San Cristóbal de las Casas, who has an in-depth knowledge of what is really going on in Chiapas, because he has lived there since 1960 and has himself received some of these desperate accusations. Why has he systematically hidden them or, when he had no way of dodging the matter, downplayed them as much as possible? Not out of sympathy for Marcos and the Zapatistas. Though he helped them in the early years—in his praiseworthy eagerness to protect the Indians from the depredations of the *caciques*, he called on a group of militant Maoists as advisers!—he later kept them at arm's length, not, as this book records, because of differences of principle, but for purposes of emulation and hegemonic competition. The bishop suffers, like Marcos, from a weakness for publicity and is as sensitive as a blushing violet to political opinion.

The book exudes affection and admiration for Mexico, a country whose spell is certainly difficult to resist. At the same time, a righteous wrath burns in its pages at the way events in Chiapas have been twisted and cannibalized by those who shamelessly seek Third World Robin Hoods to placate their consciences, alleviate the political boredom induced by humdrum democracies, or slake their thirst for revolutionary romanticism. The description of an idiot in Bermuda shorts called John Whitmer, who gave up anthropology in Connecticut in order to serve as a Zapatista commissary and to vet the political orthodoxy of journalists who come to Chiapas, is, in and of itself, a clear denouncement of the species. He is just one of the many in this book who sadden and irritate those of us who really do want to see Mexico free at last from the manipulative and abusive—and often brutal—PRI political monopoly that has functioned for more than seventy years. The first and indispensable requirement for improving the living conditions of the Chiapas Indians and the Mexican people in general is the democratization of the country's political life, the opening up of its society, the reinforcement of its institutions, and the establishment of a justice system that protects all of its citizens from the abuse of any kind of power, without exception.

Subcomandante Marcos has not aided this process of Mexican democratic reform in the slightest; he has hampered and confused it, leaching legitimacy from the democratic opposition and giving the system he claims to combat excuses for continuing to remain in power. Of course, the virtual hero he is today might be killed tomorrow, either by his adversaries or by some envious ally, and he might then take his place in the pantheon of heroes and liberators: history is peppered with these prestidigitations. But as this book proves many times over, that is not the fate he deserves. More appropriate might be that augured by the offers he has received from two of his most enthusiastic admirers: the filmmaker

Oliver Stone, who would like him to star as himself in a film, and Oliviero Toscani, Benetton's top adman, who sees him as a model in a "United Colors" ad campaign. Toscani's triumph will be the image of the *subcomandante*—mask on, machine gun over his shoulder, pipe in his mouth—in the center of a company of armed Indians in uniform gazing trustingly into the glow of the sun on the horizon.

Berlin, March 8, 1998

Painting to Survive

ॐ ॐ

Frida Kahlo is extraordinary for many reasons, among them the fact that the fate of her painting demonstrates the tremendous revolution a good biography can sometimes spark in matters of artistic judgment. And by the same token, just how precarious artistic judgments have become in our day.

Until 1983, Kahlo was known only in Mexico and to a limited international community of art lovers, more as a surrealist curiosity praised by André Breton, and as the wife of Diego Rivera, than as an artist whose work deserved respect in and of itself and not as an appendix to a movement or a mere complement to the work of the famous Mexican muralist. In 1983, Hayden Herrera's book *Frida: A Biography of Frida Kahlo* appeared in the United States. Her fascinating account of the life and artistic odyssey of the Mexican painter, read everywhere with well-warranted absorption, had the virtue of catapulting Kahlo into the epicenter of curiosity within the planet's artistic hubs, beginning with New York; soon her works had become some of the most famous and sought-after in the world. For the last ten years or so, those rare paintings reaching the auction floors of Sotheby's and Christie's have sold for the highest prices ever commanded by a Latin American painter, including, of course, Diego Rivera, who is more and more often identified as Frida Kahlo's husband.

What is most notable about the sudden and inexorable rise in prestige of Kahlo's painting is the unanimity of opinion on which it is based. She is praised by critics serious and frivolous, clever and foolish, formalist and political, and at the same time that she is installed as an icon of the feminist movement, she is seen by conservatives and antimodernists as a reminder of the classical among the excesses of the avant-garde. But what is perhaps most astonishing is that her reputation was cemented even before her paintings could be seen, since besides the fact that she painted few of them (fewer than one hundred) many—the best—were until recently firmly ensconced in a very strict private collection, to which only a handful of mortals had access.

This story could certainly give rise to an interesting reflection on the vagaries of the wheel of fortune that today raises artists up or silences them and blots out their work for reasons often having little to do with its true merits. I mention this only to add that in this case, for mysterious reasons—fate, justice, the whims of a playful god—instead of resulting in one of those familiar if absurd false canonizations of fashionable artists, Hayden Herrera's biography and its aftereffects—everything about Frida Kahlo's fate is incredible—have served to put one of the most captivating figures of modern art in her rightful place, four decades after her death.

My enthusiasm for Kahlo's painting is of very recent origin. It derives from a trip I took a few weeks ago to the Alpine community of Martigny, a Swiss town that in two thousand years of history seems to have witnessed just two noteworthy events: the passage through town of the Roman legions—they left behind some stones that are now exhibited with excessive veneration—and the present exhibition devoted to Diego Rivera and Frida Kahlo, organized by the Pierre Gianadda Foundation. The show is a model of its kind, in the quality of the selection and in the skill with which the paintings, drawings, photographs, and text have been arranged, immersing the spectator for hours in the world of both artists.

The experience is conclusive: although Rivera had more technical skill and ambition, was more wide-ranging and curious, seemed more universal in his appeal because he reconciled the main artistic currents of his era and his own historical circumstances, and left a vast oeuvre, Kahlo, despite the occasional clumsiness of her hand, her pathetic lapses into gruesomeness and self-pity, and also, of course, the grating naïveté of her ideas and proclamations, was the more intense and personal artist—I would say the more authentic, if that term weren't rife with confusion. Overcoming the almost indescribable limitations that life dealt her, Kahlo was able to create a consummately coherent body of work, in which fantasy and invention are extreme forms of introspection and self-exploration and the artist extracts in each painting—each drawing or sketch—a horrifying testament to suffering, desire, and the most terrible vicissitudes of the human condition.

The first time I saw Kahlo's paintings was twenty years ago, when I visited the Blue House, her museum-home in Coyoacán, with a Soviet dissident who had spent many years in the gulag and got chills at the sight of Stalin's and Lenin's faces on those canvases, painted in loving medallions over the hearts or foreheads of Frida and Diego. I didn't like them either, and from that first contact my impression was of a rather crude, naïve painter, more picturesque than original. But her life had always fascinated me, thanks first to some texts by Elena Poniatowska; later, when I read Herrera's biography, I was just as enthralled as the rest of the world by the superhuman energy with which this daughter of a German photographer and a Mexican Creole, struck down at the age of six by polio and at seventeen by the terrible traffic accident that shattered her backbone and pelvis—a pole of the bus she was riding in entered her neck and came out her vagina—was able to survive not just those two incidents but also the resulting thirty-two operations and the amputation of a leg. Despite it all, and despite having to remain immobile for long periods of time, sometimes literally hanging from ropes and wearing suffocating corsets, she loved life fiercely and managed not only to marry, divorce, and remarry Diego Rivera—the love of her life—but to have many affairs with men and women (Trotsky was one of her lovers), travel, engage in politics, and, above all, paint.

Above all, paint. She began just after her accident, leaving an obsessive record on paper of her battered body, her rage, her suffering, and the visions and delirium that her misfortunes inspired in her, but also her will to keep living and to squeeze all the juice—sweet, acid, or poisonous—out of life. That is what she did until her death, at the age of forty-seven. Her work, viewed chronologically as it appears in the Martigny exhibition, is a spellbinding autobiography in which each image, while chronicling some horrific episode of her physical or romantic life—her abortions, her sorrows, her wounds, her lovers, her mad desires, the extremes of desperation and impotence in which she foundered at times—also functions as exorcism and curse, a way of freeing herself from the demons that tormented her: she transferred them to the canvas or paper and brandished them at the spectator as accusation, insult, or heartrending plea.

The tremendous gruesomeness of some of the scenes and the shameless vulgarity of the depictions of the physical violence that human beings suffer or inflict on others are always bathed in a delicate symbolism that rescues them from ridiculousness and renders them troubling denouncements of pain, misfortune, and the absurdity of existence. It is a kind of painting that resists being called beautiful, perfect, or seductive but that nevertheless is deeply affecting and moves one to the core, like Edvard Munch or the Goya of the *Black Paintings* or like the music of Beethoven in his last years or certain poems by César Vallejo on his deathbed. Something in her work goes beyond painting and art and touches on the indecipherable mystery of life, that bottommost depth where, as Georges Bataille says, contradictions disappear, the beautiful and the ugly become interchangeable and interdependent, and so do pleasure and torture, weeping and rejoicing, the hidden root of experience that nothing can explain but that certain artists who paint, compose, or write as if immolating themselves are capable of making us feel. Frida Kahlo is one of those special cases that Rimbaud called "les horribles travailleurs." She didn't live to paint, she painted to live, and that is why in each of her paintings we can hear her pulse, her secretions, her howls, and the ceaseless tumult of her heart.

To come up from this plunge into the depths of the human condition onto the streets of Martigny and the clean and bovine slopes that surround the city on this cold and sunny afternoon is an unbearable anticlimax. No matter how diligently I do what I am supposed to do as a tourist—visit the Roman stones, fill my lungs with bracing air, gaze at the fields and the cows, and order fondue—the memory of the stark and piercing images I've just seen gives me no respite. They are always with me, whispering to me that all the placid, benign reality surrounding me now is nothing but illusion and appearance, that real life cannot shut out everything left behind in those flayed bodies and bloody fetuses, in the men like trees and women like plants in the painful imaginings and exultant howls of the exhibition. From it, as rarely happens these days, one emerges better or worse but certainly different from when one went in.

Martigny, March 1998

The Language of Passion

उर्ह ह्रे

When André Breton died, Octavio Paz said in his tribute that to speak of the founder of surrealism without using the language of passion was impossible. The same could be said of Paz himself, since he lived his whole life, and especially his last decades, enmeshed in controversy, inspiring intense loyalty or fierce rejection in those around him. The polemic surrounding his writings will persist, since his work is deeply embedded in the century in which he lived, a century torn by ideological strife and political inquisitions, cultural guerrilla warfare and intellectual fury.

Paz lived his eighty-four years splendidly, caught up in the maelstrom of his time thanks to a youthful curiosity that he preserved till the end. He participated in all the great historical and cultural debates, aesthetic movements, and artistic revolutions, taking sides and explaining his preferences in essays often dazzling for the excellence of their prose, lucidity of their judgment, and vastness of their learning. He was never a dilettante or a mere observer but always an impassioned actor in what was happening around him, and he was a rarity among his colleagues, unafraid of swimming against the current or braving unpopularity. In 1984, shortly after a group of absolute idiots in Mexico burned him in effigy (chanting, in front of the U.S. embassy, "Reagan, robber, friend of Octavio Paz") for his criticism of the Sandinista government, I ran into him: instead of being depressed, he was as gleeful as a schoolboy. And three years later, in the middle of a scuffle at the International Congress of Writers, I wasn't surprised at all to see him rolling up his sleeves as he headed into the fray. Wasn't it foolish to think of getting into a fistfight at the age of seventy-three? "I wasn't going to let anybody hit my friend Jorge Semprún," he explained.

It is dizzying to run through the subjects of his books: the anthropological theories of Claude Lévi-Strauss and the aesthetic revolution of Marcel Duchamp; pre-Hispanic art, the haiku of Bashō, and the erotic sculptures of Hindu temples; Spanish Golden Age poetry and English lyric poetry; the philosophy of Sartre and Ortega y Gasset; the cultural life of the viceroyalty of New Spain and the Baroque poetry of Sister Juana Inés de la Cruz; the intricacies of the Mexican soul and the mechanisms of authoritarian populism established by the PRI; the direction of world affairs after the fall of the Berlin Wall and the collapse of the Soviet empire. The list, if extended to include prologues, lectures, and articles, could go on for many pages, and it is no exaggeration to say that every one of the great cultural and political developments of his time engaged his imagination and inspired stirring reflections. Though he never lost the passion that seethes between the lines on even his calmest pages, Octavio Paz was first of all a thinker, a man of ideas, a formidable intellectual agitator in the tradition of Ortega y Gasset, who had perhaps the most lasting influence on him of the many writers from whom he profited.

Doubtless he would have liked posterity to remember him first and foremost as a poet, since poetry is the prince of genres, the most creative and the most intense, as he himself proved in his lovely readings of Francisco de Quevedo and Xavier Villaurrutia, of Luis Cernuda, Fernando Pessoa, and so many others and in his admirable translations of English, French, and Eastern poets. And he was certainly a magnificent poet, as I discovered when I was still a student, reading the blazing verse of *Sunstone*, one of the books I kept by my bed in my youth and always reread with immense pleasure. But I have the sense that a substantial part of his poetry, especially the experimental works (*Blanco*, *Topoemas*, and *Renga*, for example), succumbed to that eagerness for the new that he described in his Harvard lectures, *Children of the Mire: Modern Poetry from Romanticism to the Avant-Garde* (1974), as subtly undermining the lasting value of works of art.

In his essays, however, he was perhaps even more daring and original than in his poems. Because he covered such a broad spectrum of topics, I can't give my opinion on all of them with the same authority, and some are light and superficial. But even the pages he dashed off on India or love, which express nothing very personal or profound, say what they do say with such elegance, clarity, intelligence, and polish that it is impossible not to read them all the way through. He was a top-notch prose stylist, one of the most engaging, clear, and luminous ever in Spanish, a writer who handled language with magnificent certainty, making it express everything concrete or fantastic that occurred to him— sometimes truly wild trains of reasoning, like those that crackle in *Conjunctions and Disjunctions*—with a wealth of shadings and subtleties that make his texts impressive balancing acts. But unlike José Lezama Lima, he never resorted to *jitanjáfora* (as Alfonso Reyes dubbed pure verbal exercises without sinew or bone), even when he gave himself over to wordplay. He loved the meaning of words as much as their music, and when words flowed from his pen, they were always obliged to say something, to appeal to the intelligence of the reader as well as to his sensibility and his ear.

Since he was never a Communist or a fellow traveler, and

never had qualms about criticizing intellectuals who, whether out of conviction, opportunism, or cowardice, were complicit with dictatorships (in other words, four-fifths of his colleagues), a picture of him as conservative and reactionary was painted by those who envied his talent, the prizes showered on him, and his constant presence at the center of events. It is one I fear will be a long time in fading: the carrion seekers have already begun to devour his remains. But the paradoxical truth is that in political affairs, from his first book of essays in 1950, *The Labyrinth of Solitude*, to his last on the subject, *Pequeña crónica de grandes días* (Small Chronicle of Great Days; 1990), Paz's thought was always closer to democratic socialism than to conservatism or even the liberal doctrine of our age. From the surrealism-influenced Trotskyist and anarchist sympathies of his youth he proceeded to the defense of political democracy, or rather, pluralism and the state of law. But he always had an instinctive distrust of the free market—he was convinced that broad realms of culture, like poetry, would disappear if their existence depended solely on the free play of supply and demand—and he therefore came out in favor of prudent state intervention in the economy to correct social imbalances and excessive inequalities (the perennial argument of social democrats). That someone who thought this way, and who strongly condemned all armed U.S. actions in Latin America, including the invasion of Panama, should have been equated with Ronald Reagan and made the victim of an inquisition staged by the progressive left speaks volumes about the levels of sectarianism and idiocy that have taken over political debate south of the Rio Grande.

It is true, however, that his political image was slightly tarnished in recent years by his relationship with various PRI administrations, for the benefit of which he moderated his critical stance. This was neither gratuitous nor, as has been alleged, a capitulation to the praise and tribute heaped on him by those in power with the intent of bribing him. He was obeying a conviction, one I believed was mistaken—it was the source of the only dispute that cast a slight shadow over our long friendship—but one Paz defended with coherent arguments. Ever since 1970, in *Posdata* (Postscript), his splendid analysis of Mexico's political realities, he had maintained that the ideal way for the country to begin inevitable democratization was through evolution, not revolution, a gradual process of reform undertaken from inside the existing Mexican system. This was something which, according to him, had begun under the administration of Miguel de la Madrid and gathered critical momentum later under his successor, Carlos Salinas. Not even the great corruption scandals and crimes of Salinas's administration led Paz to revise his thesis that the PRI itself—this time under the then-president Ernesto Zedillo—would put an end to the political monopoly of the ruling party and bring democracy to Mexico.

Many times over the years I asked myself how the Latin American intellectual who had most bluntly autopsied the phenomenon of dictatorship (in *The Philanthropic Ogre*, 1979) and the Mexican version of authoritarianism could display such naïveté in this case. One possible answer is the following: Paz sustained his thesis less because he believed in the PRI's ability to metamorphose into a genuinely democratic party than because he actively distrusted the alternative political forces, the PAN (National Action Party) and the PRD (Democratic Revolutionary Party). He never believed that either group was capable of realizing the political transformation of Mexico. The PAN seemed to him a provincial party, Catholic in origin, too conservative. And the PRD was a collection of ex-PRI members and ex-Communists, without democratic credentials, which upon gaining power would probably restore the authoritarianism and cronyism that it pretended to combat. Let's knock on wood that events won't confirm this somber prophecy.

Since everyone is saying so, I, too, feel impelled to declare that

Octavio Paz, poet and writer open to all the vagaries of the spirit, and citizen of the world if ever there was one, was at the same time a quintessential Mexican—though I confess I haven't the slightest idea what this means. I know many Mexicans, and no two of them are alike, which means that as far as national identity is concerned, I wholly concur with something Paz himself once said: "The famous search for identity is an intellectual pastime, and sometimes also the occupation of sociologists with time on their hands." Except, of course, that being a quintessential Mexican means loving Mexico intensely—its landscape, history, art, problems, and people—which, incidentally, would also make Malcolm Lowry and John Huston Mexicans. Paz loved Mexico and he spent a great deal of time pondering it, studying its past and discussing its present, analyzing its poets and its painters; in his immense body of work Mexico glows with a fiery light, as reality, myth, and a thousand metaphors. Evident as it may seem that this Mexico is the fantasy and invention of the imagination and pen of an extraordinary writer rather than the unadorned and prosaic Mexico of impoverished reality, such a truth is only transitory. If we may be sure of anything, it is that the gap between the two will slowly close with the inexorable passage of time and that the literary myth will enfold and devour reality. Sooner rather than later, from inside and out, Mexico will be seen, dreamed, loved, and hated as Octavio Paz portrayed it.

Berlin, May 3, 1998

The City of Nests

✦ ✦

A s part of the celebration of the centenary of Bertolt Brecht (1898–1956), the Salzburg Festival is putting on a lavish production of *The Rise and Fall of the City of Mahagonny*, the opera in three acts that Brecht wrote in 1930 with music by Kurt Weill (1900–1950). The staging by Peter Zadek is excellent, the Vienna Radio Symphony Orchestra directed by Dennis Russell Davies is magnificent, and the spectrum of voices is impeccable, with members of the cast including Dame Gwyneth Jones, Catherine Malfitano, Jerry Hadley, Udo Holdorf, and Wilbur Pauley.

But perhaps even more interesting than the grandiose spectacle unfolding on the stage of the Grosses Festspielhaus (with no fewer than one hundred extras and several multitudinous choirs) is the sight of the thousands of spectators crowding the orchestra section and balconies, the gentlemen in tuxedos and the finely attired ladies glinting with jewels and trailing exquisite scents, who have paid between three and five hundred dollars a seat to come and enjoy a work conceived by its authors, in the vortex of the great ideological battles of the Weimar Republic in the twenties, as a blazing indictment of the North American capitalist utopia, the deceptive dream of material success at the reach of one and all, and the insatiable cult of the dollar, the new Mammon of the twentieth century, its alienating false promises concealing a nightmare of exploitation, erosion of tradition, mafia rule, and gangster violence.

To judge by their expressions of respectful concentration, maintained for the three hours the work lasted, and the enthusiasm with which they applauded the musicians, actors, singers, and dancers, very few of the spectators—top executives, successful professionals, wealthy landlords, bankers, high-level bureaucrats, jet-set beauties, the very incarnations of triumphant capitalism in its most satisfied and least tormented form—noted the delicious irony of which they were the unconscious protagonists. There they sat, sedately enjoying a beautiful work intended as an artistic bombshell by a writer and a musician who hated people like them with all their might and employed every ounce of their enormous talent to eradicate them, along with the system that allowed such people to reach the privileged heights of the comfortable life and artistic luxury they were enjoying, light-years away from the starving masses, who, like the naïve Alaskan pioneers imagined by Brecht, dream of one day reaching Mahagonny, "city of nests," as the widow Leokadia Begbick calls it, where everyone will be able to find a corner of happiness, success, and peace where they will feel safe and content, like pigeon chicks under the mother bird's wing. Because they swallow this lie and then later try to rebel against it, the unhappy Jimmy Mahoney and his beloved Jenny Smith are dealt the punishment that free-market societies inflict on those who resist it: he gets the electric chair, and she is sent to a brothel.

In the exquisite performance program (it, like the glass of champagne at intermission, costs ten dollars), illustrated with grim portraits by Lucian Freud advising those in the know of the terminal and bilious sadness with which capitalism infects human beings, a series of texts have been collected. Obviously presented with the best of intentions, they spare no examples or arguments in their intent to prove that the U.S. culture of gangster-businessmen, alcoholics, pimps, and predators denounced by Brecht and Weill in their opera sixty-eight years ago remains for the most part unchanged, although appearances might suggest otherwise, and that therefore the moral arguments and political philosophy that permeate *The Rise and Fall of the City of Mahagonny* are still pertinent. To this end, Eduardo Galeano explains that the Pinochet regime in Chile was born out of the economic theories of Milton Friedman; and Serge Halimi, drawing on the work of Karl Polanyi (which he appears not to have fully understood), calls for a new social utopia to replace the one shattered with the Berlin Wall and for challenges to the "utilitarian utopia" of Adam Smith. I very much doubt that these earnest intellectuals could ever persuade the crowd surrounding me of the intrinsic evils of the free market, or that the laborious statistics compiled by Jan Goossens with the help of Noam Chomsky ("In the United States, one percent of the population possesses 39 percent of the wealth") at the end of the program might cause them the slightest remorse or win a single one of them over to the proletariat's cause. Furthermore, I'd wager that not one person has bothered to read the program meant to rouse their consciences.

In fact, if this performance of *Mahagonny* proves anything at all, it isn't that Brecht's political ideas have survived the catastrophe of statism and Marxist collectivism. Rather, it's that his literary genius was subtler and deeper than the ideology that motivated him and that he was able to free a work like this from stereotypes and commonplaces and make it express, as if between the lines of the conscious political message, more original and enduring ideas and myths and images whose historical and moral import qualifies the explicit ideology and even contradicts it. The city of Mahagonny, which, by posing as the model of a perfect society, wrecks the dreams and lives of poor, naïve people like Jimmy Mahoney and Jenny Smith who come to it in search of happiness, is nothing like the North American society Brecht had in mind when he wrote his work, the United States of jazz and skyscrapers that bewitched the German intelligentsia between the wars as surely as it repelled them. Rather, circumstances have lent the city more and more of a resemblance to societies like Russia's, which, upon awakening from the alienation of the socialist paradise that pretended to do away with greed and egoism in human relationships, found itself in a true hell of anarchy, corruption, social violence, economic tyranny by mafias, and a no-holds-barred struggle for money (preferably dollars). If prostitution has anywhere become the last possible refuge from hunger and frustration for penniless girls, as in the Mahagonny controlled by the insatiably greedy widow Begbick and her assassins, it's not New York or Los Angeles—where prostitutes make more than writers and don't even pay taxes—but Fidel Castro's Cuba, where the struggle for greenbacks has taken on the same ferocious and inhuman character it possesses in the Brechtian city.

The work Brecht wrote in 1930 and Weill set marvelously to music by blending popular melodies with American rhythms in a modernist display that also reclaims the best elements of traditional German opera—present in the ironic allusions to Beethoven's *Fidelio*—is no longer what it first was, a critique of capitalist utopias and the belief in unlimited economic progress; it is now simply a critique of any social utopia that pretends to recreate heaven on earth and establish the perfect society. Such societies don't exist, at least not in this world of infinite human diversity, in which all attempts to impose a single form of happiness on everyone have always failed and brought most people serious misery and unhappiness. Whether we like it or not, those of us who refuse to give up the stubborn search for absolutes, full realization, and earthly paradise will discover that the only real and widespread progress—economic, social, moral, and cultural—has always rewarded modesty, not ambition. The winners are those societies that set as their goal not perfection but steady if partial progress, the renouncing of utopias, and the ascension to what Camus called "the morality of limits," a delicate and beautiful way of understanding democratic mediocrity and pragmatism.

At the debut of *The Rise and Fall of the City of Mahagonny*, on March 9, 1930, in the city of Leipzig, the angry reaction of some in the audience led to violence; almost two years later, in December 1931, when Brecht and Weill managed to find a Berlin businessman who dared to produce the work in the German capital, the scandal was also enormous. How things have changed since that bellicose and romantic time, when plays and operas transfixed people or drove them to shouts and blows. Things have improved in many ways since those days, when Stalinists and Nazis shot and beat each other to death around the Brandenburg Gate and democrats shivered, impotent and afraid, sensing the coming apocalypse. But in one way at least those times were clearer than these. Back then, when the bourgeoisie went to the theater, they knew what they liked and what they didn't like, and made their preferences known by clapping or stomping. Now they don't know, and the few who still distinguish between their artistic likes and dislikes no longer have the courage to show it. Here, at the Salzburg Festival, the fear that they will be called philistines and reactionaries makes them applaud everything that the rebellious Gérard Mortier puts before them: the excellent *Mahagonny* tonight, for example. But yesterday they clapped just as politely for a *Don Carlo* by Verdi in which Philip II appeared in a flirtatious little Andalusian hat and Don Carlo and Don Rodrigo were disguised as flamenco dancers (there was also a procession of hooded inquisitors, condemned men on a pyre, peasants with sickles and hammers, and García Lorca–esque Civil Guard officers). They'd probably applaud me, too, if I climbed onstage and sang, to music by Luigi Nono, the *Communist Manifesto* in the key of G.

Fuschl, August 1998

The Unborn Child

&t f&

The Chamber of Deputies in Spain has just rejected an amendment of the abortion laws, by a margin of one vote. To the three circumstances in which a pregnancy may be terminated (rape, malformation of the fetus, or danger to the mother's health), the amendment proposed the addition of a fourth, allowing abortion for social or psychological reasons. This is similar to what is permitted by all countries in the European Union except Ireland and Portugal; with minimal variations, their legislatures allow voluntary abortions within the first three months of gestation.

The outcome of the vote was a great victory for the Catholic Church, which took action on all fronts to prevent the law from passing. An alarming document called "Permission to Kill Even More Children" was released by the Episcopal Conference and read by twenty thousand parish priests during services; there were rogations, marches, meetings, and a flood of letters and calls to members of the Chamber (a campaign that proved effective, since four members yielded to the pressure and changed their votes). Many Catholic intellectuals, headed by Julián Marías—for whom the social acceptance of abortion is one of the greatest tragedies of the century—took part in the debate, reiterating the Vatican position that abortion is a crime committed against a helpless being and therefore an intolerable atrocity not just from a religious perspective but also from the standpoint of morality, civilization, and human rights.

Enlisting citizens in civic actions in defense of their convictions falls within the bounds of democratic practice, and it is natural that Spanish Catholics should agitate so belligerently in support of an issue that intimately affects their beliefs. On the other hand, those who favored the proposed fourth clause—in theory, half the country—remained silent or presented their case with extraordinary timidity, thus betraying an unconscious discomfort. This is natural as well. Abortion, after all, is not an action that delights or satisfies anyone, beginning with the women who find themselves obliged to turn to it. For them, and for all of us who believe that its decriminalization is just and that the Western democracies recognizing that fact—from the United Kingdom to Italy, France to Sweden, Germany to the Netherlands, the United States to Switzerland—have done right, it is an unhappy last resort, something to be accepted as a lesser evil.

The major fallacy of the anti-abortion argument is that its proponents reason as if abortion didn't exist and would only begin to exist from the moment the law was passed. Those who argue this way confuse decriminalization with the encouragement or promotion of abortion, and that is why they are able to act with clear consciences as "defenders of the right to life." In reality, however, abortion has existed from time immemorial, in countries that prohibit it as well as countries that permit it, and it will continue to be practiced whether or not the law tolerates it. Decriminalizing abortion simply means allowing women who can't or don't want to give birth to end their pregnancies under certain basic safety conditions and according to certain guidelines rather than letting it happen as it does wherever abortion is illegal, in an unofficial and precarious manner that risks women's health and may lead to criminal charges.

Decriminalization would also alleviate the discrimination that now exists in this area. Where abortion is prohibited, only poor women really feel the law's effect. The rest have access to abortion as often as necessary, by paying clinics and private doctors to perform it with discretion or by traveling abroad. Women with scarce resources, on the other hand, are obliged to turn to abortionists and underground healers, who exploit them, botch the operations, and sometimes kill them.

It is absolutely pointless to argue whether the unborn child, the few-weeks-old embryo, should be considered a human being—possessing a soul, as the religious see it—or only an incipient life-form, because there is no way to answer the question objectively. This is not something that science can determine; or rather, scientists can only pass judgment one way or the other, not in the name of science but in the name of their beliefs and principles, just like laypeople. Of course, the conviction of those believers who maintain that the fetus is already a human being invested with rights and that its existence should be respected is perfectly honorable. It is also honorable for them to make their cause public and try to win supporters, in accordance with their beliefs.

It would be a terrible outrage if a mother were required by law to abort her child, as happened in Indira Gandhi's India and still happens in China. But isn't it just as wrong for her to be forced to have children she doesn't want or can't have because of beliefs she doesn't share, or beliefs she may share but is compelled by circumstances to transgress? This is a delicate subject, and one that cuts to the very marrow of democratic culture.

The crux of the problem concerns the rights of women, whether one of those rights is the power to decide to have a child or not and whether that decision should be made by political authorities. In advanced democracies, and as a result of the growth of feminist movements, awareness has begun to spread, though not without enormous difficulties and arduous debate, that it is the person who is living the problem deep inside herself, and who must bear the consequences of the decision, who has the right to choose.

It is not a decision that can be made lightly, but a difficult and often traumatic one. An immense number of women find themselves pushed to abort for precisely the reasons covered by that fourth proposed clause: their living conditions are such that bringing a new mouth home means condemning the new being to an unworthy existence, to death in life. Since this is something that only the mother herself can judge with full knowledge of the circumstances, it makes sense that she should decide. Governments can counsel her and fix certain limits—like requiring the abortion to take place within a certain period after conception, stretching from twelve to twenty-four weeks (in the Netherlands), and obliging a period of reflection between the decision and the act itself—but they may not replace her in the momentous matter of choice. This is a reasonable policy that will sooner or later be adopted in Spain and Latin America as advances are made in the democratization and secularization of society (the two are inseparable).

Though decriminalizing abortion may be one way of addressing a serious problem, that doesn't mean the circumstances giving rise to it can't be effectively combated in other ways. A very important tool is sex education, of course, in schools and at home, so that no woman gets pregnant out of ignorance or because she has no access to contraceptives. One of the greatest opponents of sex education and birth-control policies has been the Catholic Church, which until now, with a few dissenting voices in its midst, accepts the prevention of pregnancy only by use of the so-called rhythm method and fights hard in the countries where it has greatest political influence—which still include many in Latin America—against any public campaign intended to popularize the use of condoms or the Pill.

A final reflection, inspired by the above, is in order on a delicate topic: the relationship between the Catholic Church and democracy. The former is not a democratic institution, as no religion is or ever could be (with the possible exception of Buddhism, which is more a philosophy than a religion). The truths that it defends are absolute, since they come from God, and transcendent moral values can't be the object of concessions or dialogue with opposing values and truths. So long as the Catholic Church preaches and promotes its ideas and beliefs far from political power, as part of a society governed by a secular state, and in competition with other religions and irreligious or antireligious thought, it coexists perfectly with the democratic system and does it a great service, furnishing many of its citizens with the spiritual dimension and moral structure that, for a great number of human beings, are only conceivable through the medium of faith. And there is no solid or stable democracy without an intense spiritual life at its core.

But if this tricky balance between the secular state and the Church shifts, and the Church infiltrates the state or, even worse, takes it over entirely, democracy is threatened in the short and the long term in one of its essential attributes: pluralism, or coexistence in diversity and the right to difference and dissidence.

At this point in history, it is improbable that the scaffoldings of the Inquisition, scene of the roasting of so many impious enemies of the only acceptable truth, could rise again. But even if matters are not taken to such Talibanic extremes, it is certain that women would give up the ground they have gained in free societies and be relegated to the secondary status they have always been assigned by the Church (a male-oriented institution if ever there was one) as afterthoughts and daughters of Eve.

London, October 4, 1998

New Inquisitions

❦

The Labour Party leader Ron Davies, secretary of state for Wales in Tony Blair's cabinet and his own party's candidate to lead the first Welsh Assembly, suddenly resigned from his ministerial post a few days ago. The resignation surprised everyone, not least because of the reasons stated in Davies's letter to the British prime minister. Recognizing his "serious lapse of judgement," the member of Parliament and minister confessed that the previous evening he had accepted a dinner invitation in a park in the south of London—Clapham Common—from an unknown Rastafarian who, once he had gotten into Davies's car and directed him to pick up a pair of accomplices, threatened him with a knife and stole his car, cell phone, parliamentary pass, briefcase, and IDs. To prevent the episode from harming the government, Davies was giving up his political career.

Davies is short and stocky, fifty-two years old, the son of a factory worker, and makes appearances dressed as a druid at the folk festivals of his Welsh homeland, where, due in part to his determined efforts, the Labour Party is now the major political force. He is not considered a thinker, policy man, or charismatic leader, but he is known as a tireless crusader, serious, upstanding, and loyal, one of those worker ants every political party needs in order to survive, prosper, or rise to power. How could someone with such excellent credentials and such an obvious love of politics give up everything he was and possessed simply because he was the victim of a street attack?

The truth is that with his heroic resignation Davies was trying to sacrifice himself in a preemptive strike, believing (like a man living in a dreamworld) that by renouncing politics and retreating into gray anonymity, he would avoid persecution by the press pack. Rather than putting them off, however, his strange resignation maddened the bloodhounds of the press, setting them immediately on his trail. Forty-eight hours hadn't gone by before the guts of the poor former minister were fare for the ghoulish appetite of the millions of readers of the trashy newspapers commonly known in the United Kingdom as tabloids, because many, though not all, are printed in tabloid format.

The Mail on Sunday got a hot scoop (for which it surely paid a tidy sum): an exclusive interview with Ron's first wife, Ann. She revealed the anxiety and doubts that assailed her after their wedding, in 1972, when she realized how little sexual interest she awakened in her husband, who would forget to make love to her for long periods, once of several months and finally for two years on end. A novice in these delicate matters, Ann didn't know what to do. She bought perfumes and daring nightgowns, but nothing happened. And she was so terribly, terribly naïve that she suspected nothing when the listless Ron spent his Sundays at the Turkish baths in Newport, returning home happy and relaxed.

But as always, the *News of the World*, the most-read paper in Great Britain—and maybe Europe or anywhere else—delivered the most lurid revelations (in a printing of four million copies). Its editors presented evidence that Clapham Common, the park where Davies met the Rasta who invited him to dinner, is a well-known cruising spot for homosexuals, as is Battersea Park, where the minister and his companion picked up the two accomplices. It also printed declarations from witnesses who claimed to have seen Davies several times over the past few years at other gay hangouts, like the bathroom stalls of a gas station on Highway 4, the outskirts of Bath, Caribbean haunts in the London neighborhood of Brixton, and a public restroom in downtown Cardiff. Another tabloid boasted of having obtained sworn statements from two prostitutes—whose names it was reserving for the moment—who said they had provided professional services to the deputy.

Davies, from the Welsh refuge to which he fled with his second wife and his daughter in an attempt to escape the onslaught, released a statement that was as useless as it was pathetic, denying any accusations of "improper conduct" and begging that he and his family be left in peace now that he had decided to step off the public stage. And in a gesture of extreme desperation, he appeared in Parliament, where he shakily read a text telling how his father had abused him as a child and, in a postcript to a cryptic sentence ("We are the product of our genes and our experiences"), pleaded for understanding.

Ron Davies, my friend, there is no chance of that. Only the irruption of a new, even juicier scandal will bring an end to the inquisition. Clench your fists, swallow the bitter draft, sell your soul to the devil, and auction your story to the tabloids. They'll pay a fortune for it, and you won't even have to write it yourself, since a peerless scribbler, possibly a graduate of Oxford or Cambridge, will do the work for you. You'll have to hurry, though, because a week from now your story will be old news, worth nothing anymore.

I don't read the tabloids; in fact, they disgust me so much that in the subway, or on the bus I take every afternoon to and from the British Library, I get a cramp in my neck from trying not to read them in the hands of my traveling companions. And yet I know the sad story of the much-abused Ron Davies in graphic detail. How can this be? Very simple: because it is a falsehood of Pinocchio-size proportions that the tabloids have a monopoly on treachery, gossip, malice, and scandal. The virus of sensationalism now infects the very air breathed by the British newspapers, and not even those passing as sober and serious—*The Times*, *The Daily Telegraph*, *The Independent*, *The Guardian*—are immune to it. True, important matters still prevail in their coverage, and in them one can still find substantial articles, intellectual debate, and essays on science, the humanities, and the arts. But none of them can keep from echoing all the perverse stories unearthed by the prying into the private lives of public figures that has destroyed Ron Davies. And this is so because the demand for the product is universal and irresistible. The news organ that systematically abstained from supplying scandal to its readers would go bankrupt.

This can't be called a problem, because problems have solutions and this doesn't. It is a reality of our time from which there is no escape. In theory, the law should set limits beyond which the reporting of information ceases to be of public interest and infringes on a citizen's right to privacy. For example, the actors Tom Cruise and Nicole Kidman have just won a suit against a London tabloid, in which an imaginative scandalmonger made up a completely baseless story about them (full of kinky sex, of course). A settlement like this is only within the reach of celebrities and millionaires. No ordinary citizen could risk embarking on a process that, besides drowning him in seas of litigation, would cost him many thousands of pounds if he lost. And judges, too, basing their decision on sound judgment, resist handing down sentences that seem to restrict or abolish the indispensable freedom of expression and information that democracy guarantees.

Tabloid or yellow journalism is the twisted stepchild of the culture of freedom. It can't be suppressed without dealing the latter a mortal blow. Since the cure would be worse than the disease, it must be endured, as victims endure certain tumors because they know that if they tried to have them removed, they might die. We have not been brought to this pass by the shady machinations of greedy newspaper owners who recklessly exploit their readers' base desires. That is the effect, not the cause.

The root of the phenomenon is the banalization of the reigning culture of entertainment, whose supreme value is now diversion or amusement, trumping any other form of knowledge or pastime. People pick up a newspaper, go to the movies, turn on the television, or buy a book in order to enjoy themselves, in the most frivolous sense of the word, not to be plagued by worries, problems, and doubts. Their only aim is to amuse themselves, to forget about serious, weighty, disturbing, or difficult things, and to lose themselves in light, pleasant, superficial, happy, healthily stupid diversions. And could anything be more entertaining than spying on someone else's private life, surprising the neighbor in his underwear, discovering the improprieties of random strangers, or watching seemingly respectable model citizens dragged through the mud?

The tabloid press doesn't corrupt anyone; it was born corrupt, product of a culture that, instead of rejecting rude interference into people's private lives, demands it, because the fun of poking around in other people's dirt makes life more bearable for the worker with the nine-to-five job, the bored professional, and the tired housewife. Former minister Ron Davies was the victim not of journalistic slander but of frivolity, the ruling deity of postmodern civilization.

London, November 1998

The Weaker Sex

❧ ❧

The photograph I have in front of me could be a still from a horror movie. It shows six girls from Bangladesh, two of them mere children, with their faces destroyed by sulfuric acid. One was blinded and hides her empty eye sockets behind a pair of dark glasses. It wasn't an accident in a chemistry laboratory that turned them into scarred ghosts of their former selves; they are victims of a mix of cruelty, idiocy, ignorance, and fanaticism.

With the help of humanitarian organizations, they have left their country and come to Valencia, where they will be operated on and treated at the Aguas Vivas Hospital. But it is enough to see their faces to realize that no matter how skillful the work of the surgeons and psychologists, the lives of these girls will always be utterly wretched. Dr. Luna Ahmend of Dhaka, who is accompanying them, explains that it is very difficult to put an end to the practice of throwing sulfuric acid into women's faces in Bangladesh, where 250 cases are recorded each year. It is resorted to by husbands who are angry because their brides haven't brought them the expected dowry and by prospective grooms rejected by the women they were promised in family agreements.

Sulfuric acid may be bought at gas stations. The perpetrators are rarely arrested; if they are, judges are usually bribed to acquit them. Being found guilty isn't a serious matter either, since the fine a man pays for turning a woman into a monster is barely four or five dollars. Who would grudge such a modest sum for the delicious pleasure of a revenge that not only disfigures but socially stigmatizes its victim?

This story is a good match for another that I learned about last night from a British television program on female circumcision. It is well known that female circumcision is broadly practiced in Africa, especially among Muslims, although sometimes also among Christians and pantheists. But I didn't realize that it is performed in civilized Great Britain, where anyone who mistreats a dog or a cat is sent to prison. Not so the person who mutilates a young woman, removing or cauterizing her clitoris and cutting off the outer lips of her vagina, so long as he has a medical or surgical degree. The operation costs forty pounds and is perfectly legal if it is done at the request of the girl's parents. The television program was made because a law is being proposed in Parliament to outlaw the practice.

Will it pass? I ask myself this after noting the infinite caution with which the spokesperson for the human rights organizations supporting the prohibition presented her case. She seemed much more concerned about sparing the feelings of the African and Asian families living in the United Kingdom who circumcise their daughters than in denouncing the savagery her organizations are trying to eradicate. In contrast, the person debating her showed no reluctance or scruples in claiming the right of the African and Asian communities of Great Britain to preserve their customs, even when, as in this case, they clash with "the principles and values of Western culture."

She was a Somalian leader, dressed in splendid ethnic garb—

multicolored tunics and veils—who expressed herself eloquently, in impeccable English. She didn't question a single one of the horrifying statistics compiled by the United Nations and different humanitarian organizations testifying to the scope and consequences of this practice on the African continent. She admitted that thousands of girls die as a result of infections caused by the barbarous operation, which is almost always performed by healers or witch doctors in entirely unhygienic conditions, and that many other adolescents are severely traumatized by the mutilation, which ruins their sex lives forever.

Her utterly inflexible line of defense was cultural sovereignty. Has the colonial era ended or not? And if it has, why should the arrogant and imperial West decide what is good or bad for African women? Don't they have the right to decide for themselves? In support of her thesis, she presented a survey taken of the female population of Somalia asking whether the circumcision of girls should be prohibited. Ninety percent responded that it shouldn't be. She explained that such a deeply rooted custom shouldn't be judged abstractly, out of the particular context of the society in question. In Somalia, a girl who reaches puberty with her sexual organs intact is considered a prostitute and will never find a husband, which means that whether or not she was a prostitute before, that is how she'll end up. If the great majority of Somalians believe that the only way of guaranteeing the virtue and sexual chasteness of women is by circumcising girls, why should Western countries interfere and try to impose their own standards of sex and morality?

It is possible that the excision of the clitoris and the outer lips of the vagina forever deprives girls of sexual pleasure. But who is to say that sexual pleasure is something desirable and necessary for human beings? If a religious civilization rejects that hedonistic and sensual vision of existence, why should others oppose it? Just because they're more powerful? Anyway, isn't sexual pleasure something that only concerns the woman in question and her husband? At the end of her speech, the belligerent ideologue made a concession. She said that in Somalia they are trying now, through ad campaigns, to persuade parents that instead of going to amateurs and shamans, they should take their daughters to clinics and public hospitals to be circumcised. That way fewer girls will die of infections in the future.

The fascinating thing about this speech wasn't what the speaker was saying but her absolute blindness to the fact that almost all the documentary's witnesses to the hideous aftereffects of female circumcision weren't arrogant European colonialists but African and Asian women who had experienced the same kind of physical and psychological suffering as political prisoners subjected to the bloodiest of torture. All of them—well educated or not—fervently protested the injustice that had been inflicted on them when they were unable to defend themselves, when they couldn't even imagine an alternative for women, a life without sexual mutilation. Were these Somalian, Sudanese, Egyptian, and Libyan women less African than the speaker for having rebelled against a brutal manifestation of "African culture" that had ruined their lives?

Multiculturalism was not born in Africa, Asia, or Latin America. It came into being far from the Third World, in the heart of the prosperous and civilized West—on American and western European university campuses—and its tenets were developed by philosophers, sociologists, and psychologists motivated by a perfectly generous idea: that small primitive cultures should be respected, that they had as much right to exist as big modern ones. They never could have imagined the perverse uses to which their idealistic doctrine would be put. True though it may be that all cultures contribute something to the enrichment of the human race, and that multicultural coexistence is a worthy endeavor, it does not follow that all the institutions, customs, and beliefs of every culture are deserving of equal respect and enjoy moral immunity by sole virtue of their existence. Every aspect of a culture deserves respect so long as it does not blatantly violate human rights, or, in other words, the individual sovereignty that no collective category—religion, nation, tradition—can trample without revealing itself as inhuman and intolerable. This is exactly the case of the torture called circumcision that is inflicted on African children. The woman who defended it with such conviction on television last night wasn't defending African sovereignty; she was defending barbarity, and defending it with arguments put in her head by the modern colonialist intellectuals of the Western culture she despises.

London, November 1998

Predators

✧ ❦ ✧

The North American writer Paul Theroux, author, among other works, of the amusing novel *The Mosquito Coast* and a number of successful travel books, discovered some time ago that a British bookseller was offering for sale several of the signed and inscribed books Theroux had presented to his friend, model, and mentor, Sir Vidia S. Naipaul. Indignant, he requested an explanation. A new humiliation was in store for him: instead of replying in person, Naipaul delegated the task to his new wife, a Pakistani journalist as blunt as she is beautiful, who dispatched Theroux in a few mocking lines. His revenge is a scandalous and extremely entertaining book, *Sir Vidia's Shadow: A Friendship across Five Continents*, which I don't advise you to buy or even flip through at a bookstore, since if you do, you won't be able to put it down until you've finished it.

Theroux met Naipaul—some ten years older than himself— three decades ago in Kenya, at Makerere University, where they both worked. Theroux grew fascinated by the talent and personality of the Indian-Trinidadian-English writer whose splendid novels *A Bend in the River* and *A House for Mr. Biswas* had already made him famous. Theroux became his disciple, chauffeur, and errand boy, and in reward for his devotion Naipaul deigned from time to time to instruct him on the secrets of literary genius and also, once in a while, as one tosses a few coins to a beggar, on his conception of the world, the human being, Africa, and history. These lessons must have been brilliant, their every detail seared into the memory of the young apprentice, because thirty-two years later he reproduces them literally, with accompanying gestures.

It goes without saying that Naipaul's opinions were unpublishable, their political incorrectness and pedantry seasoned with gross arrogance. When young African poets came to read him their poems and ask for advice, he would order them to give up writing. In some cases he would compound the insult by conceding that the supplicant "had lovely handwriting." Judge of a literary contest, he proclaimed that only a third prize should be awarded, given the quality of the entries. And to those who protested he replied, "You are trying to give the African an importance he does not deserve." Asked for his opinion on African literature, he asked in turn, "But does it exist?" He was not ashamed to declare that when its white inhabitants left, the black continent would descend into barbarity; to irritate the natives, he insisted on calling African countries by their old colonial names. And he treated his first wife, the stoical English Pat—"she had beautiful breasts," says Theroux—so harshly that in the book we always see her banished to the back seat of the car, sobbing quietly. And so on, ad infinitum.

I could write a book just as nasty as Theroux's about any of the writers I know, because at one time or another I've heard all of them say terrible things, late at night, in the heat of friendship or discussion, or at dinners where the wine flowed freely. Every single one exaggerates sometimes or boasts, makes a cutting remark or a cruel joke. My dear friend Carlos Barral, for example, a thoroughly good and generous man, would loose the most outrageous barbs after his second gin, making the wickedest pronouncements I have ever heard or read. Taken out of context, and stripped of the tone, manner, company, circumstances, and mood in which they were made, these statements change in character; they aren't funny anymore but vile, racist, prejudiced, or simply stupid. And since Theroux is an excellent writer (of the second rank), he makes his ignominious ploy work: the character Vidia S. Naipaul that his book creates is almost as repellent as the narrator (Theroux himself).

Sir Vidia's Shadow drips resentment and envy on every page, but although the reader is aware from the beginning that the author is writing wounded, not even pretending to be objective, venting his pain and rage at being betrayed by someone he idolized, he resists tossing it in the trash, as trash. Is it because he succumbs to the cunning narrator's competent magic, to the way the anecdotes are presented and entwined, colored and rounded off? That is part of it, certainly. But most of all, and perhaps unintentionally, it is because in this testament of a spurned and wrathful friend and disciple, Theroux manages to reveal the pettiness, spite, mediocre imitation, and sordid envy with which all human beings are inevitably afflicted, constant burdens that sour their lives, ruin their relationships with others, poison their souls, and cheapen or thwart their happiness.

Reading this book, I suddenly remembered an essay by Ortega y Gasset, perhaps his best, that thoroughly impressed me when I read it: it is a long prologue to a book on hunting by the count of Yebes. What initially seems a somewhat frivolous piece of writing intended as the introduction to an essay by an aristocratic friend gradually becomes a profound meditation on the ancient cave dweller crouched in the breast of contemporary man, his primal instincts and irrational predatory urges showing through in certain pursuits and behaviors. Ortega examines human beings' relationship with Nature, the dark and age-old attraction that death (one's own and that of others, experienced or inflicted) exerts, and the different terms in which humans and animals experience violence. Just as Huizinga saw in games the symbolic representation of historical evolution, Ortega, in this complex and enigmatic text, sees the different incarnations of the hunt as the sum of the human condition. Over the course of human development, from the prehistoric cave to the age of skyscrapers and airplanes, the central image is the destructive, bloody, deadly pursuit from which no civilization, religion, or philosophy has managed to free us. Man needs to kill; he is a predatory being. He began doing it millions of years ago because it was the only way for him to survive, to eat, to keep from being killed. And he has done it ever since, in every age, brutally or with finesse, directly or through proxies, with knives, bullets, rites, and symbols; if he didn't do it, he would suffocate, like a fish out of water. That is why the image of the biped in boots and a leather jacket aiming his loaded rifle at the defenseless silhouette of a deer (which some consider a gallant picture) seems chilling in this essay, like a haunting vision of the human condition.

Literature is a predatory art. It annihilates the real with symbols, constructing a mock world that it brings to fictitious life with fantasy and words, an artifice built with materials always plundered from life. But the process is usually discreet and often unconscious, since the writer seizes and steals—and manipulates and deforms—what is lived and what is real more by instinct and intuition than by conscious deliberation; later, his art, sorcery, and verbal sleight of hand draw an impenetrable veil over what has been purloined. If he is talented, the crime goes undetected.

In the case of this book by Paul Theroux, it doesn't: the operation is in plain sight. The author hasn't made the least effort to hide or justify it. He had a score to settle with an old friend, whom he loved and admired more than any other writer and who abused him instead of returning his affection. So he killed him, writing this violent and impassioned book.

Fortunately, those vanquished by literature, unlike those killed on the hunting trail, tend to enjoy good health. I hope that Sir Vidia S. Naipaul survives this dose of strychnine. He is the best living writer in the English language, and one of the greatest our age has produced. In his novels, essays, travel books, and memoirs, which are published all over the globe, the reader savors an exceptionally precise and intelligent prose, mercilessly pruned to eliminate all superfluous material. Its ironies are subtle, sometimes cynical and sometimes caustic, frequently drawing blood and revealing truths that refute or ridicule the received ideas of our time. There is no more politically incorrect writer in the literary marketplace. No one has pulverized the fallacies of Third World pietism and the posing and frivolity of European intellectual progressivism as subtly and gracefully as he has done in his novels or with the intellectual force he brings to bear in his essays, or has demonstrated more persuasively the demagoguery, craftiness, and opportunism generally concealed behind such doctrines and attitudes. That is why he tends to be universally detested, although every critic salutes his talent.

It seems that Naipaul—uncommon Hindu born on a tiny Caribbean island who, thanks to scholarships, was able to study at Eton and Oxford, the citadels of British privilege, where he endured the loneliness and discrimination afforded him by his dark skin and background (he was on the point of committing suicide, but didn't have enough coins for the gas)—is not bothered at all by the situation that Theroux's book addresses. Perhaps in order to defend himself against prejudice and misfortune, or perhaps because it is his natural disposition, he has cultivated unpleasantness with almost as much talent as literature. He is a master at rudeness and at disappointing his admirers.

I invited him to dinner once, and he told me he would think

about it. He called a few days later to find out who the other guests would be. We told him. But he still couldn't decide. He called again, for the third time, and asked for my wife, wanting her to describe the menu. After listening to her disconcerted recital, he gave his instructions: he was a vegetarian, and would only eat a particular dish (for which he gave the recipe). He added, "I always drink champagne at meals." The night of the dinner we awaited his appearance with great trepidation. But he came, ate and drank in moderation, and—wonder of wonders!— even made a reasonable effort to be pleasant to his fellow guests.

London, December 1998

The Permanent Erection

⚜ ⚜

Ever since I heard my Uncle Lucho describe the magic and revelry of Carnaval in Rio when I was just a boy, I've dreamed of seeing it up close, and if possible from the inside, in flesh and blood. And now I have. At the age of sixty-two, with frequent attacks of dyspepsia and a lumbar hernia, I may not be in optimal shape to enjoy it, but the experience has been enlightening, and I declare that if all humanity could take part, there would be fewer wars and less prejudice, racism, ugliness, and sadness in the world, although probably more hunger, inequality, and madness and a cataclysmic rise in birthrates and AIDS.

How is the experience enlightening? In a number of senses, beginning with the philological. No one who has not felt the sizzle of the Sambodrome during the parade of the fourteen Samba Schools (forty-nine thousand participants, sixty-five thousand spectators) or been at some of the 250 public balls or hundreds of spontaneous street dances springing up around the city can even dream of the rich and multifarious meanings acquired by words that elsewhere are shadowed with a suspicion of vulgarity, like "tits" and "ass." Here, they become the most splendid and generous terms in the language, each one a dizzying universe of variations on the subject of curves, sinuosities, consistencies, projections, tonalities, and granulations.

I cite these two examples so as not to speak in the abstract, but I could just as well conjure up any other organ or part of the human anatomy, since the scrap of cloth (the famous thong called "dental floss") worn everywhere during Carnaval in Rio lets people reveal themselves with a confidence, glee, and freedom that I believed had disappeared ever since Christian morality replaced paganism and tried to shroud and condemn the human body in the name of modesty. From head to toe, belly button to armpits, elbow to shoulders and neck, the people flaunt their bodies with amazing confidence and pride, proving to the ignorant—and reminding the forgetful—that no corner of the marvelous physical architecture of the human being can't be beautiful and a source of excitement and pleasure, requiring nothing like the fervor and reverence favored by tradition and romantic poetry with its careful descriptions of eyes, necks, hands, waists, and so on. Not the least of the marvels of Carnaval is the ascription of erotic appeal to body parts like fingernails and the Adam's apple, seemingly anodyne extras in the game of love ("That *menina* has a lovely skull," I heard one old man enthuse on Flamengo Beach) transformed by the rhythm, color, and contagious effervescence of the festivities, with everyone in a trancelike state of exhibitionism. It comes as no surprise, then, that the focus of the Samba School Caprichosos de Pilares this year was none other than the plastic surgeon Ivo Pitanguy, whose skill with the scalpel and rejuvenating genius have erased signs of aging on the faces and bodies of many beauties (female and male) of this frivolous era. Singing like a teenager on top of his float, Pitanguy himself, an immortal sixty-year-old whose presence and contortions drove the audience wild, brought up the rear of the Caprichosos parade.

When the euphoria, dancing, conviviality, songs, heat, and

frenzy reach combustion point in the early-morning hours, the spectacle reveals what the great pagan celebrations of the past must have been like, especially the Bacchic revels, those Dionysian cult rituals with their copious libations intended to stifle reason and the survival instinct, their orgies and bloody sacrifices. Here, the blood doesn't flow on the actual stage of the fiesta, but it surrounds it, lapping at its edges and leaving corpses in its wake (70 shot in the four days of Carnaval, which proves that Rio is a peace-loving city: in São Paulo the total was 240).

What does one death more or less matter in this mad explosion of multitudinous joy, in this performance that seems, with its separate spaces and scenery, designed to confirm Huizinga's theories on the game-based evolution of culture and history, a performance in which for four days and four nights a whole city is disguised and transformed, giving up its worries and fears, prejudices and hopes, morals and beliefs, likes and dislikes? Taking on a whole new personality—that of the disguise they are wearing—the participants abandon themselves to revelry, excess, and outrageous behavior that they would never have permitted themselves the day before and won't permit themselves tomorrow, when they recover their identities and once again become the desperate unemployed worker, the anxious secretary, the bureaucrat whose salary is shrinking every day because of growing inflation, the businessman overwhelmed by rising taxes, the professor who has been prevented from traveling abroad by the fall of the *real*, and the trade unionist who blames the crisis on the International Monetary Fund and its ultraliberal impositions.

Let us not forget that Carnaval comes this year in the middle of an economic crisis that has the international financial community biting its nails for fear of what might happen in Brazil. If the very strict fiscal adjustment program—which has allowed the Brazilian government, presided over by Fernando Henrique Cardoso, to take out loans for the astronomical sum of four billion dollars—fails, the Brazilian collapse will ruin not just Brazil but the other Mercosur countries as well, and the shock waves of the catastrophe will rock the stock markets and economies of the whole planet, as much as or more than the drums of the Samba Schools shake the hips of the dancers from Bahia. Does anyone dwell on such gloomy trivialities at this time of happy uproar? Yes, a few wretched sociologists who shout themselves hoarse in the papers criticizing the supposed "alienation" of the Brazilian people. Their fellow citizens are not worried at all, of course; they howl with laughter at the crisis and poke fun at it, exorcising it in the grotesque puppets of their allegorical floats, which are cheered madly by the crowds. And so that no one may doubt the general consensus, this year the Samba Schools spent 20 percent more than last year on costumes and floats for the parade, and the authorities increased the budget for orchestras, fireworks, performances, and prizes by several million *reals*. Does this extravagance defy all reason and common sense? Of course it does. Because this is still an authentic carnival, a carnival in the ancient and primitive sense of the word, from a time when sense and reason were still rarities and men and women practiced potlatch and were essentially creatures of emotion, intuition, and instinct, their feelings on the surface.

The best explanation I've found for what is happening this week in Rio de Janeiro comes not from Nietzsche, with his vision of Dionysian man, or even from my anthropologist friend Roberto da Matta and his magnificent essay on Carnaval, but from a Russian literary critic who never set foot in Brazil and who struggled to live and teach in a remote corner of the Russian Steppes, where he was banished by the Soviet regime: Mikhail Bakhtin. Everything I've seen and heard this astonishing week in Rio seems a living illustration of the theory of popular culture he developed in his dazzling book on Rabelais. Yes, here, from the bowels of society comes that brazen, irreverent, fiercely sarcastic response to established patterns of morality and beauty, that vociferous negation of the social categories and borders that so often divide and stratify races, classes, and individuals, in a celebration that equalizes and mixes everyone, rich and poor, white and black, employee and employer, master and servant. Prejudice and distance are temporarily wiped out, and in an ellipsis of illusion and a fantasy land of unending sex and music the "backwards world" from the poem by José Agustín Goytisolo is established, where princesses are dark and street sweepers blond, beggars happy and millionaires miserable, ugly women beautiful and beautiful women hideous, day night and night day; where those "below" triumph over those "above" and impose their carnal freedom, their sweaty materialism, their insatiable appetites, and their exuberant vulgarity as the apotheosis of life; where the "fresh offerings" of flesh lauded by Rubén Darío are universally exalted as the most valuable of human aspirations.

By confining the Samba Schools parade to the Sambodrome—the project of a progressive sociologist, the late Darcy Ribeiro—the establishment more or less got control of Carnaval and made it subject to certain conventions, but on the street it hasn't lost any of its insolent and rebellious roots or its anarchic aura, not just in the poor neighborhoods but also in the more proper ones. One night on the main street of very bourgeois Ipanema, for instance, I ran into a company of a thousand or fifteen hundred transvestites, boys and full-grown men, who, dressed as women or semi-naked, frenetically danced the samba behind a truck carrying a band and kissed, embraced, and practically made love before their amused, indifferent, or enthusiastic neighbors, who bantered with them from windows, applauded, and threw confetti and streamers.

The protagonists of Carnaval are the human body, as I have already said, and the music—enveloping, imperious, joyful, blind—in which it thrives and trumpets its desires. But at dawn, what prevails and pervades the milky morning—over and above the designer perfumes, expensive lotions, sweat, smells of cooking and alcohol—is the thick aroma of semen, of thousands, hundreds of thousands, perhaps millions of orgasms, masculine, feminine, precocious or venerable, slow or quick, vaginal or rectal, oral or manual or mental, a dense vapor of animal satisfaction that fills the air and is breathed in by the dazed, semiconscious Carnaval-goers, who, in the final moments of revelry, return to their lairs or collapse in parks and on paths for a brief rest, after which they'll be restored and ready to samba some more.

The conservatives can sleep easy: so long as Carnaval exists, there will be no social revolution in Brazil. Any plans to control the libido of its fast-growing population, already nearing 170 million, will be futile. President Cardoso will sweat blood and tears trying to impose austerity and economic discipline on the nation that elected him. And if the hell that Catholics believe in really exists, there will surely be more Brazilians there than people from every other country in the world combined (which comes as a relief for an unredeemed sinner like the author of these pages). But so long as Carnaval exists in Rio, those who have lived it or who remember it or even just imagine it will know a life better than the rubbish it usually is, a life that, for a few days—as Uncle Lucho swore—attains the heights of dreams and meshes with the magic of fiction.

Rio de Janeiro, February 1999

The Lost Battle of Monsieur Monet

❧ ❧

The democratization of culture has its inconveniences. To see a major exhibition today, one has to wait weeks or months and, on the chosen day, stand in a long line in the rain and the cold, only to view the paintings haphazardly, elbowing people and being elbowed in return. Nevertheless, I'd endure it all again in a second to visit *Monet in the 20th Century*, the exhibition now at the Royal Academy.

A good show teaches us something about an era, a painter, or a theme, enriches our vision of a work, and plucks us from everyday life for an hour or two, immersing us in a world apart, of beauty or invention. But in a few rare cases like this one, a show also tells us a lovely story—in paintings instead of words.

Three elements are indispensable in the emergence of a great creator: skill, ideas, and culture. These three components of creative work don't have to be equal; one can outweigh the others. If one is missing, however, the artist in question is only half an artist or never becomes one at all. Skill can be learned: it involves the technical expertise and craftsmanship that determine *in part* how a work of art is made, but on its own it is not enough to elevate a creation to the level of art. To master drawing and perspective and to acquire an understanding of color are necessary, even essential, but merely a starting point. The "idea," a more realistic way of referring to inspiration (a word with mystical and obscurantist associations), is what makes skill the vehicle for the expression of something personal, a work in which the artist contributes something new. The originality of the creator resides in "ideas." But it is an artist's contribution to the culture that gives weight, consistency, and durability to his inventions; in other words, the way a work is defined in the context of what has come before and the way it renews, enriches, criticizes, or modifies tradition. The story that *Monet in the 20th Century* tells is that of an expert craftsman who, on the threshold of old age, was seized by a stubborn whim that made him an extraordinary creator.

In 1890, Claude Monet, who was fifty years old and one of the most successful of the impressionist painters—connoisseurs fought over his landscapes—bought a house and some land on the banks of the Seine, in a village with no history, some seventy kilometers northeast of Paris. Over the next few years he designed an exquisite garden with climbing vines, daisies, and weeping willows and a pond that he sowed with water lilies and spanned with a little Japanese bridge. As he settled into the country retreat he had prepared for his bourgeois old age, the placid artist never suspected the consequences his move to Giverny would have for his art—and all art.

Up to then he had been an excellent painter, though predictable and not very imaginative. People loved his landscapes because they were tastefully conceived; they faithfully reproduced the French countryside on canvases that were usually small, offended no one, and complemented a room's decor nicely. But after he built the little lagoon just outside the door to his country house, and began spending long stretches watching the light shimmering on the water and the water lilies subtly changing color as the sun moved in the sky, he was seized by a doubt: what was realism?

Until then he had believed that it was, very simply, what he depicted in his paintings, the deft reproduction on the canvas of what his eyes could see. But those gleams, reflections, evanescences, glows, that whole fairylike display of shifting forms, those fleeting visual confusions that arose from the blending of flower, water, and sunlight—wasn't that reality too? So far, no artist had painted it. When Monsieur Monet decided he would try to capture that slippery and furtive dimension of the real with his brushes, he was almost sixty years old, an age at which many of his colleagues were retiring. He, on the other hand, was only just beginning to become an obsessive, revolutionary, distinguished creator.

When he made three trips to London to paint the Thames, between 1899 and 1902—the exhibition begins at this point in his life—he was already obsessed with the idea of depicting the metamorphosis of the world through changes in light. From his balcony at the Savoy Hotel he painted the river and the bridges and the houses of Parliament as they emerged from the shadows or disappeared into them, when the clouds parted and the sun shone, or when they were veiled and distorted by fog, that dense fog whose "marvelous breath" (his own words) he wanted to capture. Despite his desperate efforts to document the visual deliquescence of the city over the course of a day, the thirty-seven paintings completed on his sojourn in London already have little to do with exterior reality. What they reveal is Monet himself, unknowingly embarked on a wild adventure and gradually creating a self-contained and visionary new world of pure color, when he believed he was painting the changing faces the light gave the tangible world.

Between the ages of sixty and eighty-six, when he died (in 1926), Monet, like Cézanne, was one of those artists who, without breaking his close ties with tradition, began the great transformation of aesthetic values that would revolutionize the visual arts perhaps more than any other art, opening the door to all kinds of experimentation and to the proliferation of schools, isms, and trends, a process that extends into the present, although it is now nearly played out. The impressive thing about the exhibition at the Royal Academy is that it at once demonstrates Monet's contribution to this great change and reveals how little conscious he was of inaugurating a new era in the history of art, because of his stubborn search for a radical realism.

In fact, he always thought of himself as a realist painter, one who was determined to bring aspects of the real to his canvases that had so far been ignored and who worked along objective lines, as he had before Giverny. Although certainly more demanding and subtle than he had been before, he always considered himself a landscape painter. That is why he got up at dawn and studied the damp surface of the water lilies, the fronds of the willows, or the whiteness of the daisies for hours, so that not a single shading of their constant transformation and perpetual dance of color would escape him. That miracle, the enthralling spectacle unfolding before his poor eyes (cataracts almost prevented him from painting between 1922 and 1923), is what he wanted to immortalize in the hundreds of paintings inspired by his garden at Giverny. He spent two months in Venice in 1908, and another stretch in 1912, trying to capture the secrets and magic colors of the city in autumn. Even near the end of his life, when he was painting the series he would call the *Grandes Décorations*, enormous canvases whose orgy of colors and rainbow-hued forms are almost completely liberated from the figurative, Monet believed he was finally achieving his goal of capturing the uncapturable, of freezing in images that mad dance of transparencies, reflections, and gleams that were the source and object of his inspiration.

It was a losing battle, of course. Although Monet would never admit it, the clearest sign that he never truly felt he had managed to achieve his realist goals is the obsessive way he retouched and reworked every painting, repeating each one over and over with variations so minute that they are sometimes invisible to the viewer. Time and time again, the reality of pure forms evaded his brush, the way water runs through the fingers. But these defeats never discouraged him enough to make him give up. On the contrary, he fought to the last for his utopian dream of painting the ineffable, of trapping the semblance of air, the spirit of light, the glance of the sun in a cage of colors. What he did achieve—proof that realism doesn't exist, that it is merely an illusion, a conventional formula for expressing the simple fact that art has roots in real life but only achieves a life of its own when it creates a different world, a world that denies rather than mimics what already exists—was even more important than what he was searching for: the conceptual cornerstone on which the whole architecture of modern art would be erected. All signs indicate that the magnificent Monsieur Monet died without understanding what he had achieved, and perhaps also with the sorrow of having failed to realize his modest dream.

London, March 1999

A Death So Sweet

❧ ❧

After being acquitted four times, Dr. Jack Kevorkian, who is seventy years old and by his own admission has helped 130 terminally ill patients to die, has been found guilty at his fifth trial, by a jury in the North American state where he was born (Michigan), and sentenced to ten to twenty-five years in prison. In protest, "Dr. Death," as he has been baptized by the press, has declared a hunger strike. By a curious coincidence, the same day that Dr. Kevorkian stopped eating, the state of Michigan forbade prison authorities to force-feed prisoners on hunger strikes: now all they can do is explain to the strikers in writing the possibly lethal consequences of their decision. With impeccable logic, Kevorkian's lawyers are asking whether the state's official position on hunger strikes isn't the same as "assisted suicide"—in other words, the same crime for which the famous doctor is serving time.

Although his lack of humor and his single-mindedness have made him seem somewhat macabre in television appearances, Jack Kevorkian is a true hero of our age. His campaign in support of euthanasia has helped bring a taboo subject out from under wraps and into the public light, and caused it to be discussed worldwide. With his "crusade," as he calls it, he has opened many people's eyes to a monstrous injustice: that terminally ill patients who endure unspeakable torments and wish to put an end to their nightmarish lives are required to continue suffering because of a legalism that proclaims a universal "obligation to live." This is, of course, an intolerable violation of individual sovereignty and an instance of state interference with a basic human right. The decision whether or not to live (the fundamental problem of philosophy, as Camus wrote in *The Myth of Sisyphus*) is entirely personal, a choice the individual should be able to make freely and without coercion, with the assurance that his decision will be rigorously respected; the consequences of the act, after all, concern only the one who undertakes it.

Such is the case when those deciding to end their lives are people who are able to do it themselves and don't need to be "assisted"; this is, perhaps, the most lamentable of the tangle of hypocrisies, paradoxes, and prejudices that surround the euthanasia debate. The legal prohibition of suicide hasn't prevented a single would-be victim from shooting himself, taking strychnine, or leaping into the void after he or she came to the conclusion that life was no longer worth living. And no one who has survived a suicide attempt has been sent to jail for breaking the law that human beings must live. Only those who are not physically able to act on their will to die—terminally ill patients in a state of utter decrepitude, or in other words, those who are forced by the law to bear the most physical and psychological torment—are condemned to comply with the bureaucratic prohibition against dying by one's own hand. Dr. Jack Kevorkian had been battling this stupid cruelty for three decades, knowing that sooner or later he would be defeated. His case goes to show that on certain subjects, like euthanasia, Western civilization still carries a considerable baggage of barbarity. (Religion, that perennial adversary of human freedom, must bear the blame.) After all, it is no less inhuman to withhold death from a sane person who is requesting it because life has become a burden than it is to snatch away the life of someone who wants to live.

Nevertheless, despite the massive blindness and lack of understanding that plague any discussion of euthanasia, some steps have been taken in the right direction. The Netherlands is the world's liveliest example of a liberal democracy, in matters of drug use, the rights of homosexuals, and the social and political integration of immigrant minorities: a country that experiments, renews itself, tries out new formulas, and isn't afraid to seriously play the freedom card, in all social and cultural spheres.

I often think of a television documentary I saw in Monte Carlo two years ago, when I was judging a television competition. It was far and away the most impressive program, but since its subject was a serious affront to the religious convictions of some of my colleagues, we couldn't give it the prize, mentioning it instead in the final ruling as a notable entry in the controversial debate over euthanasia.

The characters weren't actors; they played themselves. At the beginning, an old sailor who had run a little bar in Amsterdam and who lived alone with his wife, went to see a doctor to tell him that the pain he was suffering due to an incurable degenerative disease was steadily getting worse and that he had decided to speed his death along. He had come to ask for help. Could the doctor provide it? The film tracked in meticulous detail the legal procedures that had to be followed in order for the assisted death to take place. The Ministry of Health had to be informed, the patient had to submit to a medical examination by practitioners other than the one who had diagnosed him, and his desire to die had to be approved by a Ministry officer responsible for determining whether his mental state was sound. The death takes place at last, on camera, in the sick man's home, where he is flanked by his wife and the doctor who administers the lethal injection. At every point in the process, even instants before death, the patient is informed by the doctor about the progress of his illness and asked again and again whether he is sure about his decision. At the most dramatic moment in the documentary, as the doctor administers the final injection, he tells his patient that if he changes his mind before he loses consciousness, all he has to do is raise a finger and the doctor will suspend the operation and try to revive him.

Since this documentary—which has been shown in some European countries and banned in many others, generating heated debate—was filmed with the characters' consent and is promoted by associations that defend euthanasia, it has been accused of being "propagandistic," something it certainly is. But that doesn't lessen its authenticity or persuasive power. Its great merit is that it shows how a civilized society can help a person who views death as a form of physical and moral liberation to take the final step, while at the same time ensuring that all the necessary precautions are taken so that the decision is a genuine one, made in a state of perfect lucidity, with a full understanding of its significance. And, of course, it shows how science can try to help alleviate the pain and trauma of the passage from life to death.

A horror of death is deeply rooted in Western culture, mostly as a result of the Christian idea of transcendence and the threat of eternal punishment for the sinner. In certain Asian cultures, like those steeped in Buddhism, death is understood as a continuation of life, a reincarnation in which the self is changed and renewed but never stops existing; in the West, however, death means the absolute loss of life—the only life that a human being personally lives and has evidence of—and its replacement by the vague, uncertain, and abstract life of a soul whose nature and identity are always slippery and difficult for even the most ardent believer, with his earthbound faculties, to grasp. That is why the decision to end a life is the most serious and tremendous decision a human being can make. Many times it is made in a fit of irrationality, confusion, or delirium and isn't a choice, properly speaking, but in a certain sense an accident. For someone who is terminally ill, however, that is never the case, because his very helplessness and the physical impotence occasioned by his condition grant him time, perspective, and ample circumstances in which to weigh his options calmly and decide after proper reflection. For the 130 unhappy souls whom Dr. Jack Kevorkian broke the law to help die, he was an angel not of death but of peace and compassion.

Madrid, April 1999

Fataumata's Feet

I don't know the lady, but her exotic name, Fataumata Touray, her country of origin, Gambia, and her current home, the Catalan city of Banyoles, suffice for me to reconstruct her story. It is a thoroughly ordinary and predictable tale, similar to that of millions of women like her who were born into poverty and will probably die in it. It would be foolish to say that what has just befallen her is tragic, because her entire life has merited that theatrical description. For Fataumata and her fellows, to die tragically is to die a natural death.

I don't need to visit the Josep Trueta Hospital in Gerona, where the ribs, wrists, bones, and teeth she broke jumping from a second-floor window of the building where she lived are now being soldered, to see her ebony skin, her kinky hair, her snub nose, her thick lips, those teeth that were blinding white before they were shattered, her ageless eyes, and her big knotty feet, swollen from so much walking.

It is those huge cracked feet, with their geologic calluses and purplish nails, scarred insteps, and petrified toes, that I find most deserving of respect and admiration. They have been walking since she was born far away in distant Gambia, a country few people could find on a map, since who in the world cares where it is or would ever need to know? It is to those tireless feet that Fataumata owes the fact that she is still alive, although it is hard to see what good living has done her so far. In the barbarous depths of Africa, even a running start probably couldn't save her from the female castration that is the fate of many young Muslim girls, though her feet may have helped her to escape some wild animal or plague or the half-naked and tattooed enemies who, because they worshipped a different god, spoke another language, or had inherited different customs, were determined to eliminate her, her relatives, and her tribe.

Here in civilized Spain, in the ancient region of Catalonia, those fleet feet saved her from the fire meant to incinerate her and a good number of immigrants from Gambia, a fire set by other enemies, probably also tattooed, certainly with shaved heads, and undoubtedly convinced, like their African counterparts, that Fataumata and her tribe have no right to exist, that the world—in other words, Europe, Spain, Catalonia, Banyoles—would be a much better place without her black presence. I am absolutely certain that in the precarious life she has lived since she was born, Fataumata has not once asked herself what horrible crime her tiny tribe, now on the verge of extinction, could have committed to have earned such hatred, to everywhere provoke such murderous rage.

Venturing a bold analogy, I declare that the journey of those formidable feet from Gambia to Banyoles is an odyssey as daring and remarkable as Ulysses's voyage from Troy to Ithaca (and perhaps more human). And also that what gave strength to the woman carried by those peripatetic feet as she crossed jungles, rivers, and mountains and squeezed into canoes, the bilges of boats, cells, and fetid rat-infested inns was her will to escape not from arrows, bullets, or disease but from hunger. It is hunger that those scarred feet have been fleeing ever since Fataumata saw the light (in a hammock, a clearing in the woods, or on the banks of a stream), fleeing her empty stomach and the hallucinations and cramps it brought, the anxiety and fury produced by not being able to eat and not being able to feed those little skeletons with eyes that she should never have borne.

Hunger makes miracles happen, fuels the imagination, and encourages resourcefulness, driving human beings to attempt the most daring feats. Five centuries ago, thousands of Spaniards as hungry as Fataumata left Extremadura, Andalusia, Galicia, and Castile and set out on a violent epic quest, the conquest and colonization of America. This was without doubt an amazing undertaking, and one in which my paternal ancestors, among many others, took part: the starving Vargases, from the noble and famished land of Trujillo. If they had been able to eat and drink all they wanted and live without wondering where the next day's food was coming from, they wouldn't have crossed the Atlantic in little toy boats, invaded vast kingdoms, crossed the Andes, ransacked a thousand temples, and plied the rivers of the Amazon basin; they would have stayed home digesting their meals and getting fat, lulled by their comfortable circumstances. What I mean to say with all this is that Fataumata Touray, who was nearly burned alive in Banyoles for invading distant lands and for being of a skin color, language, and religion different from the natives, is a woman of the race of conquerors, although at first glance she doesn't seem it.

Just forty years ago, another wave of thousands and thousands of Spaniards—it is not too much to suppose that among them were some uncles, grandfathers, or even fathers of the Banyoles arsonists—spread out over half of Europe, driven by the hope of finding work, living conditions, and income that the impoverished Spain of the time (like Fataumata's Gambia today) was unable to offer them. In Germany, Switzerland, France, and England they worked hard, sweating blood and enduring endless humiliation, discrimination, and disdain because they were different, the black race of white Europe. This is ancient history now. The Spanish no longer need to go off and labor in the factories of prosperous Europe to put food on the plates of their Murcian or Andalusian families. Now they cross the Pyrenees as tourists, on business trips, to learn languages, to take courses, and to feel modern and European. That is no doubt what they are. Spain has prospered hugely since the years when, like Gambia, it exported human beings. But memory is so short, or so wretched, that many Spaniards have already forgotten how terrible it is to be hungry and how honorable and admirable it is to feel the desire to escape, to cross borders, to immigrate to other lands, to go wherever it is possible to work and to eat. And they allow themselves the luxury of hating and discriminating against (and even wanting to incinerate) those black immigrants who stain the urban landscape.

I know exactly what Fataumata Touray was doing in Banyoles without needing to exert my imagination at all. She wasn't there on vacation, enjoying the soft Mediterranean breezes, savoring delicious Catalan cuisine, or engaging in summer sports. She was— and I repeat that this is the most worthy and just of human aspirations—sweating at menial jobs to fill her stomach. In other words, she was mopping floors, picking up trash, walking dogs, washing diapers, or selling hair clips, pins, and multicolored pendants on street corners, going from house to house offering her services, sometimes even volunteering to work for nothing but a bit of food. That is what immigrants do when they don't have an education and don't speak the language: the numbing and badly paid jobs that the natives refuse to take. Fataumata must not have been doing too badly in Banyoles when, like a number of other Gambians, she decided to settle in this pretty place and put her big feet up to rest. Did she think that at last she could be at peace, relax?

No chance. Fataumata learned otherwise in the early-morning hours of July 19, when she was awakened by flames and choking smoke at the house full of immigrants where she lived on Pere Alsis Street. Her agile feet made her jump out of bed, and after she discovered that the flames had already consumed the stairs—the arsonists knew what they were doing—they propelled her out a window, into thin air. Those feet saved her from a horrible death. What matter the damage to her hands and feet and the injuries that may prevent her from ever chewing again if the alternative was a fiery end? In a way, one might even say that Fataumata is a lucky woman.

This is a common story at the end of the second millennium in Europe, where the burning alive of immigrants of exotic skin color or religion—Turks, blacks, Gypsies, Arabs—is becoming an ever more popular extreme sport. It has been practiced in Germany, France, England, and Italy, in the Nordic countries, and now in Spain, too. To voice any alarm at it seems to be in poor taste, proof of paranoia or sinister political intentions.

One is required to keep calm and follow the example of the mayor of Banyoles, Pere Bosch, and the counsel for the government of Catalonia, Xavier Pomés. Both, with enviable composure, have emphatically denied that what happened was a racist act. Pomés has added, firmly and in an almost offended tone: "One can't speak of xenophobia in the capital of Pla de l'Estany." Excellent: the reputation of that civilized region remains untarnished. But how, then, to explain the motives of those who, with full premeditation and malicious intent, set fire to the house where Fataumata and her countrymen were sleeping? "An act of vandalism" (in other words: a bit of mischief, a nasty prank).

Oh, thank goodness. The youths who tried to burn Fataumata

Touray to a crisp aren't racists or xenophobes. They're vandals. Or rather, unruly, naughty, spoiled boys. They were bored by the quiet nights of the capital of Pla de l'Estany and wanted to have a little fun, try something new and exciting. Isn't it typical for young people to break the rules and rebel? They went too far, certainly; there's no sense in trying to justify what they did. But there's no point, either, in blowing out of proportion an incident in which no one even died. This explanation—doubtless inspired by noble patriotism—has an Achilles' heel. Why didn't these terminally bored young men, who weren't racist in the least, burn down the house of the mayor, Pere Bosch? Why didn't these boys, without a xenophobic bone in their bodies, raid the home of the head counsel, Xavier Pomés, with their gallons of gasoline? Why did they choose Fataumata's hovel? I know the response very well: pure coincidence. Or maybe: because immigrants' houses are made not of stone but of lesser materials, so they catch fire and burn more easily.

Will these explanations make Fataumata Touray feel better? Will she endure her probable lameness and scars with a lighter heart, knowing that her arsonists aren't racists or xenophobes but just bad kids? Everything is possible in this world, even that. But I'm entirely convinced that she won't stick around to live side by side with the unknown arsonists in the capital of Pla de l'Estany. As soon as she leaves the hospital, her wise feet will set out walking again, running as fast as they can with no fixed destination, along the dangerous, bonfire-dotted roads of Europe, cradle and emblem of Western civilization.

Marbella, July 1999

The Suicide of a Nation

৶ ৸

W
hat is happening in Venezuela is sad but not surprising. It has happened many times over in the history
of Latin America, and at the rate some of the New
World countries are going, it will happen again: disappointed
with a democracy that was unable to meet their expectations and
that sometimes caused their standard of living to dip, broad sectors of society have turned their eyes to a demagogic strongman,
who is taking advantage of his popularity to seize full power and
set up an authoritarian regime. Peruvian democracy perished the
same way, with the April 1992 coup engineered by President Fujimori and the armed forces in thrall to General Bari Hermosa and
Captain Montesinos; now Venezuelan democracy has begun to
disappear under the populist autocracy of Lieutenant Colonel
Hugo Chávez.

There is no denying that democracy in Venezuela wasn't
working right. The best proof is that a convicted felon, traitor to
his Constitution and uniform, is president of the country. Instead
of still being in jail, serving out the sentence for his 1992 mutiny
against the legitimate government he had sworn to uphold, Lieutenant Colonel Chávez has been anointed by the majority vote of

his countrymen. It was President Rafael Caldera who set him free after he had spent barely two years in prison, in a gesture that was intended to be magnanimous but was in fact irresponsible and sui-cidal. Upon leaving his cell, the paratrooper peacefully and elec-torally set about completing the task of demolishing the state of law, civil society, and freedom that the Venezuelan people had heroically regained by toppling the dictatorship of Marcos Pérez Jiménez forty-one years earlier.

Caldera's act wasn't just a betrayal of the voters, the majority of whom still supported the democratic system at the time and had condemned the coup attempt modeled on the Peruvian takeover. It was also a betrayal of the officers and soldiers of Venezuela's armed forces, who, faithful to their duty, refused to support the 1992 putsch and—some losing their lives in the process—defeated the rebels, thus providing Latin American mil-itary establishments with an example of civic conduct. What must those constitutionalist soldiers think today about what is happen-ing around them, as they watch the former putsch leader rise and appoint his co-conspirators to high posts in the government and army? No doubt that with leaders like this, their democracy didn't deserve to be defended.

Since Chávez won the presidential elections and has just won a sweeping victory in the elections for the Constituent Assembly—in which his motley coalition, the Patriotic Pole, landed 120 of 131 seats—it is argued that his democratic legitimacy must be recog-nized, if grudgingly. But the history of Latin America is full of dictators, despots, and petty tyrants who were popular and who won (or would have been able to win if they had called them) the elections with which they amused themselves from time to time, to placate the international community or to feed their own mega-lomania. Isn't Castro, doyen of caudillos after forty years in power, a case in point? Wasn't General Perón? And, until recently, what about Peru's Fujimori, who (according to the polls) was rewarded with a violent upsurge in popularity when he commanded tanks to shut down Congress? The quintessential dictator, Generalissimo Rafael Leónidas Trujillo, enjoyed a popular mystique, and the Dominican people would probably have torn his executioners to pieces if they had laid hands on them the night of May 30, 1961. That such a large number of Venezuelans support the populist and autocratic follies of the laughable personage known as Lieutenant Hugo Chávez doesn't make him a democrat: it just reveals the depths of desperation, frustration, and civic ignorance to which Venezuelan society has fallen.

Clearly, the political leaders of the democracy must shoulder a good part of the blame for this situation. Though its oil deposits should make it one of the richest countries in the world, Venezuela is today one of the poorest, thanks to the reckless squandering of the substantial income produced by its black gold, a sport engaged in by all the country's democratic administrations without exception. Worst of all, though, was that of Carlos Andrés Pérez, who in his first term in office managed to dissipate the eighty-five billion dollars in oil profits that had swelled the nation's coffers. What happened to that astronomical sum? A considerable part was certainly stolen, inevitable in a state made gigantic and interventionist by nationalizations where the path to economic success led not through the market—and its consumers—but through the perquisites, privileges, and monopolies granted by the principal protagonist of economic life: the politician in power. And the rest was spent on subsidies for everything, even water and air, so that Venezuela not only had the cheapest gasoline in the world—it cost less to buy than it cost to transport it to its places of sale—it also allowed itself the luxury of importing 80 percent of the foodstuffs it consumed, one year becoming the world's principal importer of Scotch whiskey.

The pipe dream Venezuela was living, lulled by the subsidies system, ended when oil prices took a nosedive. It was a brutal awakening. The administration—which, even more ironic, was Carlos Andrés Pérez's second—found itself obliged to lift controls on prices, which rose to the stratosphere. The people, taken by surprise and not understanding what was happening, flooded into the streets to loot the supermarkets. After the bust, or *caracazo*, as it is called, things continued to get worse until the arrival of the lieutenant colonel paratrooper, who has assured Venezuelans that the country's sad state of affairs—the gross domestic product has fallen 9.9 percent in the last three months, and in the same period the recession wiped out half a million jobs—will come to an end when its corrupt political parties disappear, the thieving members of parliament go home, and a new Constitution guarantees him the power to rule unchecked (and to arrange for his own reelection). To make their work easier, Chávez has given the brand-new members of the Constituent Assembly a draft of the Constitution's essential points and a peremptory order to approve it in three months. One has to ask why he is wasting his time, and why he doesn't just enact it *ipso facto*, without waiting for a rubber stamp from the robots.

According to the details leaked so far, this new Constitution is a concoction reflecting the ideological confusion that Commander Chávez displays in his much-praised speeches: Venezuela will have a "planned" and "market" economy, and businessmen who don't reinvest their earnings in their native land will be considered traitors. "Usury and unwarranted markups in price are prohibited," as are "any kind of dealings that interfere with the integrity of free competition"! Why doesn't this punctilious Constitution also prohibit poverty, illness, masturbation, and melancholy?

Chávez, like many members of the species he represents—the

military caudillo—has the frequently recycled idea that Venezuelan society is in bad shape because it doesn't work like a barracks.
This seems to be the only clear model of social organization delin-
eated in the dangerous speechs he gives announcing the future
Bolivarian Republic of Venezuela. It is why he has filled so many
public offices with soldiers, militarized public education, and decided that from now on the armed forces should assume an or-
ganic role in the social and economic life of the country. He is
convinced that the officers' energy and discipline will bring order
where there is disorder and honor where immorality reigns. His
optimism would have been nipped in the bud if he had studied the
history of Latin American military regimes and noted the consequences that convictions like his have had for the victim-countries
in question. He needn't have looked any farther than Peru, where
the military and social dictatorship of General Juan Velasco Al-
varado (1968–1975), which did more or less what he proposes to
do in Venezuela, left the country in ruins, without an institutional
framework, desperately poor, and saddled with an army that,
instead of reforming civil society, was viscerally corrupted by
its sojourn in power. (The repulsive cases of Bari Hermosa and
Montesinos would be inconceivable without that disastrous episode.)

Peru's fate doesn't much concern the international community,
which observed the establishment of the picturesquely authoritarian and corrupt regime now in power there with ironic curiosity,
and at times a certain complacency. But Venezuela's oil reserves
make it too important for the rest of the world to watch with arms
folded while it slides into demagoguery and ignorance, the abyss
toward which Hugo Chávez will steer it if he puts his plans into
effect. In Venezuela's case, it is likely that international financial
organizations and the West, beginning with the United States—
which imports a fair bit of Venezuelan oil and is conscious of the

destabilizing effect that a dictatorship submerged in economic chaos would have on the whole region—will redouble their efforts to moderate the willful, vertically structured, and centralized plans of the stentorian caudillo and demand a modicum of sense from him in his economic policies. In this area at least, then, perhaps all is not lost for the long-suffering people of Venezuela.

But the international community couldn't care less whether or not democracy survives in Venezuela, which means it won't lift a finger to prevent the systematic dissolution of civil society and the dismantling of the basic practices of democratic life on which the former coup leader has embarked with the enthusiastic and blind collaboration of so many unwitting Venezuelans. A sinister night has fallen on the land from which Simón Bolívar and his troops sallied forth to liberate Latin America, and I fear it will be a long time before it lifts.

Marbella, August 1999

The Alexandrian

❧ ❧

The apartment in Alexandria where the poet Constantine Cavafy (1863–1933) lived the last years of his life is in a run-down building in the center of the city, on a street that was called Lepsius when the neighborhood was inhabited by Greeks and Italians and is now called Charm-el-Sheik. Some Greeks are still in the area, to judge by a few signs in Hellenic script, but what predominates everywhere is Arabic. The neighborhood has deteriorated and is full of cramped alleyways, houses in ruins, and potholed paths, and—a typical sign of poor neighborhoods in Egypt—the residents have turned the roofs into stinking garbage dumps. But the beautiful little Orthodox church that the faithful attended in Cavafy's time is still there, and the graceful mosque, too, and the hospital, although the brothel that operated on the ground floor of his building has disappeared.

The apartment is a small museum in the care of the Greek consulate, and it must not get many visitors, to judge by the sleepy boy who opened the door for us and stared at us as if we were Martians. Cavafy is practically unknown in the city immortalized by his poems, which are, along with the celebrated library burned to the ground in antiquity and Cleopatra's love affairs, the best thing that has happened to it since it was founded by Alexander the Great in 331 B.C. No streets are named after him and no statues memorialize him. Or if they exist, they don't appear in the guidebooks and no one knows where to find them. The apartment is dark, with high ceilings and gloomy hallways, and it is furnished as circumspectly as it must have been when Cavafy set up house here with his brother Peter in 1907. The latter lived with him for just a year, then left for Paris. From that moment on, Constantine lived here alone; and, it seems, with unfaltering sobriety, so long as he remained within his apartment's thick walls.

This is one of the settings for the less interesting of Cavafy's lives, one that leaves no impression on his poetry and is difficult for us to imagine when we read about it: the life of an immaculately attired and unassuming bourgeois who was a broker on the cotton exchange and worked for thirty years as a model bureaucrat in the Irrigation Office of the Ministry of Public Works, where, as a result of his punctuality and efficiency, he rose to the rank of deputy manager. The photographs on the walls pay testimony to this civic prototype: the thick tortoiseshell spectacles, the stiff collars, the tightly knotted tie, the little handkerchief in the top pocket of the jacket, the vest with its watch chain, and the cuff links in the white shirt cuffs. Clean-shaven and well groomed, he gazes seriously at the camera, like the very incarnation of the man without qualities. This is the same Cavafy who died of cancer of the larynx and is buried in the Greek Orthodox cemetery of Alexandria, among ostentatious mausoleums, in a small rectangle marked by marble tombstones, which he shares with the bones of two or three relatives.

In the small museum there is not a single one of the famous broadsheets on which he published his first poems and which, in insignificant printings—of thirty or forty copies—he parsimoniously distributed to a few chosen readers. Nor are there any of the pamphlets—there were fifty copies of the first, seventy of the second—in which on two occasions he gathered a handful of poems, his only works published in anything approaching book form in his lifetime. The secrecy in which this august poet shrouded the writing of poetry didn't only have to do with his homosexuality, a shameful failing in a public functionary and petit bourgeois of that time and place who in his poems expounded with such surprising freedom on his sexual predilections; it had also, and perhaps especially, to do with his fascination with the clandestine, the underground, the marginal and *maudit* life that he slipped into from time to time and that he lauded with unparalleled elegance. Poetry, for Cavafy, like pleasure and beauty, could not be brought publicly to light, nor were such things within everyone's reach: they were available only to those daring enough to seek them out and cultivate them as forbidden fruits, in dangerous territory.

Of this Cavafy there is only a fleeting trace in the museum, in a few undated little drawings scrawled in a school notebook, the pages of which have been pulled out and stuck up on the walls without any kind of protection: boys, or maybe the same boy in different positions, showing their Apollonian silhouettes and erect phalluses. This Cavafy I can imagine very well, and have imagined ever since I read him for the first time in the translation of his poems by Marguerite Yourcenar: the sensual and decadent Cavafy, whom E. M. Forster discreetly hinted at in his 1926 essay and who became a mythic figure in Lawrence Durrell's *Alexandria Quartet*. Here, in his city, the cafés and tavernas of his poems are still thronged, and, as in the poems, there are almost no women or heterosexual couples. I don't know this for a fact, but I am sure that staged in them still, amid the crowds of men—the air dense with the smell of Turkish coffee and the clouds of smoke expelled by showy hookah smokers—are ardent meetings, first encounters, and the monetary exchanges that precede the fevered couplings of lovers of convenience in cheap rooms, their sordidness and filth setting off the allure of exquisite bodies. I'd even venture to say that I've witnessed it, on the terraces of The Corniche or in the smoky hovels that surround the textile market: a gentleman with a small sniffing nose, eager lips, and lustful little eyes, at nightfall in the warm glow of the first stars and the sea breeze, spying on the strapping young men who stroll with their buttocks cocked, in search of clients.

Unlike the men—or, perhaps more accurately, adolescents—who love each other with serenity and ease in Cavafy's poems, and enjoy sexual pleasure with the clear conscience of pagan gods, Cavafy surely found these loves extremely difficult and troubling, suffused at times with terror and always with frustrated hopes. The astounding thing about his erotic poetry is that these episodes—which must have been few and experienced under the terrible strain of one who always kept up the appearance of respectability in his public life and evaded scandal in any way he could—are transformed into a kind of utopia: a supreme way of living and relishing life, of escaping the bounds of the human condition and achieving a superior form of existence, of attaining a kind of secular spiritual state. In this state, through the pleasure of the senses and perceptions and the appreciation of physical beauty, a human being ascends, like the mystics in their divine trances, to the height of the gods, becoming a god himself. Cavafy's erotic poems burn with an unbridled sexuality, but despite that and their romantic trappings of decadence and perdition, they are curiously cold, maintaining the rational distance of an intelligence that governs the outpouring of passion and the feasting of the instincts. At the same time that he represents this ardor in verse, he observes it, studies it, and, with form as his tool, perfects and eternalizes it.

His themes and his sexual inclinations are infiltrated with

nineteenth-century romanticism—excess and transgression, aristocratic individualism—but at the moment he takes up his pen and sits down to write, a classicist surges from the depths of his being and seizes the reins of his spirit, obsessed with harmony of form and clarity of expression, a poet convinced that deft craftsmanship, clarity, discipline, and the proper use of memory are preferable to improvisation and disorderly inspiration in reaching absolute artistic perfection. He achieved that perfection: as a result, his poetry is capable of resisting the test of translation—a test that almost always vanquishes the work of other poets—so that it makes our blood run cold in all its different versions, astounding even those of us who can't read it in the demotic Greek and the Greek of the diaspora in which it was written. (By the way, the most beautiful translation into Spanish I've read of Cavafy's work is that of twenty-five poems by the Spaniard Joan Ferraté. It was published by Lumen in 1970, in a handsome edition illustrated with photographs, and, unfortunately, so far as I know, it hasn't been reissued.)

This is the third Cavafy of the indissoluble trinity: the one outside time who, on the wings of fantasy and history, lived simultaneously under the yoke of contemporary Britain and twenty centuries in the past, in a Roman province of Levantine Greeks, industrious Jews, and merchants from all over the world, or a few hundred years later, when the paths of Christians and pagans crossed and recrossed in a heterogeneous society where virtues and vices proliferated and divine beings and humans were almost impossible to tell apart. The Hellenic Cavafy, the Roman, the Byzantine, the Jew, leaps from one century to the next, from one civilization to another, with the ease and grace of a dancer, always maintaining the coherence and continuity of his movements. His world is not erudite at all, although traces of his characters, settings, battles, and courtly intrigues may be picked up in history ɔooks. Erudition sets a glacial barrier of facts, explications, and references between information and reality, and Cavafy's world has the freshness and intensity of life itself, not life as it is lived in nature, but the enriched and deliberate life—achieved without giving up living—of the work of art.

Alexandria is always present in his dazzling poems, because it is there that the events they evoke take place, or because it is from the city's perspective that the deeds of the Greeks, Romans, and Christians are glimpsed or remembered or yearned for, or because the poet who invents and declaims is from there and wouldn't have wanted to be from anywhere else. He was a singular Alexandrian and a man of the periphery, a Greek of the diaspora who did more for his cultural homeland—for its language and ancient mythology—than any other writer since classical times. But how can a poet so thoroughly of the Middle East—so identified with the smells, tastes, myths, and past of his country of exile, that cultural and geographic crossroads where Asia and Africa meet and are absorbed into each other as so many other Mediterranean civilizations, races, and religions have been absorbed into it—be so easily assimilated into the history of modern European Greek literature?

All of those civilizations left traces on the world created by Cavafy, a poet who was able to make another, different world of all that rich historical and cultural material, one that is revived and renewed each time we read him. Modern-day Alexandrians don't read his poetry, and the vast majority don't even know his name. But when we come here, the most real and tangible Alexandria for those of us who have read him is not the beautiful beach, or the curve of the seaside promenade, not the wandering clouds, the yellow trams, or the amphitheater built with granite brought from Aswan, or even the archaeological marvels of the museum. It is Cavafy's Alexandria, the city where sophists discuss

and impart their doctrines, where philosophers meditate or
lessons of Thermopylae and the symbolism of Ulysses's voyage
Ithaca, where curious neighbors come out of their houses to watc
Cleopatra's children—Caesarion, Alexander, and Ptolemy—on
their way to the Gymnasium, where the streets reek of wine and
incense when Bacchus passes by with his entourage just after the
mournful funeral rites of a grammarian, where love is a thing between men, and where suddenly panic swells, because a rumor
has spread that the barbarians will soon be at the gates.

Alexandria, February 2000

The Life and Trials of Elián

❧ ❧

I n the sad adventure that the Cuban boy Elián González has been living ever since he was left adrift in the middle of the Caribbean at the mercy of sharks, then miraculously saved by a fisherman who brought him to Miami, the great victor has been Fidel Castro. Even those of us who believe him to be one of the most repugnant dictators ever produced by the authoritarian fauna of Latin America must take off our hats to him: in the forty-second year of his absolute rule over the unhappy island of Cuba, the longest-lived tyrant of the Western Hemisphere has managed to manipulate Elián's case with such cold clarity and incredible cynicism that for several months no one has mentioned the autocracy he has made of his country or the catastrophic economic situation of the Cuban people. The only subject of discussion has been the child-martyr and the legal and political controversy surrounding his fate, with the Cuban exile community publicly condemned as intolerant extremists who have no respect for the law and with the government and justice system of the United States cornered into seeming agreement with Castro and accession to his wishes. To such a pass have we come: Fidel Castro, backed by the United States, plays the defender of parental custody and the champion of a poor father whose son is about to be snatched from him by the Nazi-fascist bandits of Miami.

Nevertheless, instead of becoming indignant, we should try to examine these events with a cool head. It seems hopeless, at this point, to recall that the person at the heart of this story is a young child of divorced parents who has just lived through one of the worst experiences imaginable—flight from Cuba in utterly precarious circumstances, shipwreck, the death of his mother and almost all the other fugitives, and long hours afloat on the high seas clinging to an inner tube—which ought to have earned him a minimum of consideration, since it is obvious that anyone who has been through such an ordeal is in delicate shape, with profound trauma ahead of him. But that has not been the case, since from the very beginning Fidel Castro, then the Miami exile community, saw the boy as a weapon to be used in a political battle to score points against their adversaries. The fatal error of the Miami exiles, who fell naively into the trap set for them by the dictator, was to accept a political struggle over a matter that should have remained on a strictly legal plane. Since it was logical to conclude that parental custody rights, which are universally acknowledged, would prevail before a court of law, it was imprudent to turn the argument that Elián should stay in the United States into a campaign in the fight against the dictatorship, since the battle would be difficult, if not impossible, to win. This has been borne out so far, and will probably be confirmed when the Atlanta jury delivers its final verdict: that Elián should be returned to the person who exercises the unquestioned right of paternity over him.

That this conclusion was predictable and that it is lawful don't make it right. I believe it is wrong, and immoral, because, given the very special circumstances of Elián's case, the person to whom the United States will turn the boy over isn't his father but Fidel

Castro, the only person who really has custody over all the Cubans on the island, as the historian Manuel Moreno Fraginals explains in an admirable article refuting the propagandistic book by García Márquez on the subject. But this is an ethical and political truth, and the courts in democratic countries judge not on the basis of political and moral realities but according to the law, although the latter might contradict and make a mockery of the former, as has happened in this case. With the great instincts of a political animal who never strays from the central aim of his existence—clinging tooth and nail to the absolute power he has wielded for more than four decades—Fidel Castro realized the good he could get out of Elián, and moved to act.

To understand that his concern was not the welfare of a helpless child, we need simply cast a glance at his record. Just seven years ago, in 1993, untroubled by the least twinges of conscience, the Cuban dictator ordered the sinking of the tugboat *March Thirteenth*, in which many defenseless Cubans were trying to flee the island; among those who died were nearly a dozen children, some of them just a few months old. And the Cuban writer César Leante has recently testified, drawing on the evidence of his own children's lives, to the kind of childhood and adolescence afforded by the Castro regime, with its rigidly run schools, obligatory work camps, three years of military service, and international military expeditions ordered to satisfy its leader's megalomania. So there is room to doubt that the massive mobilizations unleashed by Fidel Castro over the last few months in "defense" of Elián González were occasioned by his altruistic desire to defend fatherhood. They are really a psychological maneuver intended to distract those on the home front and a clever attempt to provoke the exile community in Miami into taking positions that will hurt its image and seem to confirm the extremism and insularity attributed to it in Cuban propaganda. In both objectives, the dictator has triumphed.

From the outside, the mass gatherings that took place ⟨ ⟩ day all over the island demanding the return of Elián had ⟨ ⟩ same pitiful appearance as the grandiose demonstrations of Stali⟨ ⟩ ist Russia, Hitler's Germany, Maoist China, or Kim Il Sung'⟨ ⟩ North Korea, which were intended to show the tight political unity of a people rallied behind a maximum leader but really revealed the servitude and regimentation of a society deprived of even the most insignificant measures of freedom, initiative, or spontaneity and turned into an army of automatons, blindly propelled by fear, propaganda, servility, and the demands of power. But on the inside it is likely that the spectacle took on a different aspect and that, barraged with the incessant and demagogic one-sided information delivered by a media system designed to manipulate the minds of the nation, many Cubans swallowed the official story and went out to protest of their own accord, declaring themselves against Elián's "kidnappers" and for the poor father whose child was taken from him. If even distinguished poets and a Nobel laureate put their pens at the service of this farce, what could be expected from the average misinformed Cuban, his only news that filtered down to him by the regime's propaganda machine? For several months, hunger, miserable living conditions, the shameful state of political prisoners, and the total lack of freedom and rights of citizenship were reduced to secondary importance for a nation caught up in the commotion of fighting to "free Elián."

Why did the exile community respond to this Machiavellian provocation by trying to keep the boy in Miami by whatever means it could, even against court orders and the requests of the U.S. government? Partly, it is clear, because of a genuine feeling of solidarity with Elián's mother, who lost her life trying to bring her son to a country where he could grow up free, and out of affection for the unfortunate child. But in large part, they reacted out of desperation and frustration with a regime that, despite having r⟨ ⟩

their country and turned it into a concentration camp, seems
re firmly ensconced than ever, with the international commu-
ty now increasingly indifferent to the fate of the Cuban people
and resigned to Fidel Castro as a mostly harmless pest (except in
his dealings with Cubans), even helping him to survive by sending
him masses of tourists and dollars, or establishing businesses in
Cuba that take advantage of the slave labor the regime offers, and
demanding that the United States end its embargo—after all, why
deny the Cuban dictatorship what is allowed the Chinese and
Vietnamese dictatorships? I understand very well the feeling of
impotence and rage that must sometimes overwhelm Cubans in
exile, who feel that the years are going by and their efforts to end
the tyranny stifling their country are hopeless, that the tyrant remains in power, unscathed and insolent, without giving an inch
on questions of repression or public freedoms or human rights,
and that instead it is they who are getting older or dying with a
terrible feeling of defeat.

But the political struggle must never succumb to irrationalism
and mere passion, because if it does, its ideas and principles will be
compromised. The exile community is superior to the dictatorship
because the latter is founded on arbitrariness and force, whereas
the former defends a free and lawful system in which human
rights are protected and the general good is defined by a judiciary
that freely elected authorities have the obligation to support. The
Miami exiles who unwisely challenged the government and the
courts, refusing to heed the decision that ordered them to return
Elián to his father, didn't just make a political mistake; they damaged their cause, stripping it of its greatest justification, which is
respect for the law, the basis of the democratic system. This respect can't be subordinated to claims of the justice of a cause, because if it could, society would ultimately be dominated by the
chaos, anarchy, and arbitrariness that are the ideal breeding
grounds for dictatorship.

The U.S. government's behavior in this affair has been lamentable, especially on the night of April 22, when it ordered a helmeted commando unit, armed as if to launch a bloody attack on a terrorist hideout, to assault the house of Elián's Miami relatives under cover of darkness. The *New York Times* columnist William Safire put it best: what happened there "damaged Clinton's reputation, incensed moderates, and brought shame on the United States." This explains why surveys showed that although a majority of North Americans believed Elián should be returned to his father, an even greater majority condemned as excessive the brute force used to capture the child and bring him to Washington. The photograph of the automaton-like soldier pointing a huge machine gun at a terrified Elián, who shrinks in the arms of the fisherman who saved his life, will haunt Clinton as surely as his tendency to lower his pants in the company of Arkansas state employees and White House interns; it will certainly help the Republicans beat the Democrats in the next elections, and possibly prevent Hillary Clinton from winning the New York Senate seat she is running for against Mayor Rudolph Giuliani. It is quite a paradox that the president under whose administration the United States achieved the greatest economic prosperity in its history will be remembered primarily for making passes at women working under him and for sending a fearsome military commando unit to capture a little boy in shorts as if he were a highly dangerous assassin, in a house where the FBI found no weapons, where not a single bodyguard was present, and where no one put up the slightest physical resistance to the raid. When, thrilled by what had happened, Fidel Castro proclaimed that for the first time in forty years the United States and Cuba had experienced a truce and a rapprochement that night, he was telling a disturbing truth.

This whole sad story vividly illustrates an ancient maxim: dictatorships have an indisputable advantage over democracies when differences are hashed out on legal grounds, because the law imposes rules that democracies must respect and that limit their actions but that dictatorships ignore, except in specific cases when they suit the dictators' purposes. In Elián's case, a bright light has been shed on the way the laws of a democratic society can serve the interests of a despot who uses them to inflict a setback on his adversaries and briefly lend himself a veneer of legitimacy. Parental custody is a respectable cause, even when, as in this case, it only gives Cuban totalitarianism some breathing room and sullies the political image of the Miami exile community.

What will Elián's fate be if he returns to Cuba? It's not hard to imagine. For a while, so long as Fidel Castro can still get some political mileage out of him, the playacting will continue. The prodigal child will be the object of popular adoration, the little pet of the regime, and a photograph of him, smiling in the arms of the magnanimous commander—maybe tugging on his beard with his little hands—before a crowd leaping and shouting with joy, will be broadcast around the world. Then, too, perhaps a distinguished writer with many awards to his name will write a long article about the wonderful, painstaking psychological work undertaken by a handful of teachers, analysts, and doctors of the revolution to help little Elián regain his mental and emotional balance after the terrible ordeals he was subjected to by imperialist treachery. In his beautiful house with a pool, Elián will be convinced that life is much more comfortable and luxurious in Cuba than in Miami, and he'll have a wonderful time in his place of honor at parades when the masses wave and chant his name. Then, sooner or later, while he is still a child or perhaps when he is an adolescent, Elián will no longer be of use to the great dissembler, and he'll experience another of those radical shifts that will have marked his life since he was born: the return to anonymity, the grayness and scarcity and limited existence that is the shared fate of the immense majority of his countrymen, and the apathy and resignation required for survival in societies ravaged by a dictator. Or—who knows?—maybe he will defect to the ranks of the silent and growing rebellion that leads many of his countrymen to do daring things that might land them in jail, like joining human rights activist groups, or circulating information, or even stepping onto a raft and setting off to sea once more, as his mother did with him in her arms years before, prepared for anything—to drown or be eaten by sharks—just to escape the enslaved country to which the judges, leaders, and soldiers of the most powerful democracy in the world returned him, in strict accordance with the law.

Madrid, April 26, 2000

Pernicious Futility

⚜ ⚘

The last time the Organization of American States did anything worthwhile was almost half a century ago, at the end of the 1950s, after Generalissimo Trujillo's attempt to assassinate Venezuelan president Rómulo Betancourt, when it agreed that all its member nations should break diplomatic and business ties with the Dominican dictatorship, a measure that meant the beginning of the end of Trujillo's regime. Since then, it has been an absolutely pointless organization, incapable of contributing anything whatsoever to the preservation or promotion of democracy and human rights on the continent, the goals it was created to meet. All the important steps taken in that direction, like the peace negotiations that ended the civil wars in Central America or facilitated the transition from authoritarianism to democracy (in Chile, for example), were initiatives of the United Nations or the great Western powers, with the OAS playing no role but that of an extra. This is why it is so utterly lacking in prestige, seen as a moldering establishment crammed with diplomats sent by their governments as if into early retirement, for a rest cure, or to discreetly nurse their cirrhosis on the banks of the Potomac.

The problem is that for some time now, no longer content with being irrelevant, the OAS has become frankly pernicious, turning into an institution that acts only in order to undermine the already shaky bases of legality and freedom in Latin America and to supply alibis and excuses for its executioners. Without the OAS, for example, it is likely that the Peruvian dictatorship ostensibly headed by Fujimori (but secretly run by the murderer, torturer, thief, and drug traffickers' accomplice Vladimiro Montesinos and a military inner circle under his command) would never have existed, or would in any case have disappeared after the grotesque farce of an election perpetrated last May 28, which every international body of observers, beginning with the OAS's team itself, headed by the Guatemalan former minister Eduardo Stein, refused to endorse because of its failure to adhere to the most elementary standards of orderliness and fairness.

The OAS's harsh report, signed by Stein and attesting to the absolute impossibility that the second round of elections could be legitimate under the conditions established by the regime, was seconded by identical opinions issued by missions from the Carter Foundation, the National Democratic Institute for International Affairs, and Transparency International and other delegations of observers sent to oversee the Peruvian election. Not a single one of them recognized the election as legitimate, and all left the country so as not to justify by their presence the scandalous charade that purported to extend the existence of the authoritarian Peruvian regime by five more years. (The opposition candidate, Alejandro Toledo, also withdrew from the rigged contest.) In the circumstances, it seemed obvious that the OAS would stand by the conclusions of its own envoys and refuse to recognize the blatant farce, condemning it and demanding new elections under strict international observation, as the Peruvian people and many democratic governments from all over the world had requested.

And yet nothing of the sort happened at the meeting of OAS foreign-affairs ministers in Canada, despite the urging of four governments acting with true democratic intent, which should be noted here (Costa Rica, Canada, the United States, and Argentina), since their decency and responsibility stand in healthy contrast to the ugly spectacle of cowardice, duplicity, and outright collusion with the Andean dictatorship that the others represented. The agreement that was signed would have delighted Pontius Pilate: a commission would be sent to Peru, consisting of the Canadian foreign minister Lloyd Axworthy and the secretary-general of the OAS, César Gaviria, to determine whether Fujimori's government was adopting the necessary measures to reestablish democratic legality in Peru. Is this for real, or is it a joke of cosmic proportions?

César Gaviria, besides being mediocrity incarnate—he amply proved it when he was president of Colombia and has more than confirmed it as the head of the OAS—boasts a record of initiatives and gestures in support of the Peruvian dictatorship (he effectively schemed to get the OAS to legitimize the last two mock elections held by the Fujimori-Montesinos duo) that morally disqualifies him from forming part of the team. His opinion is easily foreseen: amid clouds of legalistic jargon, he will make the astute observation that the regime, without having eliminated corruption entirely, is making worthy efforts to "overcome the inefficiencies of the last elections and to direct the country once and for all along the true path of . . ." and so on.

Lloyd Axworthy is another matter. He represents one of the most genuine and admirable democracies in the world today and has battled with conviction and energy to get the member countries of the organization to remain faithful to the OAS charter, which his Latin American colleagues have so cavalierly disregarded, and condemn in no uncertain terms the electoral fraud of May 28; he has demanded new, and this time clean, elections in Peru. That none of the countries except the United States, Argentina, and Costa Rica followed his lead must have surprised him. Nevertheless, a bit of digging reveals that in some cases the OAS ministers harbor very solid and comprehensible reasons (though not justifiable ones, of course) for their Pontius Pilate–like actions. How could the PRI government in Mexico support a censure of electoral fraud when it is likely to engage in the same thing itself on July 2 in order to block the victory of the opposition candidate Vicente Fox and ensure that of the PRI candidate Francisco Labastida? Wouldn't it have been foolish for the Venezuelan government to condemn electoral fraud when it was about to attempt the same thing in its own elections, also on May 28, but was prevented from doing so at the last minute by the courts, which postponed the voting? By helping Fujimori, the Venezuelan, Mexican, Ecuadoran, and Paraguayan pseudo democracies are taking preventive measures: they want to keep the international community from calling them to task, too, tomorrow or the next day, for civic trickery or crimes committed by their governments. And to do so, they rend their nationalist garments, as usual, and raise the fearful specters of "respect for sovereignty" and "our fraternal obligation to stand united against foreign interference." One hears these buffoons of democracy speak and wonders how they differ from the representatives once sent to the OAS by the governments of Somoza, Pérez Jiménez, Odría, and Trujillo.

More difficult to understand, certainly, is the attitude of those governments that are neither dictatorships nor aspiring dictatorships like Mexico and Venezuela but fairly respectable democracies: Uruguay, for example, or Chile, or even Colombia, in its state of deterioration. I read somewhere that their reluctance to explicitly condemn the Peruvian dictatorship is due to "progressivist" reservations: the U.S. Congress and government have come out emphatically against Fujimori's electoral fraud, and they don't want to seem too supportive of the United States. Since idiocy is also a factor to be taken into account in political life, one can't discard this interpretation of the regrettable behavior of the Uruguayan, Chilean, Colombian, and (worst of all) Brazilian ministers at the meeting in Canada. But it is worth scrutinizing the meaning of such attitudes: these countries are purchasing the appearance of independence and progressivism by abjectly validating a regime born out of a military coup that since 1992 has been destroying every forum for freedom and law in Peru, plunging large sectors of the population into poverty, controlling the dissemination of information, perverting justice, committing horrendous human rights abuses, and establishing a new model of dictatorship for the twenty-first century that has already begun to be imitated in other Latin American countries.

It isn't hard to imagine the dialogues that members of the OAS commission will have with the Peruvian authorities in their attempt to verify the "progress" of democracy in Peru. "Do you promise that no journalists will ever be tortured again the way Fabián Salazar was tortured on the eve of the elections by a National Intelligence Service (SIN, the Peruvian Gestapo) commando, who took a saw to one of Salazar's arms so that he would turn over videotapes showing the National Election Board and the cream of the establishment taking orders from Montesinos?" "It will never happen again." "Do you promise not to register Fujimori's candidacy in the 2005 elections by forging a million signatures the way you did in these elections?" "That was an involuntary lapse, merely attributable to underdevelopment, and it won't be repeated." "Will you return the television channels and radio stations that you stole from Baruch Ivcher and Genaro Delgado Parker because they criticized the regime?" "That matter is in the hands of the Ministry of Justice, whose independence is sacred to the regime." "Will you allow public stations to broadcast news about the opposition—and not exclusively news that supports the regime's propaganda—at least every once in a while?" "We respect the freedom of the press too much to interfere with the policies of our stations, whose love for the regime is so great that they are unwilling to spread the lies of its enemies. But as a token of good will, we'll ask them to consider your request." "Will you promise not to take over the newspaper *El Comercio*, which you've been threatening in a number of ways ever since it stopped supporting the regime and began devoting space to criticism?" "We respect the peaceful expression of different opinions. Of course, we could do nothing if the Ministry of Justice finds in favor of those who have lodged multiple complaints against it, or if SUNAT (the tax bureau) precipitates the bankruptcy of the cable station Channel N (property of *El Comercio*), the only television station in the country that broadcasts news that hasn't been dictated by Montesinos." "When SIN commandos assassinated students and professors at La Cantuta, massacred residents of Barrios Altos after confusing them with Shining Path guerrillas, butchered Mariela Barreto, and tortured and raped Leonor La Rosa, leaving her the battered wreck she is today, it made Peru look very bad abroad. It looks even worse when international law-enforcement agencies arrest one of those criminals, like the torturer and rapist Major Ricardo Anderson Kohatsu, and the Peruvian government saves him by giving him diplomatic immunity. Isn't there anything you can do about this?" "Difficult, considering that these people have already been granted amnesty in token of the good fellowship that should always reign among Peruvians. But they are being watched, and the next murder, torture, kidnapping, or rape they commit, the weight of Fujimori's justice will fall on them and it will be implacable. Word of honor!"

Madrid, June 2000

Index